GENTLEMEN
AND
SLEDGERS

Rob Smyth is a former
Guardian and *Telegraph* sports
journalist and the author of
*The Spirit of Cricket: What Makes
Cricket the Greatest Game on
Earth*, and the co-author of
*Danish Dynamite: The Story of
Football's Greatest Cult Team*.

GENTLEMEN
AND
SLEDGERS

A HISTORY OF THE ASHES
IN 100 QUOTATIONS AND
CONFRONTATIONS

ROB SMYTH

HEAD
of ZEUS

Head of Zeus Ltd
Clerkenwell House
45–47 Clerkenwell Green
London EC1R 0HT

WWW.HEADOFZEUS.COM

For Mum and Jay

CONTENTS

THE AGE OF BRADMAN
1930–1948

THE AGE OF ATTRITION
1950–1968

THE AGE OF THE FAST MEN
1970–1989

AUSTRALIA ASCENDANT
1989–2003

2005 AND ALL THAT

INTRODUCTION

On its first day of release in 1997, Oasis's third album *Be Here Now* sold 350,000 copies. I wasn't among the buyers, though I could relate to those who wanted – no, needed – to Have It Now. Four months earlier, I walked into HMV Hanley and saw an expensive Japanese import of Radiohead's *OK Computer*, about which my youthful self had been impossibly excited. It was still three weeks before its UK release. My eyes bulged and my wallet soon contracted.

That sense of can't-sit-still anticipation has inevitably been eroded by a combination of the instant gratification of the digital age and life's law of diminishing enthusiasm. But there remains one prospect that age cannot wither, and which unfailingly still causes the heart to race and excitement to mount: and that is the build-up to an Ashes series. The contest between England and Australia could bring out the excitable child in an 110-year-old. You can't illegally download it before its official release; you can't pay extra to get it early.

There is nothing in life to compare with the feeling on the first morning of an Ashes series – even if, for England fans, there is often not so much anticipation as anticipointment, to use the portmanteau word coined by the comedian Paul Whitehouse to describe his experiences as a Tottenham Hotspur football fan.

England lost each of the first eight Ashes series I watched, by a combined score of 30–7. It was eight years before I saw England win a live Test and sixteen before I saw them win a series. Yet like all the other members of that generation – not so much Generation X as Generation FFS (so frequently did we lament England's inadequacies) – I knelt once more at the altar of pain at the start of each series. And the eventual fulfilment, on 12 September 2005, of long-cherished hopes of an England series victory – a date as treasurable as a wedding day or a child's birthdate – makes that day a shoo-in for inclusion in the XI happiest days of my life when I'm in my dotage.

Australians will have similar stories and similar dates: 1 August 1989, perhaps, or 17 December 2013. This book is not an Anglocentric view of the Ashes. One of cricket's greatest gifts is that it teaches you to see sport with two eyes, and this is an impartial celebration of sport's greatest rivalry. Although the pages about Adelaide 2006 may, I freely admit, be stained with English tears.

The 'miracle of Adelaide' was also the match in which Shane Warne first called Ian Bell 'the Shermanator'. That is quote No.92 in this book, which tells the history of the Ashes through the quotations and confrontations that have defined each series. The quotes vary from the apocryphal to the legendary to the unfamiliar, with some discovered during happy hours trawling the archives at the British Library, or browsing books I had picked up for 30p in a second-hand shop because you just never know when they might come in handy. . .

I might need to trawl second-hand computer shops for a new asterisk key after the battering mine took during the writing of this book. There has been plenty of lively language in the course of the 133 years of the Ashes, a contest between bat, ball and mouth.

But, come on, would you really have it any other way? In 2006–07, Richie Benaud signed a book for one of the sons of the *Guardian* cricket correspondent Mike Selvey. 'Always enjoy the game no matter what.' The great man understood the Anglo-Australian rivalry as well as anybody. Whether your team wins, loses or is hammered 5–0, you cannot fail to enjoy Ashes cricket.

Rob Smyth
April 2015

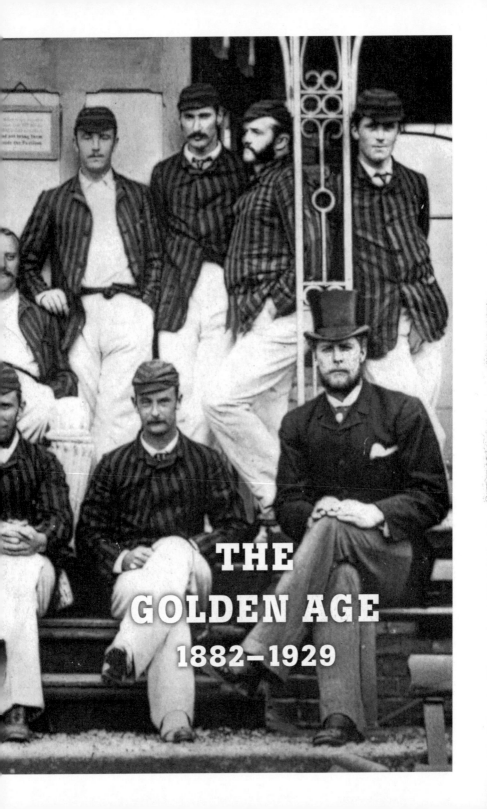

THE GOLDEN AGE
1882–1929

1882

In Affectionate Remembrance

OF

ENGLISH CRICKET,

WHICH DIED AT THE OVAL

ON

29th AUGUST, 1882,

Deeply lamented by a large circle of sorrowing
friends and acquaintances.

R.I.P.

N.B.—*The body will be cremated and the
ashes taken to Australia.*

[REGINALD SHIRLEY BROOKS,
SPORTING TIMES,
2 SEPTEMBER 1882]

FREDERICK SPOFFORTH WAS MAD AS HELL and he was not going to take it any more. Australia had been swindled by England's W. G. Grace at a crucial stage of the Test match at The Oval and Spofforth, known as 'The Demon' because of his infernal fast bowling, was not inclined to turn the other cheek. He walked into England's dressing-room and called Grace 'a bloody cheat'. And that was just the start. Spofforth, who forensically deconstructed batsmen's techniques for a living, now did the same to Grace's character; a letter from a team-mate said he addressed Grace in 'the best Australian vernacular' for a full five minutes. And he didn't mean 'G'day, mate.'

Spofforth then stalked out of the dressing-room, saying: 'This will lose you the match!' Moments later, before England started their second innings needing 85 for victory, he boomed to his team-mates: 'This thing can be done!' The burgeoning cricketing rivalry between England and Australia would never be the same again.

That rivalry had started five and a half years earlier. Just as it's hard to comprehend that life existed before the Internet, so there really was Test cricket before the Ashes. The inaugural Test match, as anybody who doesn't wish to be guffawed out of the Lord's Long Room knows, was played between Australia and England at the Melbourne Cricket Ground in 1877. The English-born Charles Bannerman made a monumental 165 out of a first-innings total of 245 for Australia, who won eventually by 45 runs.

Eight further Tests were played before Australia's trip to England in 1882, a four-month tour that included 36 matches – only one of which was a Test. In those days they had warm-down matches too.

Australia had lost their only other Test in England, two years earlier. There was a sense of invincibility wafting around England. Defeat was not just unthinkable, it was nigh-on incomprehensible – even more so when Australia were bowled out for 63 on the first day. England fared little better, only just scraping into three figures, but a meagre first-innings lead of 38 was surely worth plenty more in a low-scoring dogfight.

The turning point of the match – and, go on, let's get carried away, the history of cricket – came with Australia 114 for six in their

**'The Demon' Spofforth,
destroyer of England in 1882.**

second innings. Sammy Jones, the Australian all-rounder, completed a single and trotted out of his crease to do some gardening. While he was inspecting the state of his lawn, his house was burgled by Grace, who broke the stumps. The umpire Bob Thoms gave Jones out; one report suggests he did so with all the enthusiasm of a man taking his beloved poodle for a valedictory visit to the vet's, muttering sadly: 'If you claim it, sir, it is out.'

Spofforth, who had declined the opportunity to run out the England captain Albert 'Monkey' Hornby for backing up too far earlier in the match, was especially indignant at such gamesmanship. Grace was used to doing unto the laws of the game as Uri Geller does unto spoons, and triumphing as a result, but on this occasion he had urinated on the wrong nest.

At the end of the innings, with Australia bowled out for 122, Spofforth walked into the England dressing-room and said his piece. Grace was largely unperturbed. He was a man for whom conflict was a performance-enhancing drug, and he went on to make a masterful, ship-steadying 32 to take England to 56 for three, 29 runs from victory.

It was then that Grace drove Harry Boyle, Spofforth's trusty sidekick, to mid-off, and the match began to change. Spofforth was rarely less than formidably accurate, but his determination made him positively metronomic. He and Boyle bowled ten consecutive maidens before the important wicket of Alfred Lyttleton, bowled by a beauty from Spofforth: England were 66 for five, with 19 needed.

Spofforth took three more quick wickets, which gave him seven in the innings and 14 in the match. The tension was such that one spectator mistook his umbrella handle for a Toblerone and started to chew through it, while another reportedly had a fatal heart attack. England had opened the celebratory champagne. Not in hubris, but because the No.11, the Yorkshire slow bowler Ted Peate, was so nervous that his team-mates decided to give him a glass or two before he went out to bat.

There was panic everywhere: the England captain Hornby unwisely held back Charles Studd as insurance. Studd, an all-rounder and future Christian missionary, had batted No.6 in the first innings and had made two hundreds against Australia during tour matches that summer. This time he came in at No.10 and had faced only five balls without scoring when Boyle dismissed Billy Barnes. England were nine down and 10 runs short of victory.

There were three balls of the over remaining, after which Studd would be on strike. The new batsman Peate took two and then missed a wild swipe. Off the final ball, Peate launched into another lusty slog and was bowled. England had collapsed from 51 for two to 77 all out to lose by seven runs. The great all-rounder George Giffen said Australia were 'as irresistible as an avalanche'. Spofforth took seven for 44 and 14 for 90 in the match, though it is a curious detail that Boyle took the most significant wickets of Grace and Peate. 'I couldn't trust Mr Studd,' was Peate's explanation for his injudicious

Well, well. I left six men to get thirty odd runs and they could not get them

stroke. He was not the only one passing the buck. 'Well, well,' said Grace. 'I left six men to get thirty odd runs and they could not get them.'

The crowd's intense disappointment at England's defeat was manifest only for a split second, a fleeting wall of silence as it sank in that a fully representative England side had been beaten at home for the first time. Then the crowd ignored their partisan concerns. 'We had cheer after cheer from those healthy British lungs,' said Giffen, who possibly hadn't studied the health implications of smoking Prima Firmennaya Marka, the cigarette du jour, by the tin-load.

Australia's joy was uncontrollable. The team manager Charlie Beal accidentally knocked a gateman flying in his keenness to embrace the team, while his mother flung her arms round Giffen's neck and planted 'a motherly kiss' on his brow. England went into Australia's dressing-room with 'champagne, seltzer and lemons' and passed it round 'like a loving cup'. The captain Hornby embraced his opposite number Billy Murdoch. 'Well, old fellow, it would have been the proudest moment of my life to have won,' said Hornby, words his wife and children were doubtless thrilled to read, 'but I cannot help congratulating you sincerely on the splendid game you played and your well-merited success.'

Nobody merited congratulations more than Spofforth, whose spell went into legend. John Masefield, poet laureate from 1930 to 1967, immortalised the match in verse. There is a tendency to think of Spofforth as Dennis Lillee in a time machine. And while it's true that he started the tradition of Australian fast bowlers using the moustache as an intimidatory weapon, he was more of a subtly probing interrogator than a bludgeoning destroyer; more Jane Tennison than Gene Hunt. Yet he was truly a fast bowler in spirit, and knew how to intimidate batsmen mentally.

'He must have been a great bowler,' wrote R. C. Robertson-Glasgow, 'but his superiority over batsmen seems to have been partly the result of facial expression.' That theme was explored further by a contemporary writer: 'He had rather the type of countenance which one associates with the Spirit of Evil in *Faust*. A long face, somewhat sardonic; piercing eyes; a hooked nose; and his hair, parted in the middle, giving the impression of horns.' Not for nothing was he nicknamed 'The Demon'. Here, more than a century before the pantomime gurning, effing and blinding of the moustachioed Merv Hughes, was mental disintegration in its purest form: sledging by diabolical sneer.

The English press reacted with the thundering lack of perspective that would become a regular backdrop to Ashes defeats. The newspapers were full of soul-searching about 'the decadence of English cricket'.

He had rather the type of countenance which one associates with the Spirit of Evil in *Faust*

Reginald Brooks of the *Sporting Times* struck an enduring satirical tone. Brooks was the kind of man who gave Victorian journalism a good name: he drank heavily, he gambled, he womanised. When it came to vices, Brooks was an equal-opportunity employer. His famous mock obituary of English cricket unwittingly gave birth to cricket's most famous prize. At the time, the illegality of cremation was a major topic in England, which explains the famous end to Brooks's obituary: 'N.B. The body will be cremated and the ashes taken to Australia.'* The Ashes thus came about because of a spoof and a Spofforth.

Had cremation been legal in England at the time – it became so in 1885 – goodness knows how we would have come to refer to cricket matches between England and Australia. Whatever the way, the day W. G. Grace inadvertently raised hell by provoking 'The Demon' would still be a significant part of the legend.

---

* A similar obituary appeared in the weekly newspaper *Cricket* two days before the *Sporting Times* was published, but it made no mention of ashes and did not catch on.

1882–83

'We have come to beard the kangaroo in his den – and try to recover those Ashes.'

[IVO BLIGH,
13 NOVEMBER 1882]

NOBODY HAD A CLUE WHAT IVO BLIGH was talking about. Bligh, the Old Etonian whose England team had recently arrived in Australia, was addressing a dinner party when he made reference to Reginald Brooks' satirical obituary, and outlined his wish to restore the honour of English cricket. The Ashes would soon become an essential part of cricket's vernacular, but at that stage they hadn't even been mentioned in its bible, *Wisden*, never mind a dictionary. The assembled throng, certainly those without a keen grasp of metaphor, weren't especially enamoured with Bligh's attitude to animals either.*

Bligh's team had set out for Australia in the steamer *Peshawar* just two weeks after Frederick Spofforth had destroyed them at The Oval, with the Australian players still completing their tour matches in England. They almost did not make it to Australia; their vessel collided with another ship in the darkness of the Indian Ocean, and arrived ten days late as a result. England's fastest bowler, the Nottinghamshire left-armer Fred Morley, suffered a fractured rib during the collision, which ruled him out of the first Test and meant he was never the same bowler again.

---

* Some reports suggest Bligh expressed a wish to 'beard the lion in his den' before a member of the audience shouted 'kangaroo!'

Bligh was soon preoccupied with Ms Morphy rather than Mr Morley. Early in the tour he made the acquaintance of the first maiden of Ashes cricket – Florence Morphy, who taught music to the family of the Melbourne Cricket Club president Sir William Clarke.

England had six debutants, including Bligh, in their side for the first Test at Melbourne – a match which was originally billed as 'Mr Murdoch's Eleven v The Hon. Ivo F. W. Bligh's Team'. Australia won comfortably by nine wickets, with the medium-paced spinner Joey Palmer taking the first 10-wicket haul of the Ashes era, including seven for 65 in the first innings.

The Yorkshire off-spinner Billy Bates trumped that in the second Test on the same ground. He took the first Test hat-trick as part of astonishing first-innings figures of seven for 28, and picked up seven more in the second innings to end with match figures of 14 for 102. Bates also struck 55 batting at No.9, the second highest score of a match that England won by an innings and 27 runs. After the game, he was rewarded with a collection from the crowd of £31.

England won the decisive third Test at Sydney, despite a heroic turn from Frederick Spofforth, who took seven for 44 – the same figures he had recorded in the second innings at The Oval in 1882. Australia, needing 153 to win, were routed for 83 by Dick Barlow, who opened the batting and bowling for England in the match. He took seven for 40; it was the fifth seven-for of the three-match series, a record that endures to this day.

In statistical terms Bligh had a rotten series: he made 33 runs in five innings and did not bowl. But he was successful in his kangaroo-bearding, Ashes-recovering exploits and became indelibly associated with Anglo-Australian cricket, even though this was his only series as a Test player.

To celebrate England's Ashes victory, Bligh was given a keepsake by a group of ladies including Morphy and Janet Clarke, the wife of Sir William – a terracotta urn which contains, depending on which account you believe, a burnt bail, a burnt ball, a burnt veil or a burnt stump. The contents are immaterial: it is the little urn, just six inches tall, that matters to cricketers from Australia and England.

Bligh asked Morphy to marry him before the tour was over. Recovering those Ashes *and* meeting his bride: quite why his tour hasn't been made into a period film starring Benedict Cumberbatch and Keira Knightley is anyone's guess. In 1900, he became the 8th Earl of Darnley. The terracotta urn stayed with the couple throughout their forty-three-year marriage. When Bligh died, Morphy gifted it to the MCC.

After the presentation of the urn in 1883, England played a fourth match against Australia – an official Test, but not part of the Ashes series, the kind of eccentric detail that was commonplace in those days. Another such detail was that a separate pitch was used for each of the four innings, and Australia won by four wickets. *Wisden* called it 'the great match of the tour'.

For England, that defeat was part of an overall tour record of nine wins in eighteen matches; in those days tour matches were regarded as only marginally less significant than international matches and W. G. Grace, who was not on the tour, described England's performance as 'a trifle disappointing'. Disappointing? A tour on which England regained the Ashes? The past truly is a foreign country.

1884 to 1891–92

'When he dies his body ought to be embalmed and permanently exhibited in the British Museum as "the colossal cricketer of all time".'

[AUSTRALIAN CAPTAIN BILLY MURDOCH ON
W. G. GRACE, THE DOMINANT PERSONALITY
OF EARLY ASHES CRICKET]

MOST OF THE EARLY ASHES CONTESTS were hopeless mismatches, with one side embarrassingly superior. That side, believe it or not, was England. Ivo Bligh's mission in 1882–83 was the first of eight consecutive series wins. The tall seam bowler George Lohmann, who ended his Test career with the exceptional record of 112 wickets at an average of 10.75, took 74 cheap wickets in 14 Tests against Australia; he was an unplayable combination of accuracy, seam movement and variety. Australia had a formidable metronome of their own: Charlie 'The Terror' Turner, who claimed 101 wickets in 17 Tests at 16.53. On pure statistics, Lohmann and Turner are the greatest bowlers England and Australia have ever had.

Just as two great bowlers stood out in Ashes contests towards the end of the nineteenth century, so did two great matches. The third Test at Sydney in 1884–85 – part of the first five-match series, which England won 3–2 – was won by just six runs by Australia, with Frederick 'The Demon' Spofforth demolishing England as he had at The Oval in 1882. Two years later, on the same ground, England won by 13 runs despite being bowled out for 45, their lowest ever total, on the first day.

Batting successes were rarer, though the Australian captain Billy Murdoch scored the first Test double-century at The Oval in 1884. Two years later, on the same ground, W. G. Grace slammed 170 to complete a 3–0 whitewash.

The era is synonymous with Grace, even though he was not always in the England side because of a reluctance to tour Australia. With his long beard, Grace looked a little like Father Christmas, but really he was Father Cricket: no player has exerted a more profound influence on the game. Contradictions and charisma maketh the most interesting men; and Grace was, by turns, a brazen cheat, a power junkie, a big cuddly softie, a bully, a hypocrite, a visionary, a batting genius, obsessed with money and generous with money. Just about the only consistent thing was his beard.

He lorded over the sport like a colossus, albeit one with the morals of an alley cat. Grace, of Gloucestershire, was the first box-office cricketer and the man whose personality established cricket as England's summer sport and gave the Ashes its heightened status. 'Grace had what all kings have, power, and the story of his life is the story of the exercise of that power,' wrote his biographer Simon Rae.

> **Grace had what all kings have, power, and the story of his life is the story of the exercise of that power**

He is best remembered for three things: that beard, his plentiful stomach and his brass neck. Grace was a combination of entitlement and effrontery who treated the umpire's decision as a basis for negotiation. The stories are legion, some familiar but too good not to repeat. When he was bowled in an exhibition match, he serenely replaced the bails and announced dismissively: 'They have come to watch me bat, not you bowl.' His practice was equally sharp in the field, and it was a rite of passage for young cricketers to be stitched up by the Doctor.

Grace's reluctance to accept he was out prompted one legendary incident during a match between Gloucestershire and Essex. The fiery Charles Kortright had dismissed Grace on a number of

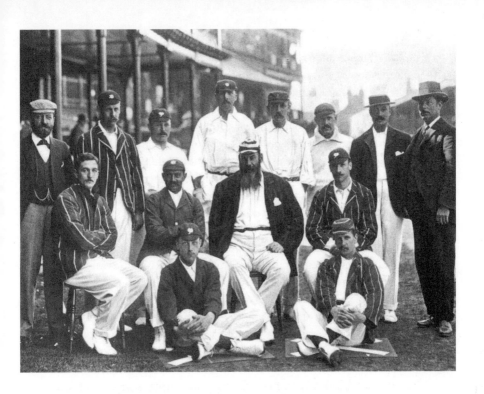

The fifty-year-old W. G. Grace (middle row, centre), playing in his final Test, leads England in the first Test at Trent Bridge, 1899. C. B. Fry and K. S. Ranjitsinhji are to Grace's right in the middle row. In the front row, in front of 'Ranji', is Wilfred Rhodes.

occasions, only for umpire Grace to reject his appeals. Finally Kortright knocked two stumps over, and Grace started to walk off. 'Surely you're not going, Doc?' said Kortright. 'There's one stump still standing!'

W. G. Grace stood alone among cricketers, and was not afraid to advertise the fact. His demands were more like those of a twenty-first-century footballer than a nineteenth-century cricketer. He

> **Surely you're not going, Doc? There's one stump still standing!**

was technically an amateur, yet earned so much more than all the professionals that this was dismissed as 'shamateurism.'

He didn't just want to have his cake and eat it. He wanted to have his cake, eat it and sell it for five times the annual wage. Yet he would regularly decline to charge poorer patients for his medical services, and was always moved by children. As a person, Grace was all things to all men. As a batsman, he was unquestionably great. Modern eyebrows might be raised at averages of 39 in first-class cricket and 32 in Tests, but these were completely different times. Grace revolutionised batting, making the world realise that front-foot and back-foot play were of equal importance. K.S. Ranjitsinhji, England's great Indian-born batsman, said he 'turned the old one-stringed instrument into a many-chorded lyre'.

England's run of Ashes success ended in 1891–92, a tour that was particularly disastrous for Grace: he irritated team-mates by demanding a tour fee of £3,000 and became increasingly unpopular with Australian fans for his haughty manner, to the point where he was barracked in Adelaide after arguing with the umpires. His first tour to Australia, in the 1870s, had followed a similar pattern. 'He was twice welcomed as a hero,' wrote Rae, 'and twice seen off on the boat home with a sense of relief.' Grace was captain when England won 1–0 at home in 1893, but did not tour Australia again; as a result, he missed out on the first great Test series.

1894–95

Give me the ball, Mr Stoddart, and I'll get t'boogers out before lunch!'

[BOBBY PEEL, FIRST TEST, SYDNEY,
20 DECEMBER 1894]

BOBBY PEEL AWOKE WITHOUT A HANGOVER. That's because he was still drunk. It was the final morning of the first Test against Australia at Sydney; the night before, he and a number of England's players had set out to find answers for their imminent defeat in the bottom of a beer bottle.

Peel, a left-arm Yorkshire slow bowler, eventually arrived at the ground so late that the start of play had to be delayed. He had no idea that an overnight storm had turned the Sydney pitch into a spin bowler's paradise, and that England had an unexpected chance of an astonishing victory. When a confused Peel saw the wet wicket, he thought somebody had watered it.

Somebody soon watered him. He was shoved under a cold shower to sober him up. Peel started to comprehend that, on an authentic 'sticky dog', he could do approximately the same amount of damage to the Australian batting line-up as he had done to his liver the night before. He may barely have known what day it was, but he certainly knew the time of day: he promised his captain, Andrew Stoddart, that he would have the match wrapped up in time for lunch, which may well have included hair of the dog.

Stoddart had taken over as England captain in the absence of W. G. Grace, who declined to tour Australia for a third time. There were nine debutants in the first Test at Sydney, five for Australia and four for England, though it was two established players who set the early tone: the all-rounder George Giffen's 161 and Syd Gregory's wristy 201 took Australia to 586. England were made to follow on after making 325, and just about stayed in the match with a determined team performance that took them to 437 all out.

Giffen, a nineteenth-century superhero, took four wickets in both innings; in total he bowled 118 overs as well as scoring 202 runs. It deserved to be Giffen's Match, and at the end of the fifth day's play it was precisely that. Australia finished on 113 for two, needing a further 64 to win, with Giffen still at the crease. A benign pitch had already produced 1461 runs, so England were resigned to their fate. Many of their players decided to deal with adversity in the timeless masculine style: by getting hammered.

Peel was one of England's most heroic drinkers* and he imbibed to his own exceptionally high standards that night. He'd had five teeth extracted before the game, so he may have been seeking anaesthetic oblivion. He duly slept the uninterrupted sleep of the truly inebriated and awoke the next morning none the wiser about the overnight storm. Most of the Australian players did not know either. They awoke seeing bright sunshine and assumed all was well. 'It's all right, boys,' chirped the fast bowler Ernie Jones, 'the weather is beautiful!'

The lugubrious Australian captain Jack Blackham knew otherwise and, according to Giffen, had a face 'long as a coffee pot'. Peel could have done with something from a coffee pot, ideally very black and of industrial strength. But the cold shower sobered him up, a bit, and he was true to his slurred word. Once play started Peel got the ball to deviate as if the pitch was corrugated, and took six for 67 as Australia collapsed from 130 for two to 166 all out. His performances in the morning session – and the session the night before – have entered into Ashes lore. Yet England's biggest match winner was the weather. As wickets tumbled, Blackham paced the team balcony, muttering 'cruel luck, cruel luck'.

---

* Three years later he would be ordered from the field by his county captain Lord Hawke – and suspended for the rest of the 1897 season – after turning up drunk for a county match. According to some reports he relieved himself on the pitch.

England's 10-run victory launched cricket's first great Test series. It was only the second five-match rubber, and established the intrinsic superiority of that particular sporting format. England went 2–0 up at Melbourne despite being bowled out for 75 on the first day; a monastic 173 from the captain Stoddart, in which risk was barely considered, never mind taken, helped them to 475 in the second innings, with all eleven players making double figures. Peel did his usual second-innings business, taking four for 77 to seal a 94-run victory. There are unconfirmed reports that he was completely sober at the time.

Australia then came roaring back with two crushing victories by 382 runs and an innings and 147 runs. In the third Test at Adelaide, the debutant Albert Trott made 38 not out and 72 not out, each time

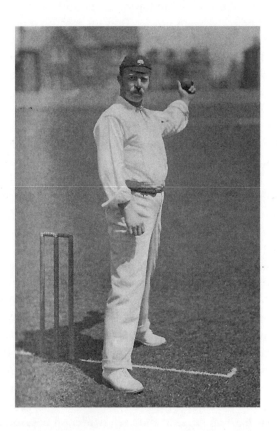

Bobby Peel, England's drunken match-winner in 1894.

batting at No.10, and then shredded England with eight for 43 in the second innings. There have been few more spectacular debuts in any sport. In the next Test at Sydney, Trott's lower-order hitting again shocked England; his 85 not out, and Harry Graham's 105, abracadabraed a score of 41 for six into 284 all out. With conditions worsening dramatically, England lost 17 wickets in three hours of mayhem on the third day: the irrepressible Giffen and the great Charlie Turner, playing his final Test, shared 15 of the 18 wickets to fall.

Australia's comeback meant record crowds for the decider at Melbourne, which was routinely described as the Match of the Century before a ball was bowled. England finally dismissed Albert Trott for 10, but Australia made an imposing 414. Archie MacLaren's sparkling 120 kept England in the game, 29 behind on first innings, and then the tireless seam bowler Tom Richardson took his fourth five-for of the series to dismiss Australia for 267. England needed 297, by some distance the highest fourth-innings target to win a Test, and were in significant trouble at 28 for two when the captain Stoddart was dismissed by the first ball of the fifth day's play.

Yorkshire's Jack Brown, who had had a poor debut series and was usually an opener for his county, came in at No.4 and launched a counter-attack of rare audacity. His 50 came in 28 minutes – the fastest in Test cricket until 2007 – and overall he struck 140 in a partnership of 210 with Albert Ward, who was a textbook straight man and ended with 93. England won by six wickets. The former *Wisden* editor Scyld Berry regards Brown's knock as 'the best individual innings ever played for England against Australia'. The Australian umpire, Thomas Flynn, said: 'I think Brown's batting about the best I have ever seen.'

Peel completed a different kind of Ashes hat-trick: having taken the match-winning wicket in the first two Tests, he hit the winning runs in the decider. It was an epic series, full of extraordinary individual performances. Giffen was the highest run-scorer (475) and wicket-taker (34) on either side, a feat even the most influential Ashes all-rounder, Sir Ian Botham, did not manage. One thing Botham did do was play hard on the field and even harder off it. Just like Bobby Peel at Sydney in 1894.

1896

'Sorry, Doctor, she slipped.'

[AUSTRALIA'S ERNIE JONES
TO W. G. GRACE, 1896]

IT TOOK A LOT TO UNNERVE W. G. GRACE. England's grand old man was now in his late forties and had seen everything, in sport and in life. Or so he thought. Then, in the summer of 1896, the Australian fast bowler Ernie Jones whistled a short ball straight through the doctor's magnificent facial fungus.

Accounts of the incident are sufficiently contradictory that we cannot be sure whether the episode occurred in the opening tour game against Lord Sheffield's XI at Sheffield Park – as seems likeliest – or during the first Test at Lord's later in the summer. Yet the incident is such an entrenched part of Ashes folklore that little distractions like facts barely matter any more. What we can say with reasonable certainty is that Jones bowled a nasty short ball, Grace threw his head back, and the ball took the top edge of the beard on its way through to the keeper. Thousands of batsmen down the years have experienced what the West Indians call 'chin music', but Grace may be the only one to receive some beard music.

There are various reports of Grace's verbal reaction, though all are along the lines of: 'What the blazes is going on, you godforsaken ne'er-do-well?' And everyone is consistent on Jones's immortal response: 'Sorry, Doctor, she slipped.' You could hit Grace about the body – as Jones often did – you could send all three stumps flying or ridicule him – as Charles Kortright did. But to defile his pride and joy was not on. It was tantamount to treason. To induce a false stroke from Grace was hard enough, but Jones went even further by inducing a falsetto. 'I vouch to you,' said C. B. Fry, 'that W. G. did rumble out a falsetto, "What – what – what."'

Thereafter Grace referred to Jones as 'the fellow who bowled through my beard', a unique sobriquet. And everyone agreed it was an extremely hostile spell – buffet bowling, but not in the usual sense. Grace was buffeted so much by Jones that afterwards his body looked like a grotesque piece of art, all black, blue and red blotches.

He and Jones came up against each other many times during the excellent 1896 series, which England won 2–1. The series included one of the first instances of a renowned batsman not walking. In the first Test, the Australian captain Harry Trott stood his ground and was reprieved by the umpire. Catches were usually taken on trust in those days and Tom Hayward was certain he had taken a clean catch. 'No one but a f****** Australian would have stood still,' was the view of one England player.

The series started spectacularly, with Australia bowled out for 53 on the first morning of the series at Lord's. England won by six wickets, with the seam bowler Tom Richardson taking 11 wickets. He added 13 more in the second Test at Old Trafford, though they were at a cost of 244 runs and Australia won by three wickets after making England follow on. 'He stood there like some fine animal baffled at the uselessness of great strength and effort in this world,' wrote Neville Cardus of Richardson after he bowled 42.3 overs without a break in Australia's second innings. Ranjitsinhji made a beautiful 154 not out on debut in that match at Old Trafford, during which he became the first person to hit – or rather stroke, this being Ranji – a hundred runs before lunch in a Test.

> **He stood there like some fine animal baffled at the uselessness of great strength and effort in this world**

The three-match series was decided on a wet pitch at The Oval. The spinners were sufficiently dominant that Richardson, who had taken 24 wickets in the first two Tests, was required to bowl only six overs in the match for England.

Joseph Darling, George Giffen, Clem Hill and Ernie Jones, stars of the Australian team at the turn of the twentieth century.

Hugh Trumble, Australia's brilliant off-spinner, picked up 12 wickets to dismiss England for 145 and 84, and Australia needed just 111 to take the match and the Ashes on the final day. The previous evening, with the weather fine, Grace went into the Australian dressing-room to congratulate them on their imminent series victory. But things changed mysteriously overnight. 'One can well imagine our surprise when we found that there had been a "local rain" of about 22 yards long and six feet wide, just where the wicket was,' said Australia's Joe Darling. The tourists were bowled out for just 44 by Bobby Peel and Jack Hearne.

Darling and Australia took their revenge by coming from behind to trounce England 4–1 in 1897–98. He made three hundreds in the series, one of which, in the third Test at Adelaide, was reached with the first six in Test cricket; in those days you had to hit the ball out of the ground for a maximum. But the best innings was played by the brilliant left-hander Clem Hill at Melbourne. At the age of twenty he made a glorious 188 out of a total of 323; nobody else made more than 64 in the match.

Yet for all the brilliant batting, Australia's victory was as notable for their work in the field, and particularly the flair of Trott's captaincy. Never mind years, he was decades ahead of his time both in field placings and bowling changes, even if no contemporary reports of his captaincy contain the word 'funky'. 'It didn't seem to matter to Mr Trott whom he put on,' said the England captain Andrew Stoddart, 'for each change ended in a wicket.'

Trott could manipulate his batsmen, too. On the 1896 tour he gave the nervous, teetotal batsman Frank Iredale a 'tonic'. It turned out to be brandy and soda. W. G. Grace could had done with something equally stiff the day he went out to face Ernie Jones.

'Put a rope around the bounder's neck and drag him out.'

MONTY NOBLE WAS PUTTING THE TEAM FIRST. He was denying his basic instincts, to hit the ball and score runs, in an attempt to preserve Australia's lead in the series. They were 1–0 up but were being outplayed in the fourth Test and had been forced to follow on, despite Noble's painstaking 60 not out. He played so well in that innings that Australia pushed him up the order and sent him straight back in when they followed on. 'You won't see me back here for some time,' he said to his team-mates as he walked out to bat again. This time he made 89; in total he batted for eight and a half hours in the match. It was like watching consecutive showings of *Das Boot*, only without the occasional levity.

Noble's performance was even more impressive given he had bagged a pair in the previous match. Not that the crowd cared for the considerable worthiness of his endeavours. During Noble's second innings the crowd started humming the 'Dead March'* and, as the dot balls mounted, one exasperated spectator suggested an innovative rope-based tactic that was not technically an option under the Laws of the game. Noble was eventually dismissed, though not in time for England to win the match. After the game he received a leather medal from an anonymous supporter. 'To M. A. Noble, the greatest

---

* This comes from Handel's oratorio *Saul* and was the solemn accompaniment at many a nineteenth- and twentieth- century state funeral.

Victor Trumper, Australia's Golden Age stylist, jumps out to drive.

Australian cricketer,' began the inscription. 'A thousand runs in a thousand years.'

Australia had gone one-up in the series in the second Test at Lord's, thanks to the brilliance of the fearsome Ernie Jones with the ball and Clem Hill and Victor Trumper with the bat. They then proceeded to draw the last three Tests relatively comfortably, even though they followed on in the last two – the first of which brought Noble's vigil.

There were some crowd-pleasing sights: J. T. Hearne took one of the better hat-tricks – Hill, Syd Gregory and Noble – in the third Test, while Trumper, twenty-one, made a divine 135 not out at Lord's in only his second Test. It was the start of a cherished thirteen-year period in which Trumper made six unforgettable Ashes hundreds. Many players have bent the contest to their will, starting with Frederick Spofforth in 1882; Trumper bent it to his skill, regularly exhibiting the most exquisite batsmanship. The worse the wicket, the more skill Trumper demonstrated. He was that rarest of batsmen: the rough-track bully. More than anybody else, Trumper captured the freedom, innocence and sheer batting talent of cricket's Golden Age, and is depicted perfectly in George W. Beldam's iconic photograph of him jumping out to drive at Lord's (see page 26).

'He had no style, and yet he was all style,' said C. B. Fry. 'He had no fixed canonical method of play, he defied all orthodox rules, yet every stroke he played satisfied the ultimate criterion of style – the minimum of effort, the maximum of effect.' During the 1899 tour W. G. Grace appeared in the Australians' dressing-room and demanded a signed bat from Trumper. Grace returned the favour before announcing, 'from today's champion to the champion of tomorrow' and sweeping out of the room.

Grace also swept out of Test cricket, playing his last Test at 50 years and 320 days (see page 15). Only one man has played Test cricket at a more advanced age – Wilfred Rhodes, who was making his debut aged twenty-one in Grace's final match.

The sides did not meet for another two and a half years until 1901–02, when Australia – as in the 1897–98 Ashes – came from behind to win 4–1. The turning point came in the second Test at Melbourne. Twenty-five wickets had fallen on a bizarre first day, but Australia's debutant Reggie Duff, held back to No.10 while batting conditions eased, made a famous century to take Australia out of reach. They squared the series and never looked back. The eventual scoreline was a little flattering. The Aussies chased a then record total of 315 to win the third Test at Adelaide by four wickets, and sneaked home in the last match at Melbourne by 32 runs.

Hill managed to pass 500 runs without making a century; implausibly, he made 99, 98 and 97 in consecutive innings at Adelaide and Melbourne. S. F. Barnes, hand-picked by the England captain Archie MacLaren, took 19 wickets in the first two Tests before injury in the third ended his part in the series. He took 13 of those in the thrilling second Test at Melbourne – a haul matched by Noble, who went on to take 32 wickets in the series, including four five-fors. English crowds did not enjoy watching his batting in 1899; nor did they enjoy reading about his bowling in 1901–02.

1902

'We'll get 'em in singles.'

[GEORGE HIRST TO WILFRED RHODES, FIFTH TEST, THE OVAL, 13 AUGUST 1902]

APOCRYPHAL STORIES AND QUOTES are a rich part of cricket, from Steve Waugh telling Herschelle Gibbs, 'You've just dropped the World Cup, mate,' in 1999 to Ian Botham saying he could 'never look Viv Richards in the eye again' if he toured apartheid South Africa.

The most famous Ashes example comes from the fifth Test at The Oval in 1902. When the last man Wilfred Rhodes joined George Hirst with 15 needed to beat Australia and barely an unbitten nail in the house, Hirst supposedly told Rhodes: 'We'll get 'em in singles.' Hirst later denied saying such a thing, yet the quote is indelibly associated with the end of one of the great Ashes series.

Eighty-three years later, that series even inspired a novel, *Sherlock Holmes at the 1902 Fifth Test*. By the time Rhodes walked to the wicket, the game was not so much afoot as nearly done, and England – despite playing some extremely good cricket – were facing a 3–0 series defeat to a brilliant Australian side.

Hirst and Rhodes had combined at the start of the series, this time with the ball. In the first Test at Edgbaston they shared all 10 wickets as Australia were skittled for 36 – with bad-wicket genius Victor Trumper making surely the best 18 in Test history and Rhodes claiming seven for 17 with his left-arm spin. Paradoxically, the match is remembered more for England's batting; the XI is regarded by many cricket historians as the strongest batting line-up England have ever fielded: Archie MacLaren, C. B. Fry, Ranji, Stanley Jackson,

Johnny Tyldesley, Dick Lilley, Hirst, Gilbert Jessop, Len Braund, Bill Lockwood and Rhodes. All made first-class centuries, and the No.11 Rhodes later became a successful Test opener.

England were denied victory in that first Test by the weather, and only 105 minutes' play were possible in the second because of rain. Australia triumphed by 143 runs in the only Test played at Sheffield's Bramall Lane, where Clem Hill made a fine 119 and Monty Noble picked up 11 wickets. England, who had to win the fourth Test at Old Trafford to maintain a chance of regaining the Ashes, made a series of changes that ranged somewhere between unfathomable and unpardonable. They omitted the stellar quartet of Sydney Barnes, Fry, Hirst and Jessop; not for the last time in an Ashes series, 'play to your weaknesses' seemed to be the England selectors' philosophy.

The captain MacLaren, whose relations with the chairman of selectors Lord Hawke were frosty at best, was not entirely enamoured. 'My god, look what they've sent me!' he said. 'Do they think we're playing the blind asylum?' Jessop later said that 'It was in the Selection Room that the Rubber was lost.'

One of the call-ups was the accurate medium-pacer Fred Tate. He was having a brilliant season for Sussex, and England thought he would excel on a wet pitch. It was a horses-for-courses selection that went

My god, look what they've sent me! Do they think we're playing the blind asylum?

horribly wrong. It did not help that Tate's call-up came so late that he couldn't find a hotel vacancy. He had to sleep in an attic and, whether because of nerves, moths or both, had around half an hour's sleep the night before his Test debut.

It is every boy's dream to make headlines in his first Test match. Tate did just that, but not quite as he would have wished. He was underbowled by MacLaren, with the pitch drying out, although that was probably a mercy on the first morning when Trumper struck a stunning century before lunch. Tate bowled only 16 out of 123 overs in the match and took just a couple of wickets. But he made an unwelcome impact with the bat and in the field.

In the second innings, fielding out of position, he dropped the Australian captain Joe Darling, who went on to make a crucial 37 in a total of 86. England needed 124 to win, and looked comfortable when they reached 36 for none at lunch. 'You old dogs, we've got you this time,' said MacLaren to the Australian team during the interval. Clem Hill later wrote that MacLaren's words were 'in the spirit of banter' – chilling confirmation that the B-word is not a new phenomenon – though there is no doubt England thought they would win. So did everyone else.

You old dogs, we've got you this time

The match bore marked similarities to the Test that started the Ashes, at The Oval in 1882, with England slowly collapsing to Jack Saunders and the inevitable Hugh Trumble. The crucial moment came when Hill took a miraculous catch. Lilley smacked Trumble towards deep midwicket, where Hill ran twenty-five yards and dived with 'not the slightest intention of bringing off a catch'. He merely wanted to stop the boundary, but the ball stuck in his hand. 'Oh, Clem, what a bally fluke!' said Lilley. 'Never on your life, Dick!' responded Hill, presumably in the spirit of banter.

England needed the last pair of Rhodes and Tate to score eight to win the match. A rain delay meant that Tate, the last man, had thirty minutes to consider the unique torture he was about to endure. He was not the only one struggling to cope. The wife of Major Wardill, sitting with Trumble's wife, was doing crochet work and stabbed a needle through the palm of her hand by accident.

Tate hit one four, and then Saunders sent his leg stump flying. Australia had retained the Ashes with a game to spare. 'Never have I witnessed such scenes of ecstasy,' said Hill. The wicketkeeper James Kelly was so delirious afterwards that he ran round the dressing-room accusing his team-mates of stealing his wicketkeeping gloves, even though they were still on his hands.

Poor Fred Tate never played for England again. History has recorded him as the definitive one-cap blunder. All the great work he did in his first-class career – 320 games, 1331 wickets at 21.55 – has been forgotten, because all anybody remembers is 'Tate's Match'; 'one of the great tragedies of the game', according to John Arlott. It is not just the kind of thing that you take to the grave; it's the kind of thing that takes *you* to the grave.

'Never mind,' Tate said to his team-mate Braund afterwards, desperately searching for consolation, 'I've got a little kid at home who will make up for it for me' (see page 53). Tate was omitted from the final Test, when Hirst and Rhodes inched England over the line despite another 12 wickets from Trumble and a first-innings deficit of 141. Hirst and Rhodes did not quite 'get 'em in singles'. But the disputed quotation does faithfully reflect the approach decided upon by the two Yorkshiremen in a mid-pitch conference. They would eschew risk and patiently drip-drip-drip their way to victory: thus there was a nudge here and a push there, but also a two after an overthrow, and even an edged boundary.

England's win did not change the result of the series, which Australia took 2–1. But any victory was precious. If the fourth Test became forever 'Tate's Match' for all the wrong reasons, the fifth became synonymous with the swashbuckling feats of a very different cricketer. That Hirst and Rhodes even had the opportunity to take England to victory with their famous last-wicket partnership was because of one of the great Ashes innings...

1902

'The human catapult who wrecks the roofs of distant towns when set in his assault.'

[RALPH DELAHAYE PAINE, 1897, ON GILBERT JESSOP, ENGLAND'S BATTING HERO AT THE OVAL IN 1902]

THE GREAT CRICKET WRITER NEVILLE CARDUS vividly recalled the moment he realised the full extent of Gilbert Jessop's batting talent. Cardus was in the refreshment room at Old Trafford, standing on tiptoe to pay for a lemonade, when there was an almighty clatter. He thought the apocalypse had come. 'It's all reight, sonny,' said a man next to him. 'It's only Jessop just coom into bat.'

Jessop, of Cambridge University, Gloucestershire and England, was a twenty-first-century cricketer who made his Test debut at the end of the nineteenth century. His ability to hit the ball into a different postcode – not to mention his brilliant fielding and stump-busting bowling – would have made him a superstar in the age of the IPL and the Big Bash.

Jessop, who was known as 'the Croucher' because of his unusual batting stance, played his defining innings at The Oval in 1902, the match also remembered for George Hirst and Wilfred Rhodes not getting 'em in singles (see page 28). Without Jessop, they would have had to get 'em in fistfuls. England were already 2–0 down going into the final Test, and were given approximately 0.00 per cent chance of chasing 263 on a spiteful wicket on the final day. The night before, Jessop decided to use self-deprecation as a means of raising morale; he cheerily boasted that he would make at least 50 the following day

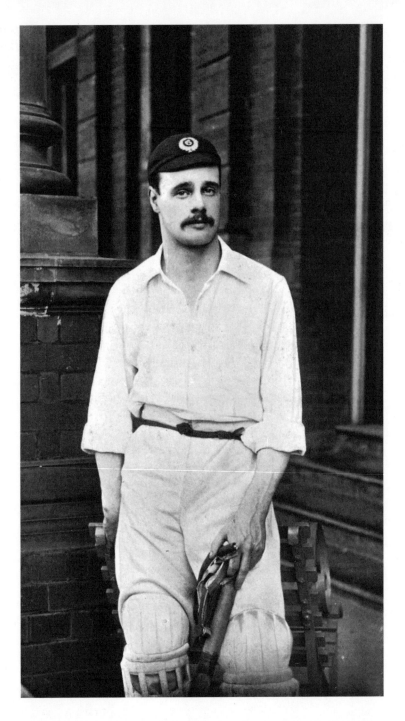

Gilbert Jessop, who smashed England to victory at The Oval in 1902.

and took bets to the contrary. His team-mates thought they were buying money.

Jessop came in at No.7, with England wobbling at 48 for five, and smashed 104 from 80 balls in 77 minutes. The fast bowlers were lofted into the pavilion on three occasions. Such hitting is familiar these days but in 1902, before Sir Ian Botham, Adam Gilchrist and Chris Gayle, it was unimaginable. 'All things considered,' said *Wisden*, which tended to consider more things than most, 'a more astonishing display has never been seen.' The great Australian bowler Hugh Trumble said, 'the only man living who could beat us, beat us.' It made an even greater mockery of the decision to omit Jessop for the previous Test.

The only man living who could beat us, beat us

Jessop was no blacksmith but an authentic batsman who simply hit the ball farther and more cleanly than anyone else. Cardus said that to call Jessop a slogger was 'libel'. The Australian Sammy Woods called him 'the most dangerous batsman the world will ever see', although it should be noted that Woods passed away before the heyday of Chris Tavaré (see page 207).

During a tour of Philadelphia in the late 1890s, the local author Ralph Delahaye Paine wrote a poem about the England team which included a tribute to Jessop:

> At one end stocky Jessop frowned,
> The human catapult,
> Who wrecks the roofs of distant towns
> When set in his assault.

Jessop put bums on seats, and then took them off those seats in excited anticipation of what might happen, or to avoid a potentially lethal leather missile heading their way. Even those buying a lemonade in the bars weren't safe. Mind the windows, Gilbert.

1903–04

'Have you got your coffin ready, Crockett?'

[AUSTRALIAN FAN TO UMPIRE
BOB CROCKETT, FIRST TEST, SYDNEY,
15 DECEMBER 1903]

IT WAS SHAPING UP TO BE ONE of the great comebacks. Australia, who trailed by 292 on first innings in the first Test against England at Sydney, had batted beautifully to reach 250 for three in their second innings. Clem Hill and Victor Trumper had looked largely untroubled in adding 59 for the fourth wicket, and Trumper had already taken 16 from the first five balls of the leg-spinner Len Braund's over.

The sixth was driven past mid-off, and the batsmen had time to come back for a fourth as George Hirst wheezed after the ball. Hirst's throw came in to the bowler Braund, who shied at the stumps and missed. The batsmen turned for a fifth, but Hill had overrun in going for the fourth and had to cover a lot of ground to reach the striker's end. The wicketkeeper Dick Lilley took Albert Relf's excellent throw and broke the stumps, and the umpire Bob Crockett gave Hill out. For possibly the only time in an Ashes Test, there were four runs and a wicket off the same ball.

Although Hill did not demonstrate any obvious dissent, you did not need to be a body language expert to discern his interpretation of the decision. The Sydney crowd generously decided to voice his dissent for him. The fact Crockett was from Melbourne didn't help. In this case, Crockett's Theme was an extended chorus of boos and abuse. The coffin is a part of cricket, in which players keep their bats and kit, but here the word took on a different meaning; the suggestion that

Crockett might have been wise to get his affairs in order before the match was soon followed by allegations of corruption: 'How much did you pay Crockett, Warner?'

That last barb was directed at 'Plum' Warner, the England captain, who discussed the situation with the new batsman, his opposite number Monty Noble. The two captains pitched their bottoms on a good length and waited for the crowd's ardour to cool.

From 112 years' distance, such an incident seems almost quaint and light-hearted. It was anything but at the time. Warner said that even Hirst and Wilfred Rhodes, the kind of men who dark alleyways were scared to have walk down them, were unnerved. In his book of the tour, *How We Recovered the Ashes*, Warner even imagined a scenario in which the War Minister would be called to send troops. 'International match now on. Crowd on hill armed to the teeth with umbrellas, bottles, melon skins and rude language, advancing determinedly on wicket. Three policemen and groundsman's dog doing good work. Umpires Crockett and Argall retreating to the mountains.'

How much did you pay Crockett, Warner?

It was enough to make a man say his prayers. But then Warner was doing that anyway. During the voyage to Australia he had asked a bishop whether it was wrong to pray to beat the Australians. 'My dear Warner,' came the reply, 'anything that tends to the prestige of England is worth praying for.' Warner's response was swift: 'I'll pray every night and morning and on the field.'

England dominated that first Test from the moment the Worcestershire all-rounder Ted Arnold dismissed Trumper with his first ball in Test cricket. Reginald 'Tip' Foster, still the only man to captain England at both football and cricket, struck a mighty 287 on his debut, a record that stands to this day. 'I have seldom seen greater contrast in a batsman,' said Hill. 'His batting for the first 80 was about the worst exhibition imaginable. . . Next day he was a different man.' After Hill's controversial run-out, Trumper compiled a sublime 185 not out, but England overcame a scare to reach their target of 194 for the loss of five wickets.

The second Test was all about the wiles of Wilfred Rhodes, who brought England victory with remarkable match figures of 15 for 124. He also had eight catches dropped. 'Please, Wilfred, give me a minute's rest,' pleaded Trumper as Rhodes landed yet another ball on a postage stamp. In a low-scoring game, there were two stunning innings: 74 out of 122 from Trumper and 62 out of 103 from Lancashire's Johnny Tyldesley. But this was undeniably Rhodes' match.

Rhodes was part of a legendary line of Yorkshire left-arm spinners – Ted Peate, Bobby Peel, Rhodes and Hedley Verity – who served England over a sixty-year period. 'Ulysses

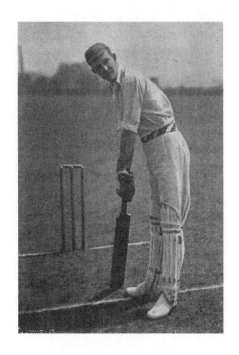

The young 'Plum' Warner, England captain on the 1903–04 tour, takes guard.

earned a world-wide reputation for his cunning,' said Warner, 'and Rhodes is the Ulysses of modern cricket.' Rhodes, like so many of the great spinners, was a master at torturing batsmen with demons that did not exist. 'If the batsman thinks it's spinnin', it's spinnin',' he would say.

Another century from Trumper helped Australia to a big victory in the third Test, but England regained the Ashes with victory in the fourth Test at Sydney. Crockett was again involved in controversy. He took the players off for around eighty minutes because of drizzle. This time, discontent manifested itself in the age-old practice of bottle-throwing, with the cycle track around the outfield made to resemble Stevenage High Street at 2am on a Sunday morning.

The match was settled when Bernard Bosanquet, the inventor of the googly, cleaned Australia up with six wickets in an hour. To say Bosanquet was erratic was an understatement; sometimes his googly bounced four times. 'He is the worst length bowler in England and yet he is the only bowler the Australians fear,' said one Australian newspaper. But his googly, which he developed while playing a tabletop game called Twisti-Twosti, was deliciously deceptive at a time when cricket was a game of almost unstinting orthodoxy – so much so that there were many calls for it to be banned. 'It is not unfair,' Bosanquet said, 'only immoral.'

Australia gained a consolation victory at Melbourne, where England were routed for 61 and 101 on a rain-affected strip. Tibby 'Terror' Cotter, a teenage fast bowler, took eight for 65 in the match, while Hugh Trumble took seven for 28 in the second innings – including his second Test hat-trick. It was his final first-class match.

The sides met again in England in the summer of 1905. Australia never quite recovered from one devastating over in the first Test at Trent Bridge. Australia were 129 for one in reply to England's 196 when the England captain Stanley Jackson dismissed the star trio of Hill, Noble and Joe Darling in the space of six deliveries. England went on to win the match, thanks to Bosanquet's eight for 107 in the second innings, and controlled the series until an innings victory in the fourth Test at Manchester gave them an unassailable 2–0 lead. 'We all admired and liked the Australians of those days,' said C. B. Fry, who scored his only Ashes century in the final Test at The Oval. 'But, by Jove, we did like beating them!'

> **We all admired and liked the Australians. But, by Jove, we did like beating them!**

The series was a triumph for Jackson. He topped the batting and bowling averages, with 70 and 15 respectively. He even won all five tosses. The Australian captain Darling was so frustrated that, for the end-of-tour fixture at Scarborough, he challenged Jackson to a wrestling match for the choice of innings. Jackson declined, won the toss again and scored a century. It was a microcosm of the summer.

1907–08 to 1911–12

'The sound of his bat somehow puts me in mind of vintage port.'

[ENGLISH AUTHOR A. A. MILNE ON JACK HOBBS'S PRE-WAR POMP]

THERE HAS NEVER BEEN A BETTER English batsman than Jack Hobbs. His nickname – The Master – said it all. A first-class average of 50.70, good though it is, is a damned lie. Hobbs was famously uninterested in his average and, in county games in particular, would often give his wicket away upon reaching a century so that somebody else could have a knock. 'Cricket would be a better game,' he said, 'if the papers didn't publish the averages.' Hobbs was the personification of modest excellence. 'A snick by Jack Hobbs,' wrote Neville Cardus, 'is a sort of disturbance of cosmic orderliness.'

He first played for England during the 1907–08 Ashes, which Australia won 4–1. He was not selected for the thrilling first Test, when Australia re-

> **A snick by Jack Hobbs, is a sort of disturbance of cosmic orderliness**

covered from 124 for six to chase 274 and win by two wickets. The England debutant George Gunn, who was not part of the original touring party but was called up at the last minute, batted beautifully for 119 and 74.

Hobbs's debut came in the second Test, which was even closer. It would have been Test cricket's first tie had Gerry Hazlitt kept his nerve. With Arthur 'Pip' Fielder dawdling over a run, Hazlitt could have thrown the ball to the keeper but instead whistled a throw wide of the stumps. It allowed Fielder and Sydney Barnes to complete the run that brought England victory after an unbroken last-wicket stand of 39. As *Wisden* later observed, the failure of a fielder to run out A. Fielder had given England a famous victory.

An even more extraordinary partnership decided the pivotal third Test at Adelaide. Australia were 180 for seven in their second innings, just 102 ahead, when a flu-stricken Clem Hill walked out at No.9 to join Roger Hartigan. The pair added 243 for the eighth wicket, with Hartigan making a century on debut and Hill hitting 160.

Up to that point the series had been spandex-tight; thereafter it was the baggiest green, despite Hobbs's astonishing 57 out of a total of 105 on a Melbourne sticky in the fourth Test. Gunn was the highest run-scorer in his debut series, just ahead of Australia's Warwick Armstrong, who finally struck his first Ashes century in his twenty-first Test against England.

Australia came from behind to retain the Ashes with a 2–1 victory in England in 1909, a series in which an increasingly desperate home side used twenty-five players. George Hirst and Colin Blythe,* the left-armers, shared all 20 wickets in England's victory in the first Test at Edgbaston, when 30 wickets fell for 346 before the opening pair of Hobbs and C. B. Fry knocked off a target of 105 on their own. The first of many Australian Test wins at Lord's in the twentieth century squared the series, after Armstrong took six for 35 in the second innings with his leg spin.

In the next Test, at Headingley, Armstrong was involved in an altercation with Hobbs, an early indication of the hard-nosed approach he would favour as captain after the First World War (see pages 46–49). With England 60 for two, chasing 214 to go 2–1 up in the series, Hobbs played a stroke to leg, set off for a run and slipped, thus dislodging the bails. He appealed that he had finished his stroke when he broke the stumps, and therefore was not out. The umpire concurred; Australia did not. Hobbs said Armstrong 'was, in my opinion, unduly argumentative', which given Hobbs's gentle nature

---

* The violin-playing Blythe would be killed by shellfire near Passchendaele in November 1917.

was the equivalent of an expletive-laden assault from most people. Hobbs was so unsettled by the rancour that two balls later he offered no stroke to a straight one and was bowled. After his dismissal, England collapsed to the pace of 'Tibby' Cotter* and the underused left-arm spin of Charles Macartney and were all out for 87.

The last two matches were drawn. Frank Laver, Australia's thirty-nine-year-old player-manager, took eight for 31 in the fourth Test at Manchester; at The Oval, Monty Noble repeated Stanley Jackson's feat of 1905 by winning a fifth consecutive toss and the stylish Australian opener Warren Bardsley became the first man to score a hundred in each innings of a Test.

Hobbs did not quite match Bardsley's feat during the next series in 1911–12, though he was the star of England's 4–1 victory. At the start of the tour, such a result was unforeseeable. When England arrived at Fremantle, Hobbs recalls 'the local urchins jeering, advising us to go home, and telling us that we didn't have a dog's chance. "Trumper is scoring hundreds," they shouted. "Armstrong is knocking them out of the ground; Cotter is doing the hat-trick every match."'

He got 'em on good-uns, he got 'em on bad-uns, he got 'em on sticky-uns, he got 'em all over the world

Hobbs performed a hat-trick of his own, with three centuries in consecutive Tests. He scored 662 runs, more than twice as many as any Australian. With the series at 2–1 and two to play, Hobbs and Wilfred Rhodes added 323 for the first wicket at Melbourne, achieving the ostensibly impossible feat of putting their foot on Australia's throat while grinding their nose into the dirt.

Rhodes liked Melbourne; this was the ground on which he had taken 15 wickets a decade earlier. He also liked his opening partner Hobbs. 'He got 'em on good-uns, he got 'em on bad-uns, he got 'em on sticky-uns, he got 'em all over the world.'

---

* Cotter, who took 89 wickets in 21 Tests, was shot dead in 1917 by a Turkish sniper at Beersheba, in Palestine, while serving with the 4th Light Horse Brigade during the First World War.

1911–12

'If we go down, at least we'll take that bugger Barnes down with us.'

[ENGLAND CAPTAIN ARCHIE MACLAREN ON SYDNEY BARNES, HERO OF THE 1911–12 ASHES SERIES]

ARCHIE MACLAREN REALISED THAT EVEN death had a silver lining. The England captain was on board the steamship *Omrah* with his team, en route to Australia for the 1901–02 tour, when they were hit by severe storms. As a number of players started to panic, MacLaren decided to console them with the thought that, if they were going to meet their maker, then so would their increasingly unpopular team-mate Sydney Barnes. This was the same Barnes who MacLaren had handpicked for their tour of Australia, even though he had played only one first-class match for Lancashire in the 1901 season. Their relationship rapidly deteriorated.

Barnes, of Warwickshire, Lancashire, Staffordshire and England, was the archetype of the awkward genius. Neville Cardus wrote that 'A chill wind of antagonism blew from him on the sunniest day.' His skill, accuracy and tirelessness made him a captain's dream when he had the ball in his hand. But at the same time he was a captain's nightmare. 'There's only one captain when I'm bowling, and that's me,' he regularly said.

When England toured Australia a decade later, in 1911–12, the actual captain was Johnny Douglas. His relationship with Barnes made MacLaren's seem like a bromance by comparison. Douglas had taken over from 'Plum' Warner when the latter succumbed to illness after the first tour match. Douglas was a middleweight boxer who won gold at the 1908 Olympics, and was far more comfortable in a boxing ring than addressing a room full of dignitaries. That was one of the requirements of the captain, however, and a reception at the Town Hall in Melbourne awaited Douglas's wisdom when England arrived. 'I hate speeches,' he said. 'As Bob Fitzsimmons once said, "I ain't no bloomin' orator, but I'll fight any man in this blinkin' country."'

There were times when it seemed Barnes might test Douglas's promise – especially when Douglas absurdly gave himself the new ball ahead of Barnes in the first Test at Sydney. It was not so much a case of putting the cart before the horse as putting the carthorse before the thoroughbred. Australia won the match by 146 runs, largely thanks to 12 wickets from 'Ranji' Hordern, first in a long and glittering line of Aussie leg-spinners.

Douglas was not in Barnes's league as a bowler. He was an early example of the 'bits and pieces cricketer': he batted a bit, he bowled a bit, he boxed a bit. But only the boxing came naturally. Douglas, whose initials were J. W. H. T., was dubbed 'Johnny Won't Hit Today' by Australian hecklers after a particularly ambient innings in a tour match at Victoria. The name stuck throughout his career.

When Barnes was given the ball in the second Test, he produced a legendary spell of medium-paced spin on the first morning, dismissing the gilded quartet of Charlie Kelleway, Warren Bardsley, Clem Hill and Warwick Armstrong at a personal cost of only one run. Australia were 11 for four, and then 38 for six. At that stage Barnes had figures of 11-7-6-5. 'This was on a perfect wicket,' wrote Jack Hobbs, 'and I look back on it as the finest bowling that I have ever witnessed.' It was even more impressive because Barnes had been unwell the night before the game; upon hearing this, the Australian batsman Syd Gregory, who was absent from the side, visited Barnes with a medicinal bottle of whisky.

The Hyde side of Barnes was seen later in the innings. During an irritating tail-end partnership between Hordern and Sammy Carter he set a different field for each batsman, an unusual and relatively time-consuming tactic. This was too much for the Australian crowd, who shouted 'Get on with the game!' Barnes – 'evidently strung up to concert pitch', said Hordern – threw the ball down, folded his arms and attempted to stare out the crowd. Even the granite-willed Barnes could not win that one. When he finally came in to bowl, the booing got even worse, to the point where Hordern pulled away and sat on his bat until the crowd calmed down.

England eventually won the match by eight wickets, with Jack Hobbs's 126 not out making light work of a tricky target of 219. Fifteen of the 20 wickets were taken by Barnes and the brilliant left-arm fast bowler Frank Foster, who were sharing the new ball in a Test for the first time. They formed a short-lived but devastating pace-bowling partnership, and shared 14 wickets in each of the next two Tests as well. England went 2–1 up with a seven-wicket win at Adelaide, though there was considerable honour in defeat for Australia. After trailing by 368 on first innings, they fought their way to 476 despite injuries forcing their batsmen Vernon Ransford and Victor Trumper to bat at No.8 and No.11 respectively.

England's series-clinching win at Melbourne three weeks later brooked no argument. They thrashed Australia by an innings, with Hobbs (178) and Rhodes (179) adding their famous 323 for the first wicket. A delightful hundred from Frank Woolley, the silky Kent left-hander, was decisive in the final match at Sydney. Barnes and Foster rounded off an outstanding series' work – 34 wickets for Barnes, 32 for Foster – by taking four apiece in the final innings. Foster added 226 middle-order runs in the series as well.

You've been asking for a punch all night and I'll give you one

Australia were well beaten. Following the third Test, the captain Hill had a brawl with a selector, Peter McAlister, although he was at least polite enough to keep McAlister abreast of imminent developments. 'You've been asking for a punch all night and I'll give you one,' said Hill before landing his first blow. He had to be restrained from throwing McAlister – who had described him as 'the worst captain in living memory' – out of a third-floor window. Hill kept his place as captain for the last two Tests, but this was to be his last series as an Australian player.

In truth there was no shame in being beaten by one of England's finest touring sides – especially as Australia had encountered Barnes at his unplayable best. He was the kind of bowler that has long since become extinct: the brisk medium-pacer who spun the ball. Anyone who suggested Barnes was a cutter rather than a spinner would be swiftly corrected, though not before they had received a murderous look.

Barnes's international statistics are extraordinary: he took 189 wickets at an average of 16.43, with 24 five-fors and seven ten-fors in just 27 Tests. Overall – including club cricket for Staffordshire – he picked up 6229 wickets at an average of 8.33. Even in 2015, there are many who will swear he was the greatest bowler of all time.

Sydney Barnes, England's bolshie bowling hero of 1911–12.

Plenty of his contemporaries certainly thought so. Foster said that 'Sydney Barnes from Staffordshire was the greatest bowler on all wickets this world has ever seen.'

He did not know it at the time but Barnes, then aged thirty-eight, would never play another Ashes Test. He appeared against Australia in the 1912 Triangular Tournament, a one-off experiment involving South Africa that was badly affected by the weather. England won the tournament after beating an under-strength Australia by 244 runs in what was effectively a final at The Oval. The outbreak of the First World War, which stopped all first-class cricket, meant that the two sides would not meet again for eight years. When Ashes hostilities resumed, another confrontational bugger would hold sway.

1921

'Please sir, you're the only decent bit of shade in the place.'

[A SMALL BOY MAKES A REQUEST OF THE VERY LARGE AUSTRALIAN CAPTAIN WARWICK ARMSTRONG, COUNTY GROUND, SOUTHAMPTON, 15 JUNE 1921]

IT WAS THE KIND OF THE SUMMER'S DAY when the skin burns in minutes rather than hours. The Australian captain Warwick Armstrong was walking round the County Ground at Southampton, enjoying an impromptu batting masterclass from Warren Bardsley and Charles Macartney in a tour match against Hampshire. Armstrong was due to bat later, and would help Australia score 569 runs on that particular day. As he continued his stroll he realised a small boy was following quietly in his wake. Armstrong, assuming the youngster was too shy to request an autograph, brusquely instructed the boy to produce his autograph book. 'I ain't got one,' he said. An impatient Armstrong asked him what he wanted, at which the boy explained that he was looking for a bit of relief from the sun.

Armstrong was a whole lot of shade. He was known as 'The Big Ship', and reports have him weighing in at, variously, 20, 21 or 22 stone. It's rather like quibbling over whether Danny Devito is 4 feet 11 inches or 5 feet. Whatever size he was, he had an aura to match, and the jokes about him throwing his weight around wrote themselves. His physical presence accentuated the impact of an already formidable character, and he was the dominant figure when the Ashes resumed after the First World War.

The MCC had turned down an invitation to tour Australia in 1919–20, fearing English cricket was not up to its pre-war standard.

It became apparent why they had done so when they reluctantly toured a year later under the captaincy of J. W. H. T. Douglas. The bowling, in particular, was on the inadequate side of hopeless. The new-ball pair in the first Test, Bill Hitch and Abe Waddington, took one for 165 in the match and were barely seen again. Hitch and Waddington sounded more like a firm of accountants than a crack bowling attack. Douglas ended up taking the new ball for most of the series.

When Armstrong set England 659 to win that first Test at Sydney, having put the game beyond them with a punishing 158 in the second innings, an appropriately merciless tone had been set. England fell embarrassingly short, losing by 377 runs, and Australia's superiority was established. Armstrong made three centuries in the series and even the fast bowler Jack Gregory hammered a hundred from No.9. That was part of a spectacular all-round performance in the second Test at Melbourne. Gregory followed his century by taking seven for 69 in the first innings. It was his debut series, yet he made an instant case for being the world's best fast bowler and ended with 23 wickets.

As the series developed, so Australia contracted Ashes fever. It is said that during the run-laden third Test at Adelaide, a wedding was interrupted so that a piece of paper could be handed round detailing Australia's recovery from a first-innings deficit. There was, of course, nothing particularly romantic about Armstrong's approach. His tough side overwhelmed England, winning four of the five Tests by thumping margins. Their principal weapon was Arthur Mailey, who was the perfect model of a leg-spinner: eccentric, whip-smart, a man who bowled with only wickets in mind.

Mailey took 36 wickets in his debut series, including nine for 121 in the second innings of the fourth Test – still the best figures by an Australian in an Ashes Test – and 10 for 302 in the match. The fact that he conceded so many runs to go with the wickets is a perfect reflection of his modus operandi. Mailey cared for economy about as much as Kim Kardashian. 'If I bowl a maiden over,' he said, 'it's not my fault but the batsman's.' Mailey, a whimsical and engaging character, went on to become a brilliant writer before opening a meat business. He placed a placard above his shop: 'Arthur Mailey – used to bowl tripe; used to write tripe; now he sells tripe.'

Warwick Armstrong and Johnny Douglas, Trent Bridge, 1921.

He was particularly successful against the England captain Johnny Douglas. On the way to Australia, Douglas told the all-rounder Percy Fender: 'You know, Fender, there is no man in England whose bowling I would rather bat against than yours; and there is no batsman in England I would rather bowl against either.' It turned out there was no batsman in England that Mailey would rather bowl against than Douglas; he dismissed him six times in ten innings.

Douglas did manage to be England's second-highest run scorer in the series, and was some way from being its most hapless performer. That honour was shared by the Australian batsman Roy Park and his wife. Park made a golden duck in the second Test at Melbourne in what turned out to be his only Test innings. Park, a doctor by trade, was said to have been up all night dealing with patients' calls. Legend has it that his wife dropped her knitting a split-second before he faced his only ball, and thus missed her husband's entire Test career as she bent down to pick it up.

The story was a footnote in a tale of almost unrelenting Australian superiority. They completed the only Ashes whitewash of the twentieth century with a nine-wicket win in the fifth Test at Sydney, where Macartney smashed a memorable 170.

There were few consolations for England. Hobbs, who turned thirty-nine during the series, stood alone on the burning deck. Only Herbie Collins scored more than Hobbs' 505 runs, and only Armstrong exceeded his two centuries in the five matches. At the age of forty-one, Armstrong made as many hundreds in the 1920–21 series as he did in his other forty-five Tests

The bat in his hand is like a hammer in the grip of a Vulcan

combined. 'Australian cricket is incarnate in him when he walks from the pavilion, bat in hand,' said Neville Cardus. 'Consider the huge man's bulk as, crouching a little, he faces the bowler. He is all vigilance, suspicion and determination. The bat in his hand is like a hammer in the grip of a Vulcan.'

His influence was such that comparisons with W. G. Grace were undeniable. Armstrong established a tradition of Australian captains doing whatever necessary to stuff the Poms, later enthusiastically embraced by Ian Chappell, Allan Border and even Michael Clarke. His *Wisden* obituary said he 'bore himself in a way likely to cause offence, but he invariably carried his desires over all opposition and sometimes with good reason'. And in 1921 in particular, he cast quite a shadow over English cricket.

1921

'With that single over, Gregory destroyed the morale of English cricket for the best part of a season.'

[RONALD MASON ON FAST BOWLER JACK GREGORY, FIRST TEST, TRENT BRIDGE, 28 MAY 1921]

THERE IS NOTHING LIKE THE FIRST MORNING of a new Ashes series. A time when it's acceptable – compulsory, even – to ignore logic and embrace optimism. England had lost 5–0 in Australia a few months earlier, but now they were on home soil and the canvas was blank. Hope sprung. . . for about half an hour. Then Jack Gregory, Australia's mean, magnificent fast bowler, produced a triple-wicket maiden that included the top-order wickets of Donald Knight, Ernest Tyldesley and Patsy Hendren, whose off stump was sent flying by a jaffa. The tone was set, and it was made of cement.

Australia's 5–0 whitewash in 1920–21 had been the first part of back-to-back Ashes series. The teams travelled on the boat together to England; the journey included entertainment from a jazz band conducted by Percy Fender and a fancy-dress ball at which Charlie Macartney came as a young lady and Hendren as Tarzan.

Gregory was used to getting in character on the field as well as off. He was an early example of white-line fever – ferocious on the field, gentle and shy to the point of reclusiveness off it. The cricket historian David Frith described him as 'a cricketing Garbo'. In that first Test at Trent Bridge, the crowd raged against his short-pitched bowling in both innings. Insult has rarely been so emphatically added to injury as when Tyldesley was smacked in the face by a ball that then deflected onto the stumps.

Gregory and his new-ball partner Ted McDonald took eight wickets apiece as England were skittled for 112 and 147 to lose by 10 wickets. Their batting – without the injured Jack Hobbs – only started to recover during the fourth Test, by which time it was far too late.

Warwick Armstrong's side won the first three Tests of the series, making it eight consecutive Ashes wins in less than seven months. England used a record 30 players in the 1921 series, including 16 debutants – taking the total of new caps to 25 in eight months – as they tried desperately to find an answer to Australia's superiority. Others were recalled for the first time since the war. Lionel Tennyson was relaxing at the Embassy Club on Old Bond Street in the early hours of 11 June when he received a telegram telling him he was needed for the second Test at Lord's later that day. By the third Test he was captain.

England were merely rearranging the deckchairs on the *Titanic*; Macartney, Australia's unorthodox batting genius, followed an amazing four-hour 345 against Nottinghamshire with 115 on the first day of the Test, setting up another big victory. Tennyson split his hand in the field during Macartney's innings and made brave scores of 63 and 36 batting down the order.

His side finally dominated a match at Old Trafford, though rain ended any hope of victory. The new captain Tennyson was the grandson of the former Poet

Hey, Tennyson, read him some of thy grandad's poems!

Laureate Alfred. As Australia's Herbie Collins meticulously constructed a five-hour 40 in a successful attempt to save the match, an increasingly exasperated spectator shouted: 'Hey, Tennyson, read him some of thy grandad's poems!' There was an instant response from Cec Parkin, the Lancashire off-spinner: 'He has done. The beggar's been asleep for hours!'

Tennyson might have been better reading the Laws of the game. Earlier in the match he attempted to make an illegal declaration late on the second day, which led to twenty-five minutes' play being lost. In the confusion, Armstrong bowled back-to-back overs from different ends. Australia drew comfortably regardless, thanks mainly to Collins infusing his bat with rigor mortis.

The series was petering out, Australia's work already done. The final Test at The Oval was such a bore that Armstrong started reading a newspaper in the outfield. For a side who had won back-to-back Ashes series 8–0, Australia did not appear to be particularly enamoured with cricket during that final Test. 'You fellows should never have played cricket if you hate it so much!' shouted the opener 'Ernie' Mayne, a member of the touring party who did not get to play a Test. 'If I were Sid Smith [the team manager], I'd bundle you moaning cows off home straight away.' It wasn't quite Tennyson, but he still made his point pretty clearly.

THE AUSTRALIAN TEAM, 1921.
Top row W. Bardsley, J. Ryder, H. L. Hendry, J. M. Gregory, E. R. Mayne, T. J. E. Andrews, S. Smith, (Manager)
2nd A. Mailey, E. A. McDonald, H. L. Collins, W. W. Armstrong (Captain), C. G. Macartney, H. Carter, J. M. Tayl
Bottom row C. E. Pellew, W. A. Oldfield.

The all-conquering Australian tourists of 1921. Jack Gregory is standing behind captain Warwick Armstrong in the back row. Ted McDonald, Gregory's fast-bowling partner-in-crime, is second from the left in the middle row, with leg-spinner Arthur Mailey to his right.

1924–25

'Never mind. I've got a little kid at home who will make up for it for me.'

ON THE FACE OF IT, ENGLAND'S TRIP to Australia in 1924–25 was little more than a continuation of their 8–0 defeat in the back-to-back Ashes of 1920–21. They were beaten 4–1 by an Australian side that had lost little power despite the retirement of their captain Warwick Armstrong. Yet there was considerable honour in heavy defeat, particularly for Jack Hobbs, Herbert Sutcliffe and Maurice Tate, and a glimpse of happier times ahead. 'There is no gainsaying the fact that a strong belief is widely entertained that the dark days are coming to an end,' said *Wisden*.

Sutcliffe, the Yorkshire opener, made 734 runs with four centuries, including three in a row. Hobbs also played beautifully – he and Sutcliffe batted all day in the second Test at Melbourne, eventually adding 283 – but there were times when it almost felt England's tail started at No.3. They tried many things, including moving all eleven players into a different position in the batting order for the second innings at Adelaide. But Australia had the happy habit of batting their way out of trouble – never more so than on the first day of that third Test at Adelaide, when Jack Ryder smacked 201 not out batting at No.7 to lead a recovery from 119 for six to 489 all out. Australia eventually won a classic match by 11 runs, with England falling just short of a target of 375.

England's spirit made them a popular side, and there was recognition that they had been extremely unlucky with injuries, most notably during that thrilling third Test. They made Australia work extremely hard at times. The first three Tests all went into a seventh day,* and then England won their first Ashes Test since the war when Sutcliffe and Tate inspired an innings victory at Melbourne. The New Zealand-born legspinner Clarrie Grimmett ensured the series would end 4–1 with 11 for 82 on debut at Sydney.

'Fate played you a scurvy trick,' said a report in the *Melbourne Herald*. 'You went down in glorious defeat. You're not taking "The Ashes" back to England with you but you will take a great reputation as brave fighters and fine sportsmen.'

It was a very high-scoring series, with thirteen hundreds in the first three Tests alone. Two were made by the Victorian run-machine Bill Ponsford in his first two Tests. The orgy of runs made the incisive, indefatigable bowling of Tate even more admirable. He bowled 319 eight-ball overs – easily a record for the greatest workload by a quick bowler in a Test series, 302 balls ahead of, yes, Maurice Tate, who would get through 371 six-ball overs in Australia four years later. Usually, taking the third new ball is the sign of a very hard time in the field. At Melbourne, Tate took the *eighth* new cherry, though it was because of a dodgy packet of balls rather than Australia batting for 630 overs. In five Tests Tate took 38 wickets at 23.18, still a record for an England bowler in Australia.

Tate was doing it for king and country – and his dad. Fred played one Test for England, against Australia in 1902, and went into Ashes legend for the wrong reasons: he dropped a crucial catch and was the last man out as England lost a pivotal Test by three runs at Old Trafford (see pages 29–31).

At the time, Maurice was seven, so his father's suggestion that he had 'a little kid at home who will make up for it for me' was quite the prediction. Maurice *did* make up for it, however, establishing

---

* Until 1939, a number of Tests were timeless and played until a result was achieved – or, as happened to England during their tour of South Africa in 1938–39, until the boat was due to go home.

himself as one of England's finest bowlers. 'Maurice Tate did not merely play cricket,' wrote John Arlott, 'he lived in it.' Few Poms have been as popular in Australia as Tate, whose cheery disposition would not change even after a day of the hardest yakka in the field. A QC called Philip Opas, then aged eight, recalled going to the nets before the Melbourne Test of 1924–25 to fetch balls for the England players. Tate, unprompted, invited him to come to the Test as his guest. Later in the tour Tate was invited to the Opas's for dinner, giving the family an impromptu post-prandial masterclass in how to grip the ball to bowl the outswinger.

Tate was a kind of cricketing BFG, a constantly happy soul and popular chap who, said the Australian batsman Jack Fingleton, 'has the biggest feet I've seen and the smallest voice'. He regularly abused the nails of his big toes, so heavily did those feet pound the crease, until an Adelaide room attendant came up with the idea of cutting a hole in the shoe.

He liked it down under, where the sun matched his disposition. Tate took 55 wickets in 10 Ashes Tests in Australia, as compared to 28 in 10 Ashes contests in England. An overall record 155 in 39 Tests was quantitative confirmation of his excellence. In that regard, he and particularly his father were very glad he wasn't a chip off the old block.

1926

'Well I never, it's those two again!'

[PATTIE MENZIES RE-ENCOUNTERS JACK HOBBS AND HERBERT SUTCLIFFE, SECOND TEST, LORD'S, 28 JUNE 1926]

WHEN SHE WENT TO LORD'S IN 1926 Pattie Menzies had only ever seen one day of Test cricket. The wife of the future Australian prime minister Robert Menzies, Pattie had been present at Melbourne in 1924–25, when Jack Hobbs and Herbert Sutcliffe batted all day. Eighteen months later, on the other side of the world, she was preparing herself for the action, when out strolled two familiar faces: Hobbs and Sutcliffe again. It was Groundhog Test.

When the Menzies left the ground around teatime, Hobbs and Sutcliffe were still batting. Pattie never saw another day's Test cricket, so her experience was limited almost exclusively to the sight of Hobbs and Sutcliffe scoring runs.

That Lord's Test, the second of the series after a near washout at Trent Bridge, was one for the openers. Earlier in the match the forty-three-year-old Warren Bardsley carried his bat for 193 in an innings where nobody else reached 40. The four century-makers in the match – Bardsley, Hobbs, Patsy Hendren and Charles Macartney – had a combined age of 163. 'By cripes,' said Macartney on the morning of his 133 not out. 'I feel sorry for any poor bastard who has to bowl to me today.' Macartney's was the first of three brilliant centuries in consecutive innings across three Tests. The second came at Headingley. When Maurice Tate dismissed the stand-in captain with the first ball of the match, Macartney walked out at No.3 and announced: 'Let's have it!' to Tate. For the next three hours he did just that, hitting 151 in a partnership of 235 with Bill Woodfull.

England followed on but drew the match comfortably. The quality of the batting, the weather and the fact that Tests were only three days long precluded a result in the first four matches. The series was like a largely boring film with a great ending. The last Test at The Oval was extended to facilitate a result, and England recalled their veteran spinning all-rounder Wilfred Rhodes, aged thirty-eight, after a four-year absence. They also changed captain, with the popular Kent amateur Percy Chapman controversially selected to replace the underperforming Arthur Carr.

Australia led by 22 on first innings, but then Hobbs (100) and Sutcliffe (161) took the game and the series away from them with an immense performance on a rain-affected pitch. Nobody else on either side made more than 33 in the second innings.

Rhodes and a young Nottinghamshire fast bowler called Harold Larwood completed a crushing win; Larwood, in only his second Test, took six for 116 in the match. It was England's first Ashes

Jack Hobbs and Herbert Sutcliffe walk out to bat, The Oval, 1926.

victory since the war, and as such produced an equal mixture of relief and joy. 'August 18, 1926, was a great day for English cricket – a landmark, I venture to think, in our cricket history, and if I may be allowed to say so, it brought joy to my heart,' wrote 'Plum' Warner in the *Cricketer*. 'Therefore "I die happy".' The new captain, Chapman, received not only favourable reviews for his imaginative tactics, but a congratulatory message from King George V.

It is hard to overstate the majesty and significance of the 172-run partnership between Hobbs and Sutcliffe. 'Finer cricket on a difficult wicket than Hobbs and Sutcliffe played I have never seen,' said the *Cricketer* match report. 'They have made their names immortal in the history of cricket.'

Hobbs and Sutcliffe have a good claim to be the greatest of all opening partnerships. Other opening pairs have scored more than their 3249 runs, such is the volume of cricket in the modern era, but no regular opening pair have come anywhere near their average of 88 per partnership.

There were twelve years between them and some might have thought they were geographically incompatible, coming from Surrey and Yorkshire, yet their mutual respect and understanding was almost instant. They were almost telepathic between the wickets, stealing hundreds of short singles and only once being involved in a run out. 'Hobbs is undoubtedly the sauciest run-stealer in the world today,' said an article in the *Cricketer*. 'In Sutcliffe, he has found the ideal partner in the felony, for the Yorkshireman unhesitatingly responds to his calls, showing absolute confidence in Hobbs' judgement.'

Sutcliffe had plenty of style – *Wisden* said 'his off-drive wore a silk hat' – but most of all he was a miracle of temperament, perfectly suited to batting long periods. 'Ah luv a dogfight', he said on numerous occasions, and the great Australian leg-spinner Bill O'Reilly called him 'the toughest competitor I ever faced in a Test match'. He was also one of only two men Mrs Menzies ever saw bat in a Test match. She didn't know how lucky she was.

'Dammit, we've done 'em!'

GEORGE GEARY WAS A TEENAGER the last time England had won the Ashes in Australia. He hadn't even played first-class cricket. Now he was a grizzled thirty-five-year-old, one of the world's best seam bowlers. On this day, however, it was his batting ability that was needed because England were staggering to glory. They required a world-record 332 to beat Australia and take an unassailable 3–0 series lead, but had slipped from 318 for three to 328 for seven amid an unlikely clatter of wickets. It did not affect Geary, who struck Jack Ryder through mid-on for four before exclaiming in triumph. It was not just any old triumph: England had retained the Ashes with two matches to spare, and had won an Ashes series in Australia for the first time since 1911–12.

Both sides had discovered exciting batting talents since their previous meeting in 1926. England had given a debut to Wally Hammond in the previous twelve months, while Donald Bradman and Archie Jackson were on the cusp of selection for Australia. A close series was anticipated – and then England won the first Test by 675 runs. After Patsy Hendren's tone-setting 169, Harold Larwood, Maurice Tate and the left-arm spinner Jack 'Farmer' White dismissed Australia for just 122 and 66. Bradman, on debut, made 18 and 1 and was dropped for the next Test.

It would have been worse for Australia had Hammond not warmed up with modest scores of 44 and 28. In the next three Tests he made

251, 200, 32, 119 not out and 177. Hammond's unprecedented purple patch was symbolised by one big red patch. 'Hammond's bat was unmarked,' said the playwright Ben Travers, who saw it after Hammond's 251, 'except that plumb in the middle of the sweet of the blade there was a perfectly circular indentation.'

England won all three of these matches, though the margins were increasingly tight. After a comfortable eight-wicket win in the second Test at Sydney, when they piled up a total of 636, they sneaked home by three wickets in the third match at Melbourne. That was when Geary hit the winning runs, though England would have had no chance of chasing down 332 were it not for another masterclass in bad-wicket batting from Jack Hobbs and Herbert Sutcliffe. They added 105 in horrible conditions on the sixth day, with Sutcliffe going on to make 135.

England went 4–0 up a month later, winning an Adelaide classic by 12 runs. Their victory was primarily down to two men: Hammond, who made hundreds in each innings, and White, who took 13 wickets in the match. One of those wickets was Jackson, lbw for a gorgeous 164 in the first innings. He was nineteen years old. 'This kid'll get a hundred,' said Tate after Jackson had hit his first ball for four. There were many who thought Jackson was even better than Bradman; he played just eight Tests before dying from tuberculosis at the age of only twenty-three (see pages 78–79).

Australia found gold amid the rubble of a heavy defeat. The twenty-year-old Bradman made two fine centuries, both at Melbourne in the third and fifth Tests, when he was recalled. The latter helped Australia to a consolation victory, despite England posting 519 batting first. That included 142 from Hobbs, his fifteenth and last Test century at the age of forty-six. Hendren's 95 included the only eight in an Ashes Test because of two lots of overthrows.

Hammond's wonderful series ended quietly, with scores of 38 and 19, but he had taken a shortcut to greatness. His Test average was below 40 at the start of the tour; by the end it was in excess of 70. 'The perfect cricketer, someone who did everything with the touch of a master,' said the Australian batsman Stan McCabe. Hammond's future England team-mate Len Hutton used the same P-word. 'The

England take the field, led by Percy Chapman, with a saturnine Douglas Jardine behind him, Brisbane, 1928.

most perfect batsman,' he said. 'I preferred to see just an hour of Walter Hammond to eight or ten hours of Don Bradman.'

In 1928–29 Hammond finished the series with 905 runs from five Tests at an average of 113.12, still a record for an England batsman in any Test series. At the time it was a record for all countries, yet it would not last long. The emergence of a freakish talent was about to cause Hammond and England all kinds of misery.

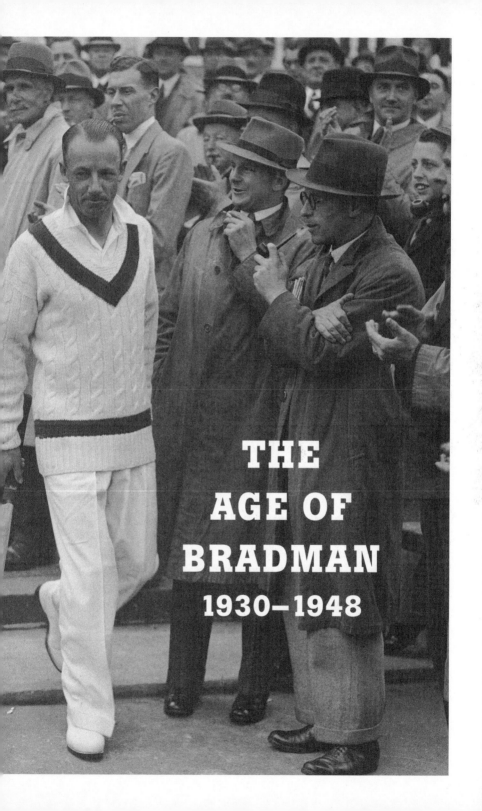

THE
AGE OF
BRADMAN
1930–1948

1930

'That wasn't a bad bit of practice. I'll be able to have a go at them tomorrow.'

[DON BRADMAN TO BILL WOODFULL, AFTER SCORING 309 NOT OUT ON THE FIRST DAY OF THE THIRD TEST, HEADINGLEY, 11 JULY 1930]

DON BRADMAN'S LEGS WERE HEAVY. It had been a full-on day at work. But his was a happy, virtuous tiredness, and he could not wait to get back to work the following morning. He had done what all batsmen need to do to feel comfortable – spent time in the middle getting used to the pitch and the bowlers. He excitedly told his captain, Bill Woodfull, about how he would really crack on tomorrow.

Bradman, the boy from Bowral, was twenty-one years old and had just made the highest score in Ashes history. He was 309 not out in the third Test against England at Headingley, having passed Reginald 'Tip' Foster's record of 287 at Sydney in 1903–04, and was just 16 away from the highest Test score of all, Andrew Sandham's 325 at Kingston in 1929–30 (although in those days Ashes cricket was so dominant that scores in other Tests did not carry the same prestige). Bradman passed Sandham's record the next day nonetheless, though he didn't really get to 'have a go at them' – he was dismissed for 334. 'It is impossible to imagine greater batting,' said the *Cricketer*.

England could not say they weren't forewarned; earlier in the year Bradman had made the highest first-class score, 452 not out, for New South Wales against Queensland. When he arrived in England he made 1000 runs against the counties even before the end of May. Not bad for a lad who many predicted would struggle on English pitches.

Australia needed all of Bradman's runs to get back in the Test series after losing the first Test at Trent Bridge. The substitute Sydney Copley, twenty-three, a member of the Nottinghamshire groundstaff, took a wonderful running catch to dismiss Stan McCabe at a time when he and Bradman were seriously threatening to chase down a target of 429. Copley played only one first-class game, against Oxford University the week after his Test heroics, yet he is one of cricket's most famous no-cap wonders. The dismissal of Bradman soon after for 131, bowled offering no stroke to a googly from Walter Robins, was less celebrated but equally important.

Australia's reply in the next Test at Lord's was formidable: Woodfull made 155 and Bradman 254 in a total of 729 for six, and they went on to win by seven wickets despite a splendid 173 from Duleepsinhji, the nephew of Ranji (see page 22), and an ultra-aggressive 121 from the captain Percy Chapman, his only Test century. The leg-spinner Clarrie Grimmett's six for 167 in the second innings took his haul to 18 wickets in the first two Tests.

But it was Bradman's innings that stayed longest in the memory. He regarded it as technically the greatest innings of his life, which automatically makes it a strong contender for the greatest innings of all – though Bradman would have told you that was played by McCabe (see page 92). 'Practically without exception every ball went where it was intended to go, even the one from which I was dismissed, but the latter went slightly up in the air and Percy Chapman with a miraculous piece of work held the catch,' he said.

The next two Tests at Leeds – in which Bradman got his 'bit of practice' – and Manchester were drawn. That meant the deciding Test at The Oval would be played to a finish, and Australia confirmed a superiority that had been increasingly apparent as the series progressed. The debonair, bibulous Chapman was replaced as captain for the Oval Test by Bob Wyatt of Warwickshire.

England started well enough, with Herbert Sutcliffe hitting 161 – just as he had in an Ashes decider on the same ground four years earlier – in a total of 405. But Bradman overcame the scoreboard pressure, and some nasty lift from the Nottinghamshire fast bowler Harold Larwood on a juicy pitch, to make 232 and give Australia a

290-run lead. Percy Hornibrook – who had taken only six wickets in eight innings in the series – claimed seven for 92 with his left-arm slow-medium to complete an innings victory. Australia regained the Ashes on their captain Woodfull's birthday.

The Oval Test was the last of Jack Hobbs's wonderful career. At the age of forty-seven he drifted gracefully from the scene, making a pair of 70s in England's first-Test victory. No England batsman has scored more Test runs against Australia. And nobody on either side has scored more Ashes runs than Bradman. Nor has anybody matched his series haul of 1930: 974 runs in only seven innings at an average of 139.14. His scores were 8, 131, 254, 1, 334, 14 and 232. It was the ultimate Ashes *mirabilis*.

> **Bradman was a team in himself. I think The Don was too good. He spoilt the game. I do not think we want to see another one quite like him. I do not think we ever shall**

For the next eighteen years, Bradman would be a chronic pain in England's collective backside, legs, brain and soul, hitting 5028 Ashes runs with 19 centuries. 'He is a text-book of batting come to life with never a misprint or erratum,' wrote J. M. Kilburn, the cricket correspondent of the *Yorkshire Post*. His appetite for runs was without precedent; he was a monument of unapologetic sporting greed, who collected runs as if he had been told they were to be rationed from midnight.

His conversion rate of fifties to double hundreds – never mind hundreds – beggars belief. Bradman reached 50 on 42 occasions in Tests. He turned 29 of those into centuries and 12 into double centuries. He passed the *Mastermind* test that distinguishes the most voracious batsmen: once he started, he certainly finished.

There is a theory and an explanation for everything these days, yet the extent of Bradman's brilliance is still one of the great brainbusters. In quantitative terms he was 40 per cent better than any other batsman who has lived. No other sportsman has exhibited anything like such superiority. It would be like Usain Bolt running the 100 metres in six seconds. 'Bradman was a team in himself,' said Hobbs. 'I think The Don was too good. He spoilt the game. I do not think we want to see another one quite like him. I do not think we ever shall.'

Bradman was a bespoke problem that demanded a bespoke solution. After his 334 at Headingley, 'Plum' Warner wrote that something needed to be done. 'England must develop a new type of bowler and fresh ideas and strange tactics to curb his almost uncanny skill.' Nobody realised quite how far England would be willing to go in an attempt to do so.

D. G. BRADMAN (N. S. WALES)

1932–33

'I've got it! He's yellow!'

[DOUGLAS JARDINE PERCEIVES A CHINK IN DON BRADMAN'S ARMOUR, EARLY 1930s]

DON BRADMAN'S TSUNAMI OF RUNS in 1930 had a traumatic impact on England's cricketing psyche. In that series he had been like an indestructible movie monster, bullets bouncing off him as his rivals wonder: *What does it take to kill this sonofabitch?* It took an outsider to spot a potential weakness: the Winchester-and-Oxford-schooled Douglas Jardine, who was not part of England's Bradman-battered line-up that summer.

While Bradman was flaying England, Jardine, the epitome of the Spartan amateur, had been attending to business matters and playing nine first-class games for Surrey. By the summer of 1931, he was captain for England's three-match series against New Zealand. Watching footage of Bradman's 232 in the deciding Test at The Oval in the company of some MCC committee members, Jardine experienced a eureka moment: in between the pulls, drives and cuts with which Bradman demolished England's attack, he believed he had seen evidence of how to make Australia's run-machine malfunction. 'I've got it!' he exclaimed, quite possibly interrupting a number of discreet post-prandial naps. 'He's yellow!'

Although Bradman made a series-winning 232, he had moments of discomfort on a lively pitch from which the ball lifted sharply, most notably against the fast bowling of Harold Larwood. Jardine noticed that Bradman had flinched and backed away to some deliveries. To Jardine, this was almost as good as discovering the meaning of life. In fact, there were times when it seemed that stopping

Bradman *was* the meaning of Jardine's life. He was determined to beat Australia by foul means or fouler. When Rockley Wilson, a first-class cricketer* who taught Jardine at Winchester, heard that his former pupil had been appointed as captain for the 1932–33 Ashes tour, he said: 'Well, we shall win the Ashes but we may lose a Dominion.'

Before setting out for Australia, Jardine met the Nottinghamshire fast bowlers Larwood and Bill Voce and their county captain Arthur Carr at the grill

Well, we shall win the Ashes but we may lose a Dominion

room in the Piccadilly Hotel, where they had a few drinks and discussed how his plan might work. It's tempting to say that Jardine was the brains and Voce and particularly Larwood his muscle. But the tactics Jardine had in mind required exceptional ability as well as physical strength.

All were agreed that the key was not just hostility but unfailing accuracy, without which Bradman would take the bowling apart. 'Cricket fans today can have no idea how dynamic this little chap was,' said Larwood. 'Bradman would murder you if you gave him any stuff that was even slightly loose.' The approach, which would become known as Bodyline, was agreed. Jardine resented that term, preferring to call it leg theory and describing it as 'this most highly skilled form of bowling'. Larwood in particular was a class act: quick, nasty, tireless and unfailingly accurate.

Leg theory was an established tactic, occasionally used in county cricket to dry up runs, but it generally involved deliveries of good or full length rather than balls bowled at the body. Jardine remixed the concept with added aggression, short-pitched bowling and as many as six fielders close in on the leg side waiting for catches as batsmen attempted to protect themselves by fending deliveries away from their body – deliveries that Larwood later described, with a fair bit of relish, as 'rib-roasters'. If the batsman tried to hook or pull, there would be fielders positioned in the deep for a catch as well.

---

* Wilson played one Test, at Sydney, in 1920–21.

Even before Bodyline, Jardine did not suffer Australians gladly. He was christened 'Sardine' when he toured with England in 1928–29; during the same trip, when Jardine was jeered by the crowd, Patsy Hendren said: 'They don't seem to like you very much, Mr Jardine.' 'It's f****** mutual,' came the reply. When he was barracked for slow-scoring by the crowd in one match, the wicketkeeper 'Stork' Hendry offered his sympathies, only to find that Jardine was not exactly simpatico: 'All Australians are uneducated and an unruly mob,' Jardine replied. During the Sydney Test, Hendry was warned by Hendren that Jardine had spiked his drinks-break refreshment with whisky.

His desire to find an antidote to Bradman simply compounded his distaste for Australia. 'We have to hate them,' he said to the fast bowler Gubby Allen. 'That's the only way we're going to beat them.' If the television programme *Room 101* had existed back then, Jardine's list might have been something like: 1. Don Bradman, 2. Australian cricket fans, 3. Australian journalists, 4. Australia.

'He is a queer fellow,' said the tour manager 'Plum' Warner of Jardine. 'When he sees a cricket ground with an Australian on it, he goes mad.' Especially when it had a particular Australian on it. During the Bodyline tour, Warner wrote to his wife that Jardine was occasionally using 'awful words' when talking about Bradman. Given that he sometimes used 'bastard' as a term of affection, the mind boggles as to what exactly Jardine said.

The more Australia raged against Jardine, the more his resolve strengthened. There were scarcely any consequences that would

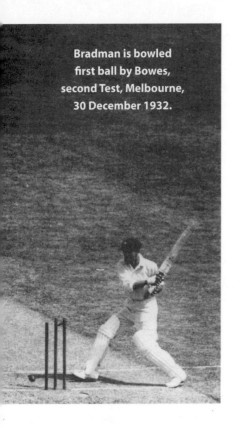

Bradman is bowled first ball by Bowes, second Test, Melbourne, 30 December 1932.

disturb his desire to win the Ashes – whether serious injury, or metaphorical murder. Jardine was worried about the potential impact of Chuck Fleetwood-Smith, a vulnerable but dangerous leg-spinner, and decided that England had to go after him in a tour match to ensure he would not be selected for the Tests. 'I want you to murder him,' he said to Wally Hammond. 'We don't want him ever to play for Australia. Now is the time to destroy him.' Hammond duly took Fleetwood-Smith to the cleaners and he was not picked for another three years.

Jardine was a one-man siege mentality. When he was asked if he could name his team early because of newspaper deadlines, his response was not something that will be included in a guide to media training. 'Do you think we've come all this way to provide scoops for your bloody newspaper?' He could be equally cutting towards his own team. When the Nawab of Pataudi, who was opposed to Bodyline, declined to field in the leg trap, Jardine said: 'I see His Highness is a conscientious objector.' Allen was also against Bodyline and took 21 wickets in the series using normal methods.

I want you to murder him. We don't want him ever to play for Australia. Now is the time to destroy him

The Bodyline tactics troubled Bradman even before the Tests began, and he made scores of 3, 10, 36, 13, 18 and 23 in tour matches against England. The stress of those scores, coupled with a row with his board over a newspaper column which almost caused him to miss the entire series, led a doctor to declare him unfit for the first Test because of exhaustion.

England's tactics, though originally designed for Bradman, weren't contingent on his presence. Everyone was going to cop it. 'We're not a bad side,' said Voce to Vic Richardson before the series, 'and if we don't beat you, we'll knock your bloody heads off.' England overwhelmed Australia by 10 wickets in the first Test at Sydney, with the two Bodyline enforcers Larwood and Voce sharing 16 wickets. The only Australian to reach 50 in the match was Stan McCabe, who played the first of his two Ashes epics, 187 not out in a first-innings total of 360. It was a blistering counter-attack. McCabe had been sitting with his parents before he went out to bat and, with the top order being peppered, said to his father: 'If I get hit, Dad, stop Mum from jumping the fence.'

We're not a bad side, and if we don't beat you, we'll knock your bloody heads off

England flitted back and forth between orthodox and Bodyline fields. The fact that more than half of Larwood's 33 victims in the series were bowled out shows that he delivered plenty of stump-roasters as well as attacking the body. But the physical threat was real. 'We bade sentimental farewells to each other as each batsman made his way out to bat,' said the leg-spinner Bill O'Reilly. 'We had a genuine feeling they were making a journey from which they might be borne back on a stretcher.' Fifty years after the mock obituary that started the Ashes, *Smith's Weekly* published another mock advert:

> We conduct
> CRICKETERS' FUNERALS
> With Neatness and Dispatch
> Only Australian Materials Used
> Under Direct Patronage of the Board of Control
> JARDINE, LARWOOD & CO

It was during the first Test that Hugh Buggy of the *Melbourne Herald* coined the term 'Bodyline'. The return of Bradman for the second Test at Melbourne, three weeks after the first, was the subject of overwhelming hype. There was such a roar before his first ball that the bowler, Yorkshire's Bill Bowes, stopped twice in his run-up on the pretext of making a field change. Bradman, expecting a bouncer, pre-empted a hook stroke and walked across to the off side. The ball was much fuller and, although he almost managed to adjust, he could only drag the ball onto his stumps. There has been no more shocking golden duck in cricket.

'Have you ever heard 60,000 utter an involuntary yell of despair?' wrote Hammond. 'That "O-OOH!" will remain with me till my dying day.' After the involuntary expression of shock came the most perfect silence. Bowes broke it, ever so slightly, when he remarked 'Well, I'll be fooked' to the umpire. As Bradman walked off Bowes noticed his captain looking as gleeful as a rascal whose schoolyard nemesis had just **Well, I'll be fooked** fallen in a barrel of dung. 'Jardine, the sphinx, had momentarily forgotten himself for the one and only time in his cricketing life,' wrote Bowes. 'In his sheer delight at this unexpected stroke of luck he had clasped both his hands above his head and was jigging around like an Indian doing a war dance.'

The moment was so dramatic that it's easy to forget that Australia won the game by 111 runs. That was because of a ten-for from O'Reilly, the latest in the line of great Australian leggies, and an immensely determined 103 not out from Bradman in the second innings – the same number of runs he had made in seven innings against England on tour up to that point. It was not a fluent innings, far from it, yet that made it all the more admirable. In the context of a match that produced only two other scores over 35, never mind the personal pressure, it was a staggering performance, possibly the finest of his career. On that day, he was anything but yellow.

'I don't want to see you, Mr Warner. There are two teams out there; one is trying to play cricket and the other is not.'

[AUSTRALIAN CAPTAIN BILL WOODFULL TO THE ENGLAND MANAGER 'PLUM' WARNER, THIRD TEST, ADELAIDE, 14 JANUARY 1933]

BILL WOODFULL HAD LOST CONTROL of his body. His bat fell to the ground as his grip involuntarily relaxed and he staggered around, just about managing to stay on his feet. The Australian captain had been struck below the heart by a very fast, short ball from Harold Larwood. As he started to compose himself with help from his batting partner Don Bradman, amid a cacophony of hooting and jeering from the Australian fans, his opposite number Douglas Jardine spoke three devastatingly loaded words: 'Well bowled, Harold.' It was the moment a fractious sporting contest started to become an international incident.

Probably the most unpleasant Test ever played. Altogether the whole atmosphere was a disgrace to cricket

Wisden Cricketers' Almanack does not come with a pinch of salt attached to the inside of the yellow jacket. Few, if any, publications are as trustworthy. It is the bible of cricket, whose word is gospel. As such, its description of the third Bodyline Test at Adelaide says all we need to know. 'Probably the most unpleasant Test ever played,' was the *Wisden* verdict. 'Altogether the whole atmosphere was a disgrace to cricket.' It was the match when the Bodyline series went nuclear. Diplomatic relations were frayed to breaking point, with the two boards exchanging terse cables and the tour under threat.

The match had started well for Australia. England were 30 for four on the first morning before a middle-order rally from Maurice Leyland, Bob Wyatt and Eddie Paynter took them to 341. Australia had already lost the opener Jack Fingleton to Gubby Allen when Larwood, with the last ball of his second over, struck Woodfull in the chest.

At the time he was bowling to an orthodox rather than a Bodyline field. Jardine's praise for Larwood's bowling was primarily, if not exclusively, for the benefit of the non-striker Bradman. The gentleman was not for turning, though he had no compunction about turning the screw. In a thoroughly sinister twist, Jardine ordered his men to assume their Bodyline positions at the start of Larwood's next over. The Australian selector Bill Johnson described it as 'the most unsportsmanlike act ever witnessed on an Australian cricket field'.

Bradman failed, caught in the Bodyline trap with contemptuous ease after scoring eight, and Woodfull had his bat knocked out of his hands by a vicious delivery from Larwood before eventually falling for 22. Later that afternoon, the England management duo of 'Plum' Warner and Dick Palairet went into the Australian dressing-room to enquire about Woodfull's health. After Woodfull's famous response – which was later leaked to the press, with a list of suspects including Bradman and Fingleton – a shocked Warner departed almost in tears.

Later in the day, when the England fast bowler Bill Voce was struggling with injury, a request was put out on the public-address system for medical assistance. The crowd, erroneously thinking it was for Woodfull, reacted furiously. In those days, the practice of 'counting out' was commonplace, and the crowd decided it was time to do so to Larwood. 'One, two, three,' began the chanting. 'Four, five, six, seven, eight, nine, OUT, YOU BASTARD! Go home you Pommie bastards! Bastards! Bastards! Bastards!'

Bill Ponsford battled to 45 not out at the close, despite constant blows to the body, and resumed after the rest day. He was at the non-striker's end when the wicketkeeper Bert Oldfield suffered a fractured skull after edging an attempted hook stroke off Larwood into his face. The ball had been wide of off stump, bowled to an orthodox field, and when Larwood apologised Oldfield immediately accepted the blame for his imperfect stroke.

Not that those around the ground knew as much, or cared. Woodfull, in his suit, vaulted the pickets and ran onto the pitch shouting, 'This isn't cricket, this is war!' Larwood, anticipating a pitch invasion, inched towards the stumps so that he could grab one as a weapon if necessary. Maurice Tate – a man who saw the good in everyone and everything – disappeared from an enclosure into the dressing-room. 'I'm getting out of here,' he said. 'Someone will get killed.' The Adelaide Oval was a ring of ire: police surrounded the boundary in anticipation of a riot, with more waiting outside the ground in preparation. Jardine might have been arrested for assaulting the spirit of cricket. At the end of the day's play, the same police were needed to protect Larwood.

The crowd had barely calmed down by the time Australia were bowled out for 222, a deficit of 119. In the England dressing-room between innings, Jardine demonstratively cocked an ear. 'Listen to the bastards yelling,' he said. 'I think I'll go in myself and give the bastards something to yell at.' He put on his most outlandish Harlequin cap – 'a symbol of the despised Old School Tie back in the Old Dart,' as Larwood put it – and walked out to bat.

I wanted to hit one bowler before the other hit me

England ground their way to 412, leaving the hosts to chase an impossible 532. Bradman made a skittish 66, and hit Hedley Verity for his first Test six. He was out next ball attempting a similar shot. 'I wanted to hit one bowler before the other hit me,' he said. At the end of that fifth day's play, with Australia 120 for four and on the way to a crushing defeat, the Australian Cricket Board sent a cable to the MCC:

Bodyline bowling assumed such proportions as to menace best interests of game, making protection of body by batsmen the main consideration. Causing intensely bitter feeling between players as well as injury. In our opinion is unsportsmanlike. Unless stopped at

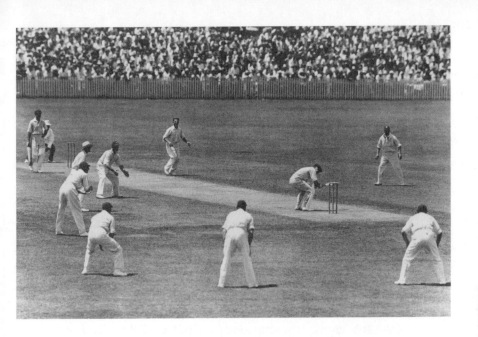

Harold Larwood bowls to Bill Woodfull with a Bodyline field, fourth Test, Brisbane, 1933.

once likely to upset friendly relations existing between Australia and England.

Four days later, the MCC replied.

We deplore your cable . . . we deprecate your opinion that there has been unsportsmanlike play. We have the fullest confidence in our captain, team and managers and are sure that they would do nothing to infringe either the laws of cricket or the spirit of the game . . . If you consider it desirable to cancel the remainder of the programme, we would consent, but with great reluctance.

The ACB eventually backed down, and the tour continued. Woodfull refused to respond with Bodyline tactics – though England did face some short-pitched bowling during tour games. Goodness knows what would have happened had he not turned the other cheek. 'If any dignity was left to Test cricket at the end of that 1932–33 season,' said Fingleton, 'it was due entirely to Mr W. M. Woodfull.'

'You can't go off while the
little bastard's in.'

[DOUGLAS JARDINE REJECTS THE
INJURED HAROLD LARWOOD'S REQUEST
TO LEAVE THE FIELD, FIFTH TEST,
SYDNEY, 27 FEBRUARY 1933]

AFTER THE BATTLE OF ADELAIDE, England needed to win one of the last two Tests to reclaim the Ashes. If the third Test was a tale of wounded Australians, then the fourth at Brisbane was a story of a sick Englishman. The Lancashire batsman Eddie Paynter was taken ill with tonsillitis during the first day's play. On the second, with England in trouble in their first innings, he got out of bed and took a taxi to the ground before going into bat at No.8. Paynter ended the day 24 not out, got a taxi back to hospital and resumed the following morning. 'It were nowt more than a sore throat,' he said. Paynter's match-turning 83, which helped England to 356 and a narrow first-innings lead, was the feelgood story of a feelbad series. Harold Larwood bowled superbly again to take seven wickets in the match, including Don Bradman in both innings for scores of 76 and 24.

Having bowled Australia out for 175, England reached a tricky target of 160 to win by six wickets and take an unassailable 3–1 lead. With Bill O'Reilly bowling beautifully, and the tension so great that the manager 'Plum' Warner left the ground, their captain Douglas Jardine went into over-my-dead-body mode, going 82 balls without scoring at one stage. Jardine said to O'Reilly that he was like 'an old maid defending her virginity'. Paynter completed a memorable personal performance by smashing a six to win the match and the Ashes. On the same day, the brilliant Australian batsman Archie Jackson died from tuberculosis at the age of twenty-three. A few hours before his death he sent a telegram to Larwood: 'Congratulations magnificent bowling. Good luck all matches.'

Although the series was won, Jardine was not inclined to give Australia's suckers anything resembling an even break. Larwood, who had a splintered bone in his left foot from pounding the un-forgiving Australian pitches, asked to be rested from the final Test at Sydney. Jardine wouldn't even consider such an idea. 'We've got the bastards down there,' he said, 'and we'll keep them there.' Larwood's main impact in that match was with the bat. He was so irked to be asked to go in as nightwatchman that he smashed 98. 'Even the next day I was batting on spleen,' he said.

It was an innings that earned Larwood an ovation from the Sydney crowd – at the start of the innings they had been imploring the bowlers to 'knock the bastard's head off' – and he would have made a Test century but for the extreme mischance of being caught out by Bert Ironmonger, the world's worst fielder. 'I never realised the approach of Australian crowds until that moment,' he said. 'It proved to me Australians like a trier, they go for the underdog, and they appreciate good cricket no matter who provides it.'

Larwood said Jardine greeted him with 'unaccustomed friendliness' after his innings. 'You little bastard, I knew you could play,' said his captain. By now Larwood was physically spent, and could barely walk during Australia's second innings. Still Jardine would not let him leave the field. If Paynter had been sick at Brisbane, then Jardine was positively twisted at Sydney. When Bradman was out, bowled by Hedley Verity, he and Larwood left the field at the same time, though they weren't exactly skipping along arm in arm. 'I half-limped alongside Bradman,' said Larwood. 'Neither of us spoke a word.'

Larwood ended the series with 33 wickets at an average of 19.51. An eight-wicket win in that final Test, sealed with a straight six from Wally Hammond, gave England a thumping 4–1 victory. Bradman ended the series with scores of 48 and 71, which meant a total of 396 runs at 56.57 – his lowest average in a Test series throughout his career. Jardine's plan had worked. And he hadn't even lost a dominion. He had, however, become almost universally hated in Australia.

1932–33

'Don't give the bastard a drink.
Let him die of thirst.'

**[AN AUSTRALIAN SPECTATOR
TO BILL WOODFULL, FIFTH TEST, SYDNEY,
28 FEBRUARY 1933]**

DOUGLAS JARDINE'S MISSION WAS almost complete. England were about to complete a crushing series victory over Australia with a win in the fifth Test at Sydney. Jardine was at the crease, savouring the moment, when play stopped for a drinks break. The chivalrous Australian captain Bill Woodfull was about to hand Jardine some water when a lone voice suggested that it might be better to let his opposite number's dehydration become terminal. Jardine, who had spent the entire series disparaging all things Australian, quietly enjoyed that particular bit of barracking. He later called it 'one of the few humorous remarks which we were privileged to hear on this tour'.

Jardine is loathed more than any German who ever fought in any war

Jardine was characterised as the archetypal English villain, cold and calculating, the kind of man who would be played by Alan Rickman.* 'Jardine is loathed more than any German who ever fought in any war,' wrote Gubby Allen in a letter during the Bodyline tour, before adding: 'Sometimes I feel I should like to kill [him] and today is one of those days.'

---

* In the TV mini-series *Bodyline* (1984), Jardine was in fact played by Hugo Weaving, who later found fame as Agent Smith in *The Matrix* and Elrond in *The Lord of the Rings*.

During the third Test at Adelaide, Jardine went to the Australian dressing-room to demand an apology because one of the Australian players had called Harold Larwood 'a bastard'. He was met by Vic Richardson. 'Okay,' he said, turning round to his team-mates, 'which of you bastards called Larwood a bastard instead of this bastard?'

When Jardine swatted a fly away from his face during one match, he was upbraided by a spectator. 'Oi, leave our flies alone, Jardine – they're the only flamin' friends you've got here.' In his book, *In Quest of the Ashes*, Jardine devoted an entire chapter to his love of Australian crowds. 'It is high time that full publicity was given to the evils of barracking,' he said. 'One would expect that any genuine enthusiast would be tempted to tell the owner of an empty head and

PLAYER'S CIGARETTES

D. R. JARDINE (SURREY)

**Douglas Jardine, England's hated captain
on the 'Bodyline' tour of 1932–33.**

a pair of brazen lungs that he was spoiling the enjoyment of others round about him by going off at minute intervals like a raucous maroon... I cannot help thinking that a psychologist would find it extraordinarily interesting to experiment with an Australian barracker'.

The treatment of Jardine was a significant landmark in the development of Aussie barracking. When England try to win the Ashes in Australia, it is not so much eleven against eleven as eleven against 23 million. They have to compete with the entire country. The process of mental disintegration begins the moment they step off the plane – or even before, in the age of social media – and continues until they step back on it.

Every England cricketer who has played in Australia has a story to tell. Kevin Pietersen says he was 'called a wanker 24/7' – and not just by his team-mates – while Stuart Broad was public enemy number one throughout the 2013–14 series because he did not walk during the preceding Ashes. When the Australian-raised bowler Martin McCague hailed a taxi during the 1994–95 series, the driver spat: 'You're that bloody English traitor. Clear off. I'm not taking you.' Four years later, John Crawley was pummelled in an assault outside a bar in Cairns.

And these incidents took place outside the ground. *Inside*, the attitude tends to vary from affectionate contempt to outright hatred. Fielding in front of Bay 13 at the MCG, in particular, has become a rite of passage for callow English tourists. David Bairstow was once pelted with beer cans in an ODI at Sydney – and Australia weren't even playing. 'A cricket tour in Australia would be the most delightful period in your life... if you were deaf,' said Larwood. He probably thought that, when the Bodyline tour finished, he would be returning to a bit of peace and quiet in England. He could not have been more wrong.

1932–33

'Why, Mummy, he doesn't look like a murderer.'

[A CHILD AFTER SEEING HAROLD LARWOOD IN ADELAIDE, MARCH 1933]

HAROLD LARWOOD KNEW HE WAS INFAMOUS. There had been a few clues, with the police escorts and the fact he had been christened 'bastard' by the Australian crowds. But the full extent of that infamy only became apparent when, towards the end of the Bodyline tour, he went to the theatre in Adelaide, the scene of the poisonous third Test. A little girl walked up to Larwood, nervously looked him up and down, and observed to her mother that the man in front of her did not look like the beastly killer who had been portrayed in the press.

> **Woodfull was too slow and Bradman was frightened. . . yes, frightened is the word. He was scared by my bowling. I knew it, as everyone did**

By that stage, Larwood was enjoying his notoriety. 'Although I was threatened with murder and told. . . what a pleasure it would be to tar and feather me, strangely, it was in many ways the most enjoyable tour I ever had. My notoriety on the field encouraged hospitality to the point where Australians off the field almost killed me with bonhomie.'

Larwood, originally gagged by his tour contract, was not allowed to talk about Bodyline until a couple of months after the tour. When he finally did so, he did not pull his punches. 'Woodfull was too slow and Bradman was frightened. . . yes, frightened is the word,' he said. 'He was scared by my bowling. I knew it, as everyone did.'

The interview brought both sympathetic and abusive mail. One piece of correspondence, from Mr J. Payne of Victoria Street, Fremantle, was particularly memorable. 'There is no doubt you are a dirty swine. . . If you were half a man you would not have used Bodyline here. . . What else can be expected from a village Bonehead like you? The Hangman's name is Larwood.'

In fact Larwood was about to be hung out to dry by the bosses of English cricket. He missed almost all of the 1933 season because of injury, but he should have been England's attack leader even in the post-Bodyline world of 1934, when Australia were next due to visit.

Harold Larwood in his Blackpool sweet shop, late 1940s.

The MCC wanted Larwood to sign an apology, believing it would improve relations before the tour. He declined, pointing out that he had been following orders, and that he had nothing to apologise for anyway. He never played for England again. The Sydney Test in 1932–33 was his last Test match at the age of twenty-eight. 'The MCC wanted someone to sacrifice,' he said, 'and I was the obvious choice.'

Larwood played for Nottinghamshire until 1938 and then ran a sweet shop in Blackpool. 'History embalmed Larwood in the Bodyline series, as though he died bowling it,' wrote his biographer Duncan Hamilton. 'As a cricketer, he is preserved only in its controversy.'

The MCC wanted someone to sacrifice, and I was the obvious choice

He received honorary membership of the MCC in 1949; it healed some of the wounds, but could not replace the lost years when he should have been adding considerably to his total of 78 Test wickets. With his business producing only modest returns, Larwood was encouraged to emigrate with his family to Australia by Jack Fingleton, one of the Australian batsmen he had terrorised during the Bodyline series. Fingleton even found him a house. In 1950, after a farewell dinner with Jack Hobbs and Herbert Sutcliffe – and 'the worst hangover I have ever had in my life' – he left for Australia, where he was greeted like a returning hero. He was leaving another great hangover, the fallout from Bodyline, behind.

Larwood spent the final forty-six years of his life in Australia and never changed his opinion on the events of 1932–33. The last line of his 1984 book, *The Larwood Story,* made things abundantly clear. 'I'm still glad to this day that I never apologised.'

1934

'I don't believe in the law of averages.'

[DON BRADMAN TO NEVILLE CARDUS, FOURTH TEST, HEADINGLEY, 20 JULY 1934]

DON BRADMAN APPEARED TO BE SUFFERING from some kind of Post-Bodyline Stress Disorder. He began the 1934 Ashes series with a run of scores more commonly associated with a frivolous dasher than the most remorseless batsman ever born: 29, 25, 36, 13 and 30. 'He was batting in a fashion that made the world wonder what had come over him,' said the England opener Herbert Sutcliffe.

In fact, although nobody realised at the time, he was suffering from acute appendicitis and peritonitis. At least he did not have to contend with Bodyline this time. Douglas Jardine had retired from international cricket, Harold Larwood was a pariah, and both teams agreed they would not use leg theory. A year later, after some controversial county matches, the MCC changed the laws to prohibit such tactics.

Bradman's modest form did not stop Australia taking the first Test of the 1934 series at Trent Bridge with a victory that was both crushing and nail-biting. They won by 238 runs yet took the final wicket with only twelve minutes to spare. Arthur Chipperfield became the first man to have the bittersweet experience of being dismissed for 99 on Test debut and Clarrie Grimmett and Bill O'Reilly – the finest leg-spin twins there have ever been – shared 19 wickets.

England's innings victory in the second Test, their only Ashes win at Lord's in the twentieth century, was the consequence of an astonishing performance from Yorkshire's left-arm spinner Hedley Verity, who took 15 for 104. Fourteen of them came on the final day, and six in the last hour of the match. Leonard Crawley, the Essex batsman who once compared Verity's bowling to a 'cup of cat's piss', was mercifully not made to drink his words.

Fifty-five years later, Verity's performance even made a TV episode of Agatha Christie's *Poirot*. Throughout the 'Four and Twenty Blackbirds' case, Hercule Poirot's sidekick Captain Hastings is aghast at missing the Test, and then pleasantly shocked at hearing of Verity's exploits. 'And after the weekend rains you are surprised, *mon ami*?' said Poirot. 'Australians are used to hard pitches. The Lord's wicket

Don Bradman hits out during the 1934 Ashes series.

would have been decidedly sticky, no? So it's not a day for the stroke play. No. It's a day for the art of spin bowling, and Hedley Verity is the greatest exponent alive.'

There were no weekend rains in Manchester during the third Test. *Wisden* said the heat was 'at times almost unbearable'; you can insert your own joke about Manchester weather here. They were not the ideal conditions in which to bowl a 13-ball over, as Gubby Allen did at one stage after a flurry of no-balls and wides. Bowlers' feet groaned throughout a match that produced 1307 runs for the loss of just 20 wickets.

The fourth Test was at Headingley, where Bradman scored 334 on his previous Ashes tour. On the first evening he rejected a dinner invitation from the writer Neville Cardus. The series was in the balance, with Australia 39 for three in reply to England's 200 all out, and Bradman told Cardus he had to make at least 200 the following day. Cardus suggested that, after the 334, the law of averages was against him. 'I don't believe in the law of averages,' said Bradman. He duly made 271 not out the next day and 304 in total. He was still struggling physically, and was so weak when he finished his innings that he had to be undressed by his team-mates and lifted onto the massage table.

After all those nothing scores in the first three Tests, it was a pretty emphatic way to return to form. He added 388 with the opener Bill Ponsford, another gluttonous run-getter, who made 181. They were the only two scores above 50 in the entire match, and England were facing an innings defeat when rain saved them on the final day.

The writer R. C. Robertson-Glasgow called Bradman and Ponsford 'the lightning of Sydney and the thunder of Melbourne'. A biblical storm came down on England in the next Test, when the pair added 451 on the first day at The Oval. It was the deciding Test, to be played to a finish, but the result was obvious after the first day. Ponsford eventually made 266, Bradman 244, Australia 701. That great old-ball attack Grimmett and O'Reilly did the rest, taking their combined series tally to 53 wickets; the other Australian bowlers took 18 between them. For the second consecutive Ashes tour, Australia regained the Ashes at The Oval on the birthday of their captain Bill Woodfull – this time with a brutal 562-run victory.

The lightning of Sydney and the thunder of Melbourne

Bradman, who despite his slow start ended the series with 758 runs at 94.75, had an emergency appendix operation while still in London. There were concerns for his life; 'there can be no doubt that for some time I hovered on the brink of eternity,' said Bradman. In the 1930s, peritonitis was often fatal. But as with the law of averages, Bradman didn't really believe in probability.

1936–37

'Oh, don't give it another thought.
You've just cost us the Ashes,
that's all.'

[GUBBY ALLEN TO WALTER ROBINS
AFTER THE LATTER DROPPED
DON BRADMAN, SECOND TEST,
SYDNEY, 21 DECEMBER 1936]

BILL VOCE KNEW HE HAD TO GO TO THE WELL one more time. He'd had a spectacular day at Sydney, bowling Australia out for 80 with the help of Gubby Allen, but Don Bradman was at the crease and England would not sleep soundly if he was still there at the close. There was every chance Bradman's innings would decide whether Australia squared the series or England went 2–0 up.

Australia were progressing well in their second innings, having followed on 346 runs behind. Bradman was batting relatively poorly, but he had reached 24 and everybody knew what could happen if Bradman got a start. Summoning up the spirit of 1932–33, Voce pounded in a short ball with all the effort he had left. Bradman hooked blindly and directed the ball straight towards Walter Robins, in position at short square-leg for precisely such a chance. The Middlesex man dropped it.

It was not a dolly for Robins, but nor was it a particularly hard chance. Dropping Bradman was cricket's equivalent of letting a serial killer escape jail, and Robins was probably seeking comfort when he apologised to his captain, Gubby Allen. If so, he did not receive it: never mind costing England the match, Allen pointed out that it might cost them the series.

Both teams had changed captain since the previous Ashes in 1934, with Bradman eventually replacing the retired Bill Woodfull* and Allen succeeding Bob Wyatt. Bradman got off to a humiliatingly bad start as Australian captain. In the first Test, at Brisbane, he made 38 and 0 as Australia were thrashed by 322 runs. Allen and Voce shared 18 wickets, and demolished the Aussies for just 58 in the second innings. A low-scoring match was notable for outstanding centuries from Maurice Leyland (his fourth in the last five Ashes Tests) and Jack Fingleton (his fourth in a row in Tests).

The second Test at Sydney got off to an equally bad start for Australia and Bradman. Wally Hammond ground them down with a patient 231 not out, which took his Test record at Sydney to 770 runs at an average of 257. England plodded to 426 for six in the first two days and declared after a thunderstorm on the third morning. Bradman went for a second consecutive duck, this time a first-baller, the second of three wickets in four balls for Voce. He and Allen were a handful on the juiced-up pitch and hustled Australia out for just 80. It could have been worse; at one stage they were 31 for seven.

Australia followed on and were eating into the deficit on a fast-improving pitch when Robins dropped Bradman. He had to sleep on his error, as Bradman ended the day on an ominous 57 not out. On the fourth morning he proceeded towards the inevitable century. Then, just before lunch, he was unexpectedly bowled for 82 by Hedley Verity. Despite a coruscating 93 from Stan McCabe, England chipped away and won the match by an innings and 22 runs. Robins had not dropped the Ashes after all.

At that stage Bradman had made 120 runs in four innings at an average of 30; the obvious conclusion, widely expressed, was that captaincy was affecting his batting. The third Test, at Melbourne, was a unique match, which has a case for being the most interesting game of cricket ever played. Bradman called it 'a sensational battle of tactics as circumstances rarely allow'. The reason for that was the impact of the rains on the uncovered pitch. He declared Australia's first innings at 200 for nine so that they could get at England on what

---

* Vic Richardson was captain for the 1935–36 series against South Africa, with Bradman unavailable.

Wisden called a 'glue-pot wicket'. When England then declared after being reduced to 76 for nine, Bradman bought his batsmen more time while the wicket improved by promoting Nos. 9–11 to one, two and three.

Australia were 97 for five, a lead of 221, when Bradman came in at No.7. He added 346 for the sixth wicket with Fingleton, the opener who had been pushed down to No.6. It was not enough just to win the game and make it 2–1 in the series. 'Bradman's aim seems not only to kill the psychological advantage which England gained in the first and second Test matches but to cremate it on a mammoth pyre of runs,' said *The Times*. He made 270 and left England an absurd target of 689. Despite yet another hundred from Leyland, they were bowled out for 323.

Bradman, the grim second-innings reaper, did it again in the next Test at Adelaide. England started well and took a slight first-innings lead of 42 after Charlie Barnett's 129. Then came Bradman with a numbingly certain 212 to give Australia control. The leg-spinner Chuck Fleetwood-Smith, who had been murdered by Hammond four years earlier (see page 71), came back from the dead to take 10 wickets in the match to complete a comfortable 148-run victory. Australia had come from 2–0 down to square the series.

Bradman ensured there would no final plot twist, hitting 169 and adding 249 with McCabe on the first day of the deciding Test at Melbourne. England were thrashed by an innings. Bradman, who had started the series so poorly, ended up with 810 runs, still a record for an Australian batsman in a home Ashes series. The captaincy did indeed affect his batting – for the better.

The story is often erroneously told that Robins dropped Bradman during the third Test, when his 270 tipped the series on its head. That would have been a great tale, but the real story is pretty good too: this is still the only instance of a team coming from 2–0 behind to win a Test series.

'Come and look at this. You've never seen anything like it.'

THE TWENTY-NINE-YEAR-OLD DON BRADMAN was as giddy and restless as a newborn pup. Stanley Joseph McCabe, his Australian team-mate, was giving a demonstration of rare genius in the first Ashes Test at Trent Bridge, and Bradman urgently implored the rest of the team to take the once-in-a-lifetime opportunity to watch his innings. It was almost too much for Bradman. 'Towards the end I could scarcely watch the play,' he said. 'My eyes were filled as I drank in the glory of his shots.'

Australia were in significant trouble after slipping to 194 for six, still 464 runs behind, but McCabe was easing into the innings that would define him. He scored 232 out of 300 while at the wicket, including 72 in the final twenty-eight minutes and 44 off three overs from the leg-spinner Doug Wright. Neville Cardus said he 'batted with the ease of a man using a master key. . . McCabe demolished the English attack with aristocratic politeness, good taste and reserve. Claude Duval never took possession of a stagecoach with more charm of manner than this.' McCabe scored 127 runs in a single session, still an Ashes record.

McCabe demolished the English attack with aristocratic politeness, good taste and reserve

'I gripped his hand, wet with perspiration,' said Bradman. 'He was trembling like a thoroughbred racehorse. I can recall saying to him after expressing my congratulations, "I would give a great deal to be able to play another innings like that." No skipper was ever more sincere in his adulation of another's skill.' Bradman was still raving about it over a decade later. 'I firmly believe it to be the greatest innings ever played,' he said in *Farewell to Cricket*. 'Such cricket I shall never see again.'

It was the finest way to start a series. England, now captained by Wally Hammond, had controlled the first Test from the start. Eddie Paynter's 216 not·out was one of four centuries in their total of 658 for eight declared. The others came from Len Hutton and Denis Compton – future greats playing their first Ashes Test – and Charlie Barnett, who nearly completed a hundred before lunch of the first day of the series. He was 98 not out and did so off the first ball after the interval.

Australia were all out for 411, which meant they would still have to follow on, but McCabe had given them a grand chance of saving the game – and added motivation to ensure his masterpiece would not be in vain. McCabe's overall Test average of 48 may be very good rather than great, but two innings – the 232 here and his 187 in the first Bodyline Test (see page 72) – showed he was not just a great batsman; he was

It would be hard to think of a greater Australian batsman. He had qualities that even Bradman hadn't got

a genius. They were JFK innings. Bradman would certainly never forget where he was. McCabe did not just do things that were beyond mere mortals; he did things that were beyond the other immortals. 'It would be hard to think of a greater Australian batsman,' said Hutton. 'He had qualities that even Bradman hadn't got.'

Australia, stirred by McCabe's batting, saved the match comfortably after centuries from Bill Brown and, inevitably, Bradman. That was the first of three hundreds in four innings for Bradman. Not for the first time in the 1930s, the series degenerated into an orgy of runs. Brown and Hammond made double hundreds in the drawn second

Test at Lord's, while Hutton had something even bigger in mind for the final Test. Overall there were fourteen centuries in five Tests – and one of those, the third at Manchester, was washed out without a ball being bowled.

The series of colossal scores with which Australia opened their programme – they registered 3954 runs in their first seven innings – revealed the batting power available. There were only three five-wicket hauls in the entire series. Two of them, crucially, were claimed by the leg-spinner Bill O'Reilly in the fourth Test at Headingley. It was the decisive match of the rubber. In a low-scoring game, Bradman's exceptional 103 on his favourite ground gave Australia a lead of 19, and then the aggressive leg-spin duo of O'Reilly and Chuck Fleetwood-Smith reduced England from 60 for nought to 123 all out. Australia had a few jitters on their way to their target of 105 but got there for the loss of five wickets.

The victory ensured Australia would retain the Ashes regardless of what happened in the final Test at The Oval. Given what *did* happen in Kennington in late August, that was a pretty good thing. The orgy of runs was about to become positively bacchanalian.

1938

'Frank, they'll get a thousand.'

[AUSTRALIAN BATSMAN STAN McCABE TO UMPIRE FRANK CHESTER ON ENGLAND'S BATTING PROSPECTS IN THE FIFTH TEST AT THE OVAL, 20 AUGUST 1938]

THEY WERE THE LAST STEPS OF THE FIRST part of Len Hutton's life. He cut the ball deftly through the slips and set off for a run; then, as it became clear the ball was going for four, Hutton turned and moved back towards his crease. The Australian captain Don Bradman approached him, grinning broadly, before shaking Hutton's hand and patting him on the back. Bradman's handshake was like official ratification: Hutton, aged twenty-two and in only his sixth Test, had just broken Bradman's record for the highest ever Ashes score.

Eight years earlier, Hutton had been a local boy among the Headingley crowd as Bradman made a record score of 334. Australia's victory on the same ground a month earlier, which put them 1–0 up, ensured they would retain the Ashes in 1938, though the notion of a dead rubber was anathema in those days. The Oval Test was a thing of great importance – not least to Wally Hammond, who was desperate to clinch his first victory against Australia as England captain.

It was apparent from the moment England won the toss and batted that Australia had the hardest yakka ahead. After bowling the second over of the match, and getting no response from the wicket, Stan McCabe suggested to the umpire Frank Chester that England might be the first team to reach four figures in a Test innings.

McCabe's hyperbolic prediction might have come true had Hammond not eventually declared at 903 for seven. The leg-spinner

Chuck Fleetwood-Smith ended with the worst figures in Test history, one for 298. As the runs piled up, his fellow leg-spinner Bill O'Reilly suggested an unorthodox tactic. 'Where's the groundsman's hut?' he said to the umpire Chester. 'If I had a rifle, I'd shoot him now.'

Australia were so put upon in the field that even Bradman had a rare bowl – and then broke his ankle while doing so. With Jack Fingleton straining a muscle, they were two batsmen light. Many suggested that Hammond, who was determined to take this unexpected opportunity to humiliate Australia, would have gone beyond a thousand had Bradman and Fingleton been fit. Even batting on past 900 was akin to giving Fort Knox a few more barbed-wire fences.

When Hutton played one frivolous drive over mid-on, Hammond stood up on the balcony and sternly instructed him to rein it in and keep going. Hutton's innings started on Saturday morning and, because of the rest day, did not end until Tuesday. He might have been out on 40, when Ben Barnett missed a simple stumping, but it was an otherwise chanceless innings.

Hammond was in the strange position of being desperate to lose his own world record. He had made the highest Test score, 336 against New Zealand in 1932–33, but if Hutton passed that he would also pass Bradman's Ashes record of 334. Bradman did lose his record. And he broke his ankle. And Australia were thrashed out of sight. It's a surprise Hammond didn't die of a massive attack of *schadenfreude*.

Len Hutton is congratulated by Don Bradman on his world-record 364, The Oval, 1938.

Hutton was 300 not out at the end of the second day's play. He was teetotal, but his team-mate

Maurice Leyland, sensing that it might be a long night, prescribed port and Guinness. It did little good. 'I should have had five or six,' said Hutton. 'With so many people telling me that I needed another 35 runs to break the record, I tossed and turned most of the night, haunted by one face. That of Bill O'Reilly. I could not shut out of my mind the thought of his charging up, ball after ball, as he always did, as though he was going to eat me. My, how that man hated batsmen. What a great competitive bowler. I've never played against a better bowler.'

Where's the groundsman's hut? If I had a rifle, I'd shoot him now

O'Reilly did dismiss Hutton that morning, but only when he had made 364, shattering the existing records of Bradman and Hammond. When he moved past Bradman – though not, at that stage Hammond – Hutton recalled how 'A perfect blizzard of cheers and applause stopped play as effectively as violent rain can do.'

Hutton reacted, both at the time and in the aftermath, with striking modesty. 'It's Pudsey has got a swelled head,' said the Mayor of Hutton's home town. On that Tuesday night, the church bells of Pudsey rang 364 times. Hutton became a hero to millions – including the cricket-loving writer Harold Pinter. In 1986 he sent a poem to his fellow playwright Simon Gray: 'I saw Len Hutton his prime/Another time, another time.' When he heard nothing back, an impatient Pinter called to find out if Gray had received it. 'Yes,' he said, 'but I haven't finished it yet.'

Australia, without Bradman and Fingleton, and with no hope of a draw in what was a timeless Test, fell to defeat by a record margin of an innings and 579 runs. The *Cricketer* magazine described the match as 'a farce', because of those injuries, and Australia had the last laugh by taking home the Ashes after a drawn series. Even so, a record win is a record win is a record win. And Hutton's innings, still a record for Anglo-Australian Tests, will be talked about as long as the Ashes are still being contested.

1946–47

'A f****** fine way to start a series.'

[WALLY HAMMOND TO DON BRADMAN
WHEN THE AUSTRALIAN CAPTAIN
FAILED TO WALK, FIRST TEST,
BRISBANE, 29 NOVEMBER 1946]

THE ENGLAND TEAM DID NOT ASK the question because they already knew the answer. Don Bradman was out, caught by Jack Ikin in the slips off Bill Voce. It was so obvious that there was no need to appeal, and they started to swap chappish handshakes. On the first morning of the first post-war Ashes Test, they had seen off the ever dangerous Bradman for a modest score of 28.

Or so they thought. Bradman stood his ground as if nothing had happened, and, though England belatedly appealed, the umpire George Borwick gave Bradman not out on the grounds that it was a bump ball. England were on the apoplectic side of outraged, nobody more than their captain Wally Hammond. It was possibly the most acrimonious and controversial start to any Ashes series.

For a short period after the Second World War, a mood of innocence, relief and generosity of spirit prevailed in life and in cricket. The Victory Tests of 1945 – when England and Australia drew 2–2 and the box-office all-rounder Keith Miller introduced himself – hinted that the game might be different in a post-war landscape. It was only the illusion of an epiphany. Noble intentions were soon sacrificed to the sour realities of Ashes cricket in the Bradman era.

Bradman had not been involved in the war; he was invalided out of the Army School of Physical Training suffering from chronic fibrositis in 1941 and spent a rather sickly war as a stockbroker. For him not much had changed; he wanted to stuff England, and to hell with any hippy vibes.

To English eyes, that was clear from the moment he declined to walk on the first morning. Bradman saw things rather differently; he said he did not walk because he could not be sure he was out. In *Farewell to Cricket*, he said all the broadcasters at the ground thought it was a bump ball, while the newspaper men were split.

With utter inevitability, Bradman went on to make 187 as Hammond and England fumed with impotent rage. Australia's total of 645 – already formidable – was worth twice that after a couple of thunderstorms turned the pitch into a beast. Bradman found the whole thing impossibly funny. 'The first time I played against England, in 1928, they scored 521, caught us on a wet wicket and got us out for about 120,' he said to Ian Johnson. 'With a lead of over 400, they batted a second time and left us over 700 to make in the last innings. Then they invented Bodyline for my special benefit. The last time I played against them, in 1938, England made over 900 before Hammond declared and I broke my ankle bowling and couldn't bat. Just this once, we have them in trouble. Do you really blame me for being so happy?'

Miller took seven for 60 in the first innings, but did not enjoy the experience. 'I was bowling on the worst sticky ever and I was frightened of hurting someone,' he said. 'Blind Freddie could have got wickets on that track.'

> I was bowling on the worst sticky ever and I was frightened of hurting someone. Blind Freddie could have got wickets on that track

Miller and Ray Lindwall, the fast-bowling duo who made their Test debuts against New Zealand a year earlier in Australia's first post-war series, quickly established themselves as a truly great new-ball pair.

They were asked by Bradman to target Len Hutton's bad arm, which had been seriously injured on a commando training course during the war; after Bodyline, it was a case of the bitten biting. Hutton said that batting in such circumstances was 'akin to being in the Blitz'. Miller was not impressed. 'Here we are after the War, everybody happy to be alive, and we have to grind them to dust. So I thought, bugger me, if this is Test cricket, they can stick it up their jumper. Don kept up this incessant will-to-win but it just wasn't my way of playing cricket.' England were rolled over for 141 and 172 to lose by an innings and 332 runs.

Bradman had another reprieve in the second Test at Sydney, when England thought he was caught at short leg on 22. He made 234, the same score as the opener Sid Barnes, with the pair adding 405 for the fifth wicket. England were again thrashed despite a twenty-four-minute 37 from Len Hutton, a cameo so audacious that it was celebrated even more than the pair of 234s. Not that it changed the outcome. Australia won the first Test by an innings and 332 runs; in the second they simply removed the two and won by an innings and 33.

Bradman 'failed' twice in the third Test at Melbourne, making 79 and 49, but there was no rest for the England attack: even the No.9 Lindwall biffed a century in a second-innings total of 536. That match was the first drawn Test in Australia for 65 years, which meant England had at least averted a possible whitewash. But the tour was an almost endless humiliation for their captain Hammond, who came up against Bradman for the final time. It was a landslide.

Bradman was the asterisk Hammond put against his own achievements, and throughout his career he was heard to exclaim 'Bloody Bradman'. Whatever Hammond did, Bradman trumped it. When Hammond made a record 905 runs in the 1928–29 Ashes, Bradman made 974 in 1930. Even when Hammond broke Bradman's record for the highest Test score, nobody really cared because it was not in an Ashes Test. If Hammond had cured the common cold, Bradman would have cured cancer.

Hammond could have done with a cure for syphilis. His increasing moodiness was originally thought to be the result of a disease caused by a mosquito bite in the Caribbean in 1926, but his biographer David Foot concluded that he contracted syphilis or another sexually transmitted disease. Hammond was a notorious philanderer, a man whose proclivities made Ron Jeremy seem a paragon of chastity by comparison. In those days, the Hammond organ referred to something other than a musical instrument. 'Wally – well yes, he liked a shag,' said his England team-mate Eddie Paynter.

There were no effective antibiotics at the time, and Foot suggests Hammond's treatment significantly exacerbated the darker side of his character. That treatment saved his life, but he emerged from the nursing home a different person. 'He was the greatest player we shall ever see,' said a Gloucestershire team-mate, 'but a funny bugger.' He didn't mean funny ha-ha.

Wally – well yes, he liked a shag

If Foot's persuasive thesis is to be believed, Hammond's life was never the same because of a debilitating combination of syphilis and Bradmania. England's Denis Compton said relations between the two 'became strained to an almost unbearable extent' during the 1946–47 tour. The fact that Hammond couldn't buy a run didn't help; his highest score in the series was 37. He retreated into himself to such an extent that, during a 700-mile journey with Hutton, he said only one thing: 'Keep an eye out for a garage; we need some petrol.'

One writer said that Hammond came 'as a cricket god, only to leave a failure both as a batsman and a captain'. His personal life was barely any better, with his divorce splashed all over the papers. Upon returning home, he married again and retired from cricket. It was a sad effing way to end a great career.

1946–47

'Sorry, Godfrey, but I have to do it – the crowd are a bit bored at the moment.'

[KEITH MILLER AFTER BOWLING CONSECUTIVE BOUNCERS TO GODFREY EVANS, FOURTH TEST, ADELAIDE, 6 FEBRUARY 1947]

THE ONE THING KEITH MILLER COULD NEVER abide was boredom. Godfrey Evans had been at the crease for an eternity in the fourth Test at Adelaide and still hadn't scored a run, so Miller decided to liven things up. He whistled a short ball past Evans' face, and followed it with another next ball. As Evans looked down the pitch in surprise, Miller explained the reasoning for his sudden assault.

Whether to please the crowd or satisfy his own daredevil spirit, Miller dealt almost exclusively in attacking cricket. His emergence as an all-rounder of rare talent and even rarer charisma was one of the happier features of the 1946–47 series.

Australia had already retained the urn going into that fourth Test at Adelaide. It ended in a draw, a match of great moments rather than a great match. In the first innings Alec Bedser bowled Don Bradman for a duck with a ball that pitched leg and hit off; Bradman deemed it the greatest delivery he ever faced. The following day was a rest day, so Bedser went to the beach at nearby Glenelg, where he was approached by a boy. 'You've spoilt my weekend,' he said. 'I could hit you. Why did you bowl out Don Bradman for a duck?'

When the match resumed, Miller struck a spectacular maiden Test century, including a six off the first ball of the fourth day's play. Both

Denis Compton, whose flair had charmed the Australian crowds, and Arthur Morris made two centuries in the match.

After two draws, Australia reasserted their authority in the final match at Sydney, winning by five wickets to take the series 3–0. Hammond missed the match with fibrositis, and was replaced as captain by Norman Yardley. Len Hutton, after making 122 not out on the first day, was hospitalised with tonsillitis and took no further part in the match. Lindwall and Doug Wright, England's talented but erratic leg-spinner, took seven wickets apiece in the first innings; another leggie, the all-rounder Colin McCool, ran through England in the second innings with five for 44.

Miller had a quiet end to the series but ended with exceptional figures in his first Ashes: 384 runs at 76.80 and 16 wickets at 20.87. He became the golden boy of Australian cricket and was nicknamed 'Nugget' as a result. 'He could bat, bowl, field and he could fly an aeroplane,' said his team-mate Bill Brown. After his experiences as a fighter pilot in the Second World War, he had an unwavering commitment to attacking, entertaining cricket. 'Pressure is a Messerschmitt up your arse,' he said in a later interview with Michael Parkinson. 'Playing cricket is not.'

Pressure is a Messerschmitt up your arse. Playing cricket is not

During the war, he broke away from his fleet to fly over Bonn, the birthplace of Beethoven. There were regular rumours of a relationship with Princess Margaret. Miller was devastatingly handsome, a Boy's Own hero with a roguish twinkle who would demonstratively flick back his luscious mane.

He was not always popular with English crowds, who took umbrage at his short-pitched bowling on occasion, but he was a fair and principled man. Never mind the spirit of cricket; Miller captured the ideal spirit of life. When Australia famously massacred Essex for 721 runs in a single day in 1948, Miller offered no stroke to his first ball and was bowled. He had no truck with what he perceived as vulgar greed, and had regular clashes with Bradman.

**Ray Lindwall and Keith Miller, Australia's brilliant
post-war fast bowlers.**

He found a kindred spirit in Compton, who became the Brylcreem
Boy and shared Miller's attitude to life and cricket. They were
idolised around the world.* Ill health in his old age failed to dull
the spirits of an authentic Australian hero. Interviewed at the age of
seventy-five, Miller said: 'No regrets. I've had a hell of a good life.
Been damned lucky.'

In his career, Michael Parkinson has interviewed over 2000 of the
world's most famous people, from Muhammad Ali to Jack Nicholson.
Miller left a greater impression on him than any. 'Were I to host a
dinner party to celebrate my last days on earth,' said Parkinson, 'Keith
Ross Miller would be at the top of my guest list.' And his presence
would ensure that the dinner would be anything but boring.

---

* When Sir Tim Rice won an Academy Award, he thanked Compton during his acceptance speech,
prompting a delicious confusion. 'We don't know who Denis Compton is,' said a Walt Disney
employee. 'He doesn't appear to be at Disney Studios or have anything to do with them.'

1948

'What's going on out here then?
Let's get stuck into 'em.'

[NEIL HARVEY TO KEITH MILLER,
FOURTH TEST, HEADINGLEY,
24 JULY 1948]

FOR A SIDE WHO HAD ALREADY REGAINED the Ashes, Australia were in quite a predicament. They were being outplayed for the second consecutive Test and the crushing superiority of the early part of the series felt a long time ago. Don Bradman's off stump had just been sent flying, and now a boy was being sent to do a job that even the greatest batsman in cricket history could not do.

Australia were 68 for three in response to England's imposing 496 in the fourth Test at Headingley when Neil Harvey, nineteen, playing in his first Ashes Test, emerged capless from the pavilion and strolled jauntily to the middle as if he was off on his paper round. His new partner was Keith Miller, the freewheeling all-rounder who had been reduced to caution by the match situation. Harvey addressed Miller, almost ten years his senior, as if they were playing a park game. The result was one of the most charming partnerships ever seen in an Ashes Test, and a tipping point in cricket history.

When Australia arrived in 1948, everybody knew they were a seriously good side. After beating England 3–0 in 1946–47 they had thrashed India 4–0 at home. England had a strong spine – Len Hutton, Denis Compton, Godfrey Evans, Alec Bedser – but Australia had an elephantine spine, and significantly better love handles too. The fact that England gave seventeen debuts in the fifteen months between Ashes series reflected the work-in-progress nature of their team.

Bradman scored his usual bucketload of runs in the last series of his Test career. The team also included the great batsmen Arthur Morris and Lindsay Hassett, the irrepressible Miller and the peerless fast bowler Ray Lindwall, all reliable sources of national pride. 'We didn't have Milton and Shakespeare but, by God, we had Bradman and that kid Ray Lindwall,' said the writer Thomas Keneally when looking back on the tour. The 'kid Lindwall' came to Test cricket late because of the war. By 1948 he was twenty-seven and at his peak, a beautifully rhythmical fast bowler whose pace and late swing were an examination that most batsmen flunked.

We didn't have Milton and Shakespeare but, by God, we had Bradman and that kid Ray Lindwall

As brilliant as Australia's bowling was, the tour is primarily associated with their batsmen. In Tests and county matches they scored runs in eye-popping quantities. 'When you're batting well,' said the opener Morris, 'you make your own rubbish.' That year, the cricket grounds of England became landfill sites. There were 47 first-class centuries in all, and against Essex they scored a record 721 runs in a single day.

Bedser was the only Englishman to take 10 wickets in the Tests, and even he took the sort of tap that would be unthinkable in future Ashes series, whereas Bill Johnston and Lindwall each picked up 27 cheap wickets for Australia. England's best player was Compton, who made two courageous hundreds. His 184 in the first Test at Trent Bridge, spread over three days because of interruptions, could not save a match that Australia won by eight wickets. The decisive moment of the match came when Compton hit his wicket trying to hook a bouncer from his mate Miller. Australia marmalised England by 409 runs at Lord's, with the openers Morris and the eccentric Sid Barnes – who ended with a career average of 63 from just 13 Tests – both scoring hundreds.

England responded by dropping Hutton for the first time in his career; his replacement, George Emmett, a brilliant hitter at county level, was sorted out by Lindwall: he made 10 and nought on debut in the third Test at Old Trafford before joining the list of one-cap wonders when Hutton was restored to the side.

Compton's second masterpiece ensured England dominated that third Test. He made 145 not out, having originally retired hurt on three after mishooking Lindwall into his face. Three hours later he returned, fortified with stitches and brandy. 'Great as Compton is, never has he been greater,' said the *Movietone News* commentator Leslie Mitchell.

The weather precluded a result but England simply continued their dominance across the Pennines a fortnight later, as if it was a continuation of the third Test rather than a new match. They were 423 for two in the first innings at one stage, with the nightwatchman Bedser making 79. Even after a first-innings collapse, the game was theirs to shape like a piece of Play-Doh when Harvey came to the crease.

Australia were still 438 behind. Crucially they had lost Bradman, whose wicket was worth about five psychologically – especially at Headingley, where his previous Test scores were 334, 304, 103 and 16. Harvey was only playing because of an injury to Barnes. Miller's mood changed with Harvey's arrival; he launched into a blazing counter-attack, pumping Jim Laker for one of the highest sixes anyone could remember.

The idea was to let Harvey settle in at the crease; instead he matched Miller stroke for stroke and smile for smile. It was playground cricket at the key point of an Ashes series. 'I don't think I have known a more enjoyable hour of cricket,' wrote the former Australian opener Jack Fingleton. His was not a lone view, or a partisan one: the great English commentator John Arlott said he could not believe it possible 'for a brain to conceive any innings which could have been greater [than Miller's]'.

The pair added 121 in comfortably under two hours. Miller fell for 58 and Harvey went on to make 112. He had never used his Slazenger bat before – not even in practice – and never used it after. The bat was a different kind of one-hit wonder. The spirit of the counter-attack was so infectious that the next batsman Sam Loxton smote five sixes before falling seven short of a maiden century. 'There goes the old man's axe through the radio,' he said as he returned to the dressing-room.

The runs, and particularly the way Australia made them, changed the mood of the match to such an extent that, even when England declared their second innings on 365 for eight to set Australia a world-record target of 404, the Aussies decided to get stuck into 'em. On a big-spinning pitch England had only a young Laker, who was hit back into county cricket with match figures of three for 206, and the part-time spin of Compton.

The England captain Norman Yardley had other things on his mind on the last day; his wife was due to give birth. Everyone else was having kittens as it was becoming increasingly apparent that the unthinkable was going to happen. England lost their way, and were hopeless in the field, yet that should not detract from the ultimate demonstration of the 1948 Australians' greatness. Morris made 182, Bradman 173 not out – between them they hit 66 fours – and Harvey arrived to hit the winning runs with just over 10 minutes to spare. He was merely finishing what he had started.

Instead of 2–1, the series was now 3–0. Crucially, Australia were still unbeaten. They stayed that way throughout the tour, in all matches – played 31, won 23, drawn 8 – and became known as the Invincibles. For some reason, very few specific teams in cricket history have a nickname; the Invincibles stand out so much that they should have their own font. The cricket world will forever be on nickname terms with them.

It is on first-name terms with the Don, also. With the series settled, attention turned to the last Test – the final match of Bradman's career. He suggested, perhaps out of politeness, that England would have won comfortably with a proper spin bowler on that last day at Headingley. On the same day, a leg-spinner called Eric Hollies was taking seven for 55 for Warwickshire against Glamorgan.

1948

'It's not easy to bat with tears in your eyes.'

[DON BRADMAN TALKS TO LEN HUTTON ABOUT HIS LAST TEST INNINGS, FIFTH TEST, THE OVAL, 14 AUGUST 1948]

DON BRADMAN WENT INTO THE FINAL Test of the 1948 Ashes with an average of 101.39. Nobody really knew or cared about those numbers; the main event was Bradman's last Test appearance. Under normal circumstances he would have had two innings, but England made that unlikely when they were routed for 52 by Ray Lindwall on the first day. At one stage Lindwall took five for eight in 8.1 overs; he ended with figures of six for 20.

Len Hutton made 30 of those, a masterful performance which was worth approximately 364 on another day. He was the last man out after an astonishing legside snaffle by Don Tallon which Bradman described as the best wicketkeeping catch he had ever seen.

By the time Bradman walked to the wicket towards the end of the first day, Australia were 117 for one and it was odds on that it would be his final innings. England gave him a guard of honour and three cheers – common for retiring greats these days, but not so much back then. The crowd, clearly experiencing a variation of Stockholm Syndrome after all the misery Bradman inflicted on them, sang 'For he's a jolly good fellow'.

Bradman, who was a fortnight away from his fortieth birthday, had become a nervous starter. The ovation compounded that. 'The reception had stirred my emotions very deeply and made me anxious – a dangerous state of mind for any batsman to be in.'

Very few people had registered that, if this was to be Bradman's last innings, he needed to score just four runs for a career average of 100; Alec Bedser said that, had he known and been bowling at the time, he would have fed Bradman a full toss.

Instead Bradman was facing Eric Hollies, the leg-spinner playing his first Test in a year. He felt Bradman couldn't pick his googly, having played against him for Warwickshire, and apparently predicted that he would bowl Bradman second ball with that same delivery. The first ball was defended, although Bradman said he barely saw it. He lunged forward assertively to the second ball, as he had thousands of times in his Test career. But this was the Hollies googly – the ball he struggled to read at the best of times, never mind with misty eyes. It came back through the gate, possibly via the inside edge, to hit the stumps. The crowd stirred from their shock to applaud Bradman from the field. 'Best f****** ball I've bowled all season, and they're clapping *him*!' said Hollies to a team-mate.

Best f**** ball I've bowled all season, and they're clapping him!**

John Arlott's radio commentary captured the disbelief. 'Hollies pitches the ball up slowly and... he's bowled. Bradman, bowled Hollies, nought. Bowled Hollies, nought. And, what do you say under those circumstances? I wonder if you see a ball very clearly in your last Test in England on a ground where you've played out some of the biggest cricket in your life, and where the opposing team have just stood round you and given you three cheers and where the crowd has clapped you all the way to the wicket. I wonder if you really see the ball at all.'

Others did not buy the suggestion that Bradman had something obscuring his vision. 'That bugger Bradman never had a tear in his eye throughout his whole life,' said Jack Crapp, who was fielding at first slip. In the press box, Jack Fingleton and Bill O'Reilly – erstwhile team-mates of Bradman who did not care for his ruthless approach – were nearly crying with laughter. It is generally suggested they did so out of sheer *schadenfreude*, though in *Bradman's War*, his book of the 1948 tour, Malcolm Knox suggests that it was 'more likely to be at the cruel irony of the cricketing gods than in mockery of Bradman'.

**Don Bradman, in his final Test innings, is bowled by
Eric Hollies for a duck; The Oval, 1948.**

Not even Bradman was spared sport's vicissitudes. His failure was a
tale of four runs, three cheers, two balls and one almighty anti-climax.
He once said he didn't believe in the law of averages (see page 86). He
certainly knew about the *lore* of averages; his career average of 99.94
is sport's most famous decimal place.

In a sense, the average is damaging, because it can obscure focus on
the sheer genius of Bradman, particularly his tap-dancer's feet and
ability to take any attack to the cleaners. Bradman was the batsman
at Lord's in 1948 when the English leg-spinner Doug Wright bowled
what he regarded as the best over of his career. 'Every ball came
out of the hand the way I wanted and pitched where I wanted,' said
Wright. 'I beat him twice. It went for 16.'

Modern eyes perceive Bradman's failure differently from those of
1948; back then, it was simply a shock to see Bradman out for a duck
in his last Test innings. He didn't get close to a second innings, with
Australia winning by an innings and 149 runs. The main reason for
that is one of the great forgotten Test knocks. The opener Arthur
Morris was once asked whether he played in Bradman's final Test.
'Yes,' he replied. 'I got 196.' The next highest score in the match
was 64. But the only score anyone remembers is Donald's duck.

THE
AGE OF
ATTRITION
1950–1968

1950–51

'Fine lettuce! Nine-pence! With hearts as big as Freddie Brown's!'

[A BARROWMAN AT SYDNEY QUAY, 9 JANUARY 1951]

IN SPORT, A REFERENCE TO FRUIT AND VEG is not generally a sign of approval. Rotten eggs are thrown at players by affronted fans; and the England football manager Graham Taylor was nicknamed 'Turnip' after failure at the 1992 European Championship. For Freddie Brown, England's captain on the 1950–51 MCC tour of Australia, however, it was only a positive thing.

Brown, the Northamptonshire all-rounder, is one of the great unlikely Ashes heroes. Born in Peru, he was thirty-nine when he was appointed captain, and had played only nine Tests in nineteen years since his debut in 1931. He had been on the Bodyline tour of 1932–33, and when he returned many Australians amused themselves by telling him that 'I knew your father when he was here eighteen years ago.'

England were in the doldrums after their shock defeat at home to West Indies the previous summer – Sonny Ramadhin, Alf Valentine and all that – but Brown infused English cricket with some much needed serotonin. He had taken over from Norman Yardley for the final Test of that summer; England did not appoint a professional captain until 1952, and Brown seemed the best option among the dwindling breed of county amateurs.

When he was offered the captaincy for the winter tour of Australia,

Brown thought he might have to say no because he had just taken on a job with an engineering firm. When he asked his new boss whether it might be possible to have some time off to captain England in Australia, the reply was non-negotiable: 'If you don't take the job, you're fired!'

England went 2–0 down in the series, though they might have won both games. They lost the second Test, an unremittingly tense, low-scoring match, by 28 runs. And the first Test on a Brisbane sticky dog was decided by the toss. *Wisden* said that 'Most Australians agreed [that England] batted better, bowled better and fielded better.' The pitch was so unplayable on the third day that 20 wickets fell for 102, with Australia declaring their second innings on 32 for seven to get England in again before the pitch eased up. Len Hutton's 62 not out on the last day, as England fell 70 short, was an astonishingly accomplished innings. Brown's 17 was the only other score in double figures.

The praise for Brown and his team was such that at times it felt like England had won the series 1–4. It was not a moral victory as such, because although the series was extremely close at the start, everybody accepted that Australia were ultimately too strong even without Don Bradman. But it was a crushing PR victory for the Poms. A modest England team – who did not help themselves by leaving players like Bill Edrich at home – played with pluck and intelligence throughout.

You've got about as much chance of taking a wicket on this tour as I have of pushing a pound of butter up a parrot's arse with a hot needle

They overcame an unlikely number of setbacks, most obviously in the third Test at Sydney when injuries to Trevor Bailey and Doug Wright left them with only three bowlers. Harsher judges would say they only had two. One of the bowlers was the debutant seamer John Warr of Middlesex, who struggled through 36 overs without reward. An Australian barracker had a fair idea what Warr was good for. 'Hey Warr!' he shouted. 'You've got about as much chance of taking a wicket on this tour as I have of pushing a pound of butter up a parrot's arse with a hot needle.'

Brown, who by now had turned forty and usually took a back seat with the ball, sent down 44 eight-ball overs of medium pace. It was the following day that a barrowman outside the Australia Hotel on Castlereagh Street in Sydney saw the opportunity to sell some special-edition lettuces.

In the next match, at Adelaide, Warr continued to toil fruitlessly. Eventually the Australian all-rounder Ian Johnson thin-edged a catch behind, only for the umpire not to spot it. As Warr's shoulders started to sag, Johnson did what Australians are not supposed to do (see page 22) and walked. The identity of the unfortunate parrot was never revealed.

The identity of the world's best batsman was clear, however: with Bradman gone, Hutton was widely recognised as the finest around. His series average of 89 was outrageous, especially as only two other Englishmen averaged as much as 20. He produced another masterpiece in the fourth Test, carrying his bat for 156 in the first innings. Nobody else made 30. In the same match, the Australian opener Arthur Morris struck 206 for Australia with nobody else passing 45, and in the third Test at Sydney Keith Miller blitzed 145 not out.

The great batsmen on both sides were driven to such heights by the quality of the bowling and the difficulty of the pitches. The Invincible seam triumvirate of Ray Lindwall, Miller and Bill Johnston shared 60 wickets at an average of 17, while Alec Bedser's interrogative seam bowling brought 30 wickets at an average of 16 for England.

Then there was the magical mystery spin of Jack Iverson. The former *Wisden* editor Tim de Lisle once wrote that England traditionally handled spin 'like soap in the bath'. They handled Iverson like a marmot in the bath. He took 21 wickets at 15 in his only Test series. England did not have a clue which way the ball was spinning. Iverson did not make his first-class debut until the age of thirty-four, having developed an unusual bent-fingered method of spinning the ball. A constant worrier, he was a mystery to batsmen and an even greater mystery to himself. He played only two more Sheffield Shield matches – and no Tests – after the 1950–51 series.

It was no coincidence that Iverson's poorest Test, in which he struggled with an ankle injury, was the one England won, the final match at Melbourne. It averted a whitewash and was Australia's first defeat in thirteen years. 'At last promise turned to fulfilment,' said *Wisden*. 'By a victory as worthily achieved as it was earned, England broke Australia's post-war run of twenty-six Tests without defeat.'

Reg Simpson, on his thirty-first birthday, made 156 not out in a first-innings total of 320 in another low-scoring game that England won by eight wickets. Brown played his part with an unlikely first-innings five-for to cap a splendid individual tour. *Wisden* said he 'brought England out of the post-war slough into which it had sunk'. He took 18 cheap wickets in the series, and his jaunty middle-order hitting also furthered his reputation. Even though England lost heavily, Brown became a hero in Australia for his good cheer and fighting spirit in the face of adversity. Australians recognised him as a fair dinkum Pom.

The final Test also brought overdue reward for Bedser, who ended a heroic series' work with five-fors in each innings. Bedser had the kind of work ethic that would be illegal in today's health-and-safety-conscious society, and bowled almost twice as many overs as any other Englishman in the series. His heart might have been even bigger than Freddie Brown's.

1953

'Bedser was really super fine/
Fourteen wickets for ninety-nine/
Alec Bedser, who taught you
to bowl Australia.'

[LYRICS FROM 'ALEC BEDSER CALYPSO'
BY LORD KITCHENER, 1953]

LINDSAY HASSETT WAS SEEING IT LIKE a football. The Australian captain had batted 397 minutes for a splendid 115 in the opening 1953 Ashes Test at Trent Bridge and looked good for many more. Then Alec Bedser produced the mother of all jaffas. It swung onto Hassett's legs before snapping sharply off the seam in the other direction to hit off stump. 'I tried to play three shots off one ball and almost made contact the third time,' said Hassett.

> **I tried to play three shots off one ball and almost made contact the third time**

Hassett's dismissal was the key moment of a stunning Australian collapse, from 237 for three to 249 all out. Bedser took seven for 55 and followed up with seven for 44 in the second innings. His match figures of 14 for 99 remain the best return by an England seam bowler in an Ashes Test. Bedser was among the greatest English-style bowlers of all, with a leg-cutter that was the definition of unplayable. He was a captain's best friend, as reliable as could be, and even received his own tribute from the renowned calypsonian Lord Kitchener after that performance at Trent Bridge.

Bedser's labours did not secure victory for England; rain washed out most of the last two days and England ended on 120 for one, 109 runs away from victory. It was an anti-climactic end to an otherwise excellent Test, a brilliant beginning to the keenly awaited 1953 series. England felt they were finally able to compete with Australia on even terms, and the thought of winning the Ashes for the first time since 1932–33 appealed even more because it was Coronation Year. However, Australia, who had won 4–1 in 1950–51, had added promising young all-rounders Alan Davidson and Richie Benaud to an already imposing side.

After their scare at Nottingham, Australia began to assert themselves, and England were indebted to Trevor Bailey for saving Tests with both bat and ball. At Lord's, in the second Test, he and Willie Watson undertook one of the great rearguards. After hundreds from Hassett and Keith Miller, England began the last day on 20 for three, chasing an unlikely target of 343. They soon lost Denis Compton but Watson and Bailey batted from before lunch until forty minutes before the close in a fifth-wicket partnership of 163.

Watson, thirty-three and an England football international, made a career-defining century on his Ashes debut. If Bailey was the Barnacle, as he was nicknamed for his adhesive qualities, then Watson was positively parasitic. The Australian batsman Colin McDonald, inverting the usual description of a one-way contest between bat and ball, said they were 'unbowlable'. Although both were eventually dismissed, England held on to reach 282 for seven. The former England bowler Bill Bowes, writing in the *Cricketer*, said it was 'a draw as glorious as any victory'. The Australian players were criticised for supposedly being in a nightclub until the early hours of the final day's play; their team manager said there was nothing to worry about and that he was 'personally satisfied that everyone was in bed by 1am'.

After a rain-affected draw in the third Test at Old Trafford, in which an absent-minded Australia collapsed bizarrely to 35 for eight in the final session, Bailey saved England again in the fourth Test at Headingley. England started the final day precariously placed on 177 for five, only 78 ahead, but Bailey batted over four hours for 38. He wasted time at every opportunity, including an appeal against the light, in bright sunshine, just before lunch. By the time the umpires had conferred, there was no time for another over. At one stage an exasperated Miller bowled a full toss past Bailey's head, then sat down in protest when the crowd jeered him. More time was wasted.

Miller was equally exasperated when the great umpire Frank Chester, in his last Test, reprieved Reg Simpson when he appeared to be run out by Hassett. Miller threw the ball into the pitch in anger. Simpson was out soon after, but Australia had lost more vital minutes.

For all that, they still had a good chance of winning the match. They needed 177 in 115 minutes and were going well when Bailey came on to bowl a different kind of leg theory. He speared the ball down the leg side from around the wicket, thereby radically restricting the batsmen's scoring opportunities. They fell 30 runs short and would almost certainly have won without Bailey's intervention.

It was just about the only time England's hopes with the ball did not depend on Bedser. He had taken six for 95 in the first innings of the game, which made him the first man to take 30 wickets in consecutive Ashes series – a feat that has not been repeated since. He ended with 39 wickets at 17.48. 'They said to me at The Oval, "come and see our new bowling machine",' he said in 1989. '"Bowling machine?" I said. "I used to be the bowling machine."'

He had his greatest success against the Australian opener Arthur Morris, dismissing him 18 times in Tests – a Test record until Glenn McGrath got to work on Mike Atherton a few decades later (see page 266). Morris was a great batsman, the Invincibles' top scorer in 1948, but his position at the top of the order exposed him to Bedser.

In 1953 Bedser dismissed Morris in the first innings of every Test. 'Again the cry went up that Arthur was my "rabbit",' wrote Bedser. 'Personally I have never seen fit to minimise Arthur's skill because I have had the fortune to get his wicket a few times. . . We have been the best of pals since we first met in 1946.'

At the end of the 1953 series, as their team-mates drank champagne, they broke off to go and get a beer together and spent the evening chatting about Morris's job as a car salesman, among other things. They tended not to discuss cricket, which on that particular day meant no talk of one of the most famous moments in Ashes history.

1953

'England deserved to win, if not from the first ball then at least from the second-last over.'

[THE AUSTRALIAN CAPTAIN LINDSAY HASSETT LAVISHES FAINT PRAISE ON HIS OPPONENTS, FIFTH TEST, THE OVAL, 19 AUGUST 1953]

DENIS COMPTON EASED BACK IN HIS CREASE and dragged the ball forcefully into the leg side. He walked towards his partner Bill Edrich, smiling gently, both hands still gripping his bat. If it all looked a little low-key, it was actually anything but. By the time he reached Edrich, hordes of supporters had run past him on their way to the pavilion. England had just won the Ashes for the first time in two decades.

It was a generation-defining moment. Thirteen years before Kenneth Wolstenholme's iconic commentary on England's 1966 football World Cup victory, cricket's Brian Johnston offered his own famous reaction to a national sporting triumph. Johnston's words are some of the most frequently misquoted in British sports commentary.

Is it the Ashes? Yes! England have won the Ashes!

It is usually suggested that Johnston said 'It's the Ashes!' when Compton ended nineteen years of Ashes misery. Johnston even wrote that himself. Yet the archive footage suggests it was slightly different: 'Is it the Ashes? Yes! England have won the Ashes!' Not that it changes the sentiment in any way, of course. This truly was a moment for English cricket to celebrate.

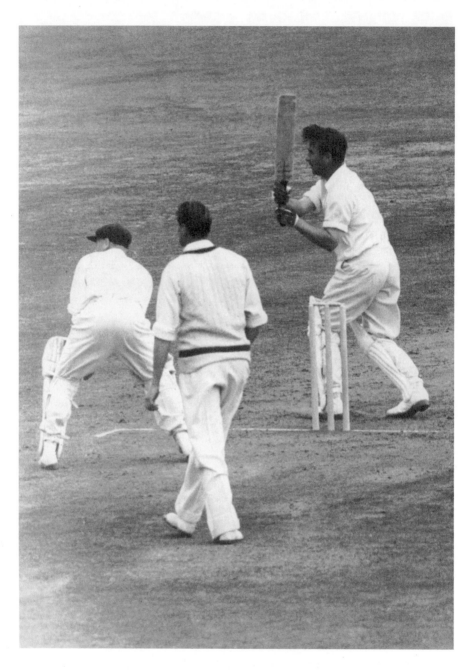

Dennis Compton hits the Ashes-winning boundary, The Oval, 1953.

For winning back the urn, the England XI who started the game went into folklore – even if they did not all receive MBEs after the series – and those of a certain vintage keep themselves warm in their dotage by reciting their names. The team for the final Test at The Oval is regarded by many as England's best ever side. Len Hutton, Bill Edrich, Peter May, Denis Compton, Tom Graveney, Trevor Bailey, Godfrey Evans, Jim Laker, Tony Lock, Fred Trueman and Alec Bedser. It was a contemporary team full of all-time greats.

May and Trueman, young players who were not yet established, had been recalled for the match as England looked for the right balance after a series in which they had often been outplayed in the first four drawn games of the series. Crucially they stuck with two spinners, Laker and Lock, while Australia had no specialist spinner after omitting the struggling Richie Benaud. It was a decisive selection error. The pitch turned increasingly as the match progressed and, after England took a slender first-innings lead of 31, Laker and Lock decided the match.

All Australia's good work in the series was dramatically undone when they slipped from 59 for one to 61 for five in their second innings, the wickets including Arthur Morris, Neil Harvey and Keith Miller. After that, there was no way Australia could get out of trouble, and Laker and Lock shared nine wickets to bowl them out for 162.

A target of 132 might have been tricky against a pair of spinners; instead it was a breeze, even against Ray Lindwall, Miller and Bill Johnston. Not to mention Hassett and Morris. Hassett came on to bowl the second-last over to which he referred after the match, and then Morris followed him with a few runs needed. Compton pulled him for four, the formal cue for the pitch to be invaded. The crowd formed a human beard at one end of the ground, chanting 'We want Len!' at the England balcony until the captain Hutton emerged.

Hassett, the Australian captain, was largely magnanimous. He gave a very generous speech, and cheerfully smashed his champagne glass on the Oval clock after toasting England's success, though he could not resist a couple of digs about who had been the better side for much of the series. In football terms, Australia only needed a draw, yet dominated most of the match before England scored a ninety-fourth-minute winner on the counterattack. Hassett also said, 'Lock threw us out,' in reference to Lock's quicker ball. When batting against Lock he was wont to shout, 'Strike one, strike two!' after certain deliveries. It was just not cricket.

It was England's first Ashes win since the end of the Second World War; the first, in fact, since the end of an even earlier war – known as Bodyline (see pages 68–85). The *Wisden* summary of the series could easily be applied to the future Ashes epic of 2005 (see pages 290–310): 'No other series of Tests captured such public attention. What with day-by-day front page newspaper articles and radio and television broadcasts there were times when industry almost stood still while the man in the street followed the tense battle between bat and ball.'

The celebrations in 1953 were more muted than those of 2005, however. Trueman, who was on National Service with the Royal Air Force at the time, went straight back to barracks at RAF Hemswell in Lincolnshire on the night of England's historic triumph. A friend once said to him, 'Bloody hell, Fred, you must have had one hell of a party after the Ashes win in 1953.' 'Party?' replied Trueman. 'You must be f****** joking. I had to be back at camp before midnight otherwise I was absent without leave.'

Unlike his fast-bowling namesake Freddie Flintoff, who caroused through the wee small hours and most of the following day after winning the Ashes in 2005 (see page 309), 'Fiery' Freddie Trueman had an early night. England had, after all, left it late enough to win the series.

1954–55

'I swear there was a new light in his eyes, as if a spark had been kindled deep down inside him.'

[LEN HUTTON ON FRANK TYSON
AFTER THE FAST BOWLER WAS KNOCKED
OUT BY RAY LINDWALL, SECOND TEST,
SYDNEY, 21 DECEMBER 1954]

THE SCENE SOUNDS A BIT LIKE SOMETHING from a schlocky horror film. A body, lying prostrate on a massage table, surrounded by wide-eyed onlookers. A sudden movement. It's alive! The eyes begin to open, and the look in those eyes is not the same as it was before. Somebody is going to pay. The body was that of Frank Tyson, the England fast bowler who was knocked unconscious while batting against Australia in the second Test of the 1954–55 Ashes. His lights had gone out, and when they came back on the wattage was significantly brighter.

His captain Len Hutton certainly thought so. 'I am not given to fanciful imagination, and the fact is that when he resumed bowling the next day he was a yard, maybe a yard and a half quicker than before. His pace on that decisive and extraordinary day in Sydney was nothing short of frightening.'

Tyson had only played one Test going into the tour, and Hutton talked him down to the Australian media. They would have believed the lack of hype after the first Test, when Tyson took one for 160 and England were trounced by an innings. Hutton infamously put Australia in at Brisbane, whereupon Australia scored 601 for eight declared, albeit with the aid of twelve dropped catches. 'Pitches

Frank Tyson, whose pace overwhelmed Australia in 1954–55, in action during the fourth Test at Adelaide.

are like wives,' said Hutton. 'You never know how they'll turn out.' England also went in without a specialist spinner, a tactic which in those days was as shocking as a miniskirt. 'Hutton is a muttonhead!' said the former England captain 'Plum' Warner back in London.

The second Test at Sydney did not start much better for England. They were bowled out for 154 on the first day and were 55 for three, still 19 behind, in the second innings when Peter May was joined by Colin Cowdrey. The two young amateurs put together a splendid partnership of 116 – more than double the next highest stand in the match – to give England hope, and May went on to make an outstanding 104.

It was just before lunch the following day when Tyson turned his back on a Lindwall bouncer and was hit on the head. He was briefly concussed before being led from the field. Improbably, after stirring on the massage table, he returned to the field to finish his innings. An affronted, aggrieved Tyson internally swore revenge, and then came down like the wolf on the Australian fold.

After one ball of Tyson's first spell in the second innings, the wicket-keeper Godfrey Evans and the slips exchanged looks and took a few paces backwards; Hutton had never seen Evans stand so far back. Tyson had taken a few steps forward, shortening his run considerably after the first Test. He had taken four wickets in the first innings, and scorched through Australia in the second, taking six for 85 as England won a thriller by 38 runs despite a glorious unbeaten 92 from Neil Harvey.

Tyson relaxed at the cinema that evening, but the images that remained with him were of Australian stumps flying. 'I hung on to the day as if reluctant it should ever end,' he said. 'One night I went to sleep an ordinary fast bowler who enjoyed playing cricket, only to wake up the next day dubbed a violent hurricane, frequenting the coasts of China and Japan – a Typhoon.' It was an enduring nickname. 'Typhoon' Tyson was the first fast bowler to give Australia the fear since Harold Larwood. Evans recalled Keith Miller coming to the crease in one Test, exchanging pleasantries and then saying, in reference to Tyson, 'I hope that bastard comes off soon!'

I hope that bastard comes off soon!

Tyson was helped considerably by his new-ball partner Brian Statham. C. B. Fry said they were 'the fastest pair of England bowlers we had ever seen'. Unlike many fast bowlers, both attacked the stumps relentlessly. 'If there has ever been a more accurate bowler than Statham,' said Tyson, 'I have yet to see him.'

Nobody had seen a faster bowler than Tyson. He produced an even more spectacular spell in the next Test at the MCG, taking a devastating shortcut through the Australian batting line-up with seven for 27 in the second innings to put England 2–1 ahead. In a game where nobody else reached 50, Cowdrey (102 in the first innings) and May (91 in the second) were again influential. Tyson scalped six more in the fourth Test at Adelaide, where England retained the Ashes with a five-wicket win. In three Tests Tyson had taken 25 wickets and turned disaster into famous triumph.

England reached their target of 94 for the loss of five wickets, despite a wonderful burst of 9-8-5-3 from the thirty-five-year-old Miller.

With the Ashes at stake, 'Nugget' ignored medical advice not to bowl fast because of a bad knee. 'The buggers have done us!' said Hutton to Denis Compton as Miller was running riot. 'Steady on, Len,' replied Compton. 'There's still me.' Compton saw England home. The retrospective rankings also show that this is the day England would have gone top of the ICC Test Championship, a position they would have held for the next four years.

The 1954–55 tour is indelibly associated with the primal menace of Tyson. Like a number of England's Ashes-winning quicks – Larwood and Simon Jones in particular – his career was cut short. He played only seventeen Tests because of injury, taking 76 wickets at the stunning average of 18.56. And, like Larwood, he subsequently emigrated to Australia.

'Speed – burning, scorching speed was his weapon,' said the great Australian all-rounder Alan Davidson. With Tyson, the biggest threat was not so much to life and limb as to off, middle and leg stump – he bowled full and straight, and a startling 43 per cent of his Test wickets were out bowled. Tyson did not have much subtlety in his bowling, but he made up for that with the sophistication of his sledging. Not for him the four-letter wisdom beloved of most; he would sledge confused batsmen with quotes from Shakespeare and Wordsworth.

Speed – burning, scorching speed was his weapon

Tyson was a unique fast bowler, whose pace – which he once estimated at well over 100mph – came from the shoulder power of a Russian shot-putter. And he knew how much his sheer pace intimidated Australia. 'No batsman likes quick bowling, and this knowledge gives one a sense of omnipotence.'

'Oh yes, there have been better fast bowlers,' he said. 'But I doubt whether there has been one who derived more pleasure from bowling fast.' Never more so than on that famous day at Sydney in 1954, when a knock on the head unleashed a hurricane.

1956

Ian Johnson: 'We need guts and determination. We can still save the match!'
Keith Miller: 'Bet you 6/4 we can't.'

[AUSTRALIA'S STAR ALL-ROUNDER REACTS TO HIS CAPTAIN'S SUGGESTION THAT THE FOURTH TEST AT OLD TRAFFORD COULD STILL BE DRAWN, 27 JULY 1956]

THE SECOND DAY OF A TEST MATCH was a bit early for death-or-glory rhetoric. But the situation left the Australian captain Ian Johnson little choice. His side were about to follow on, having been bowled out for a paltry 84 in the fourth Test at Old Trafford, in a game they could not lose if they wished to regain the Ashes. Most of the team were preoccupied with a pitch they believed had been doctored to suit England's spin bowlers, Jim Laker and Tony Lock, and Johnson was desperate for them to refocus.

His speech was stirring stuff – or it would have been, had Keith Miller not instantly countered with such undeniable pragmatism. Miller, who usually relished even the toughest challenge, looked up from the racing pages he was perusing and gave Johnson some odds of his own. If 'Nugget' Miller was waving the white flag, then Australia really were in trouble.

Although Australia had been devastated by Frank Tyson in 1954–55, their perceived vulnerability against spin was the main topic of conversation at the start of the 1956 series. That was largely the result of the Oval Test in 1953, when Laker and Lock bowled England to Ashes glory. Laker also took all ten wickets in an innings for Surrey against Australia in a tour match at the start of the 1956 summer.

England's plan was so obvious that they could have 'accidentally' shoved it under the Australians' hotel room doors the night before the game. When the series began with a rain-affected draw at Trent Bridge, all 13 Australian wickets went to the spin of Laker, Lock and Bob Appleyard.

The summer of spin had a five-day hiatus at Lord's in late June, when England made the mistake of preparing a good cricket wicket. Miller won the match with splendid fast bowling, taking the only ten-for of his Test career in a 185-run victory. Even by Miller's standards, this was heroic stuff: his new-ball partner, the debutant Pat Crawford, was injured early in the match, and Miller, at the age of thirty-six, bowled 70.1 overs in the match to end with figures of ten for 152.

An even older man had a profound influence on the third Test at Headingley. England's No.5 was the forty-one-year-old Lancastrian Cyril Washbrook, who had formed an outstanding opening partnership with Len Hutton after the war but had not played Test cricket since 1950–51. Washbrook, a selector, had to leave the room while his potential inclusion was discussed. When he walked to the wicket on the first morning, England were in huge trouble at 17 for three. 'I've never felt so glad in my life than when I saw who was coming in,' said Peter May. He made 101 and Washbrook 98 in a series-turning partnership of 187. That was more than Australia managed in either innings on a turning pitch as Laker and Lock claimed 11 and seven wickets apiece.

Australia were suspicious of a dusty Old Trafford surface even before the fourth Test began. Miller told anyone who would listen that the game would be done inside three days. Yet England posted a strong score of 459, and Australia's reply started well when they reached 48 for nought before Laker dismissed the opener Colin McDonald. Moments later, Laker bowled Neil Harvey for nought with a peach that had a similar impact to Shane Warne's Ball of the Century on the same ground thirty-seven years later (see page 245). It pitched leg, hit off, and caused Harvey to glare at the pitch in a manner that reverberated throughout the Australian dressing-room. 'I am not being boastful,' said Laker, 'when I express the opinion that this ball won the Test series.'

Although the pitch was far from easy, Australia, ravaged by psychological demons, batted appallingly to be bowled out for 84 in the first innings. Laker took nine for 37, including a spell of seven for eight in 22 balls. 'Naturally I was proud of my return of nine wickets – but it would never have been as profitable if there had been much sanity in the Australian display.'

Ken 'Slasher' Mackay said he batted like an elephant on ice. 'We were all pissed off,' said the batsman Ian Craig, 'and we dropped our bundle a bit.' When the groundsman Bert Flack went to the Australian dressing-room between innings to ask them which roller they wanted to use, a number of players put their hands around their throats in a universal gesture for imminent throttling. 'Please your f****** self,' said the captain Johnson.

It was a huge controversy. 'Thank God Nasser has taken over the Suez Canal,' said Flack, 'otherwise I'd be plastered over every front page like Marilyn Monroe.' The pitch had indeed been given a buzzcut the day before the match; Flack says he did so under instructions, though the chairman of selectors Gubby Allen denied that. 'England cheated, if by cheating you include the practice of preparing wickets to suit your own purpose,' said McDonald, who made a superb 89 in the second innings.

England cheated, if by cheating you include the practice of preparing wickets to suit your own purpose

For a time it seemed Australia would escape with a draw because of rain and McDonald's six-hour demonstration of how to bat on a raging turner. They were only two down at lunch on the final day, when Laker had a pint and a sandwich on his own in the dressing-room. The sun came out thereafter, and slowly made the pitch ever more difficult for batting. 'If I ever own a racehorse,' said Laker, 'I think I shall call it "Manchester Sun".'

Laker took all ten wickets for 53 and finished the match with time to spare. Upon taking the final wicket, he simply shook a few hands

Jim Laker walks off after taking 19 wickets, Old Trafford, 1956.

and walked off the Old Trafford pitch. 'Even when bowling out 19 Australians in a Test match. . . his demeanour implied that the whole thing was a fearful chore,' wrote Alan Ross.

It is among the more perverse statistics that Lock took only one of the 20 wickets to fall to England's spin twins. Lock bowled umpteen fast, spinning deliveries that did too much and beat everything. The more wickets Laker took, the harder Lock tried, and the more his mood darkened.

It was a strange form of humiliation for Lock. After one wicket he was heard offering congratulations, of sorts: 'Well bowled, you bastard!' In time, Lock told Laker's wife that he wished he hadn't taken that one wicket, but at the time he was furious. Lock was the ghost at the feast and did not even bother to shower before leaving the ground after the game.

It took Laker a little longer to get away. For the next few hours there were drinks, a press conference, TV and radio, and half an hour of signing autographs by his car. Then began the long, lonely drive back to Surrey; Laker could not stay overnight in Manchester, because he had to meet Australia again in a tour match the following morning. Such was the Stakhanovite nature of international tours in the 1950s. When he fancied a break on the way home, Laker stopped at a pub in the sleepy Staffordshire town of Lichfield. Kipling would surely have approved. This was how to treat triumph: with a modest handshake, a beer and a sandwich.

It was a pretty typical Tuesday night in the pub, and one particular topic dominated the conversations around the bar: the extraordinary events that had taken place at Old Trafford. The punters paid little attention to the man on his own in the corner, supping a pint and eating a stale cheese sandwich. Nobody realised that this was none other than Jim Laker, who was in the paradoxical

What a performance. I'd give anything to meet that Laker

position of being an anonymous national hero. There is a – possibly apocryphal – story that somebody in the pub said to Laker: 'What a performance. I'd give anything to meet that Laker.' Never meet your heroes; you might not recognise them.

Laker claimed seven more scalps in the final Test, a rain-affected draw at The Oval, to end the series with an Ashes-record 46 wickets at an average of 9.60. Yet his performance at Old Trafford inevitably overshadows his excellent work in the other four Tests.

Nobody has taken more than 16 wickets in a Test since, though Anil Kumble took all 10 in an innings in 1999. Even Muttiah Muralitharan and Sir Richard Hadlee, those great one-man attacks, could not get close to Laker's record. And we'll bet you 6/4 that nobody ever does.

1958–59

'Well, at least he's chucking them straight, isn't he, mate?'

[AN UNNAMED AUSTRALIAN UMPIRE DESCRIBES THE BOWLING ACTION OF THE OFF-SPINNER KEITH SLATER DURING THE 1958–59 SERIES]

ENGLAND TEAMS IN AUSTRALIA EXPECT the old enemy to throw everything at them, including the kitchen sink; but in 1958–59 the chucking was real rather than metaphorical. The left-arm fast bowler Ian Meckiff, who later become the only Australian bowler to be no-balled for throwing in a Test, was just one of a number of bowlers with dubious actions. Australia felt England had a couple of chuckers of their own in Tony Lock and Peter Loader, so they decided to lock and load with an army themselves.

Australia were given no chance before the series – even Don Bradman said he only hoped Australia could make a contest of it – and had a new captain in Richie Benaud, who was a marginal choice to replace Ian Craig. England entered the tour in a state of complacency. They had not lost a Test series for eight years and, in a reversal of some modern Ashes send-offs, were hailed as the best team ever to leave England. A nasty shock awaited them.

The first Test at Brisbane was the first to be televised live in Australia. Trevor Bailey served up a treat for the viewers, scoring the slowest fifty in Test history: it took 350 balls and 357 minutes. The innings included eight runs in the two-hour morning session on the fourth day, which in all produced just 102 runs in six hours. Bailey was not the only one to blame: Australia's Jim Burke made 28 not out in

250 minutes, and the overall scoring rate of 1.64 runs per over is the slowest for any Ashes Test. In *The Times*, John Woodcock called it 'a travesty of a game'.

Meckiff took five wickets in the match and England grumbled about his action. 'It's like standing in the middle of a darts match,' said Jim Laker to Neil Harvey at Brisbane when Meckiff and the off-spinner Burke were bowling. Once, during a match on his home ground at Sydney, a barracker shouted that every time Burke hit the stumps, somebody should 'give him a coconut'.

England rationalised the first Test defeat as a one-off. There was an it'll-be-alright-on-the-night attitude among the team, as if they could turn on their superiority whenever they needed. They did so in the second Test in Adelaide. Neil Harvey's magnificent 167, Australia's first Ashes century for eleven Tests, took his side to 255 for two, just four runs behind England. Then Brian Statham, with seven for 57, dragged England right back into the series. The last eight wickets fell for 53, and Australia's lead was 49. On a flat pitch, England had the chance to bat Australia out of the game.

The events of the next two hours are among the most jaw-dropping in all Ashes cricket. Meckiff took six for 38, including five of the top six, to rout England's illustrious batting line-up for just 87. 'I never saw anything so blatant as Meckiff's action that afternoon,' said the cricket writer Jim Swanton. 'The Australian selectors had condoned a type of bowling which every spectator knew was not justified by the law. The peal of victory had a hollow ring.'

It's like standing in the middle of a darts match

With every passing defeat, England realised a public complaint would be dismissed as the sourest of grapes. They settled for a few on-field and off-record chunters instead. They soon had more than Meckiff to contend with: the off-spinner Keith Slater made his debut in the third Test and immediately aroused suspicion. 'I vividly remember one conversation in which one of us drew attention to Slater's action,' said Fred Trueman, 'and an Aussie umpire grinned, "Well, at least he's chucking them straight, isn't he, mate?"'

England also had to contend with the blond giant Gordon Rorke. They thought he was a chucker as well, but their main gripe was about something else. It was not Rorke's drift that worried England; it was his drag. He would drag his foot after landing it behind the return crease and bowl from much closer than the usual twenty-two yards. 'Having the ball thrown at you from eighteen yards blights the sunniest disposition,' said the England captain Peter May.

The great Australian fast bowler Ray Lindwall, playing in his last Ashes series, started to feel like a dodo. 'I'm the last of the straight-arm bowlers,' he said. Rorke helped Australia win the last two Tests, at Adelaide and Melbourne, by ten and nine wickets to complete a remarkable 4–0 victory. The opener Colin McDonald made excellent centuries in both matches; there were only five hundreds in the entire series, such was the bowlers' dominance. England did not reach 300 in any of their 10 innings.

The impact of the throwing controversy was such that it is generally forgotten that Australia's best bowlers in the series were the captain Benaud and his brilliant lieutenant Alan Davidson. They took 55 of the 97 England wickets to fall, and it is hard to escape the conclusion that England would have been beaten whether Meckiff and Rorke had played or not. Benaud was a revelation in his first series as captain with his intuitive, attacking approach to the game.

Whatever the reasons, the result is one of the most surprising in Test history. England's *galacticos* of the mid-1950s were starting to look like *geriatricos* – Bailey, Godfrey Evans, Laker and Frank Tyson in particular were past their best – but that still left a number of great and very good in their pomp. Yet they were destroyed.

Meckiff became a movie monster; a reporter from the *Melbourne Herald*, after hearing thirty cricket writers question the MCC president about him in 1960, concluded that: 'Ian Meckiff is 10 feet tall, bowls at 3,000 miles an hour and tries to kill batsmen.' He eventually quit cricket after being no-balled in a Test a few years later. His son was called 'Chucker' at school. In his book *Thrown Out*, he uses capital letters to stress 'I DO NOT THROW THE BALL!' But his attitude has changed with time. 'In the cold light of everything, when it is looked at realistically, I must now concede I was a chucker.'

1961

'Stick with me, Wal, we're going to win this game.'

[AUSTRALIAN CAPTAIN RICHIE BENAUD
TO WALLY GROUT, FOURTH TEST,
MANCHESTER, 1 AUGUST 1961]

WALLY GROUT WAS AS FIERCELY PATRIOTIC as the next cobber, but he had additional motivation for wanting Australia to win the fourth Test at Old Trafford. Grout had bet a decent sum on his side winning; as wicketkeeper, he had the best view in the house of his money slipping away. Thanks to a lordly innings from Ted Dexter, the dashing middle-order batsman, England were hurtling towards a target of 256 to take a 2–1 lead in the series.

Grout was starting to lose his rag with his captain Richie Benaud, who seemed almost indifferent to what was happening. When Benaud ended another ineffectual over with a long hop that Dexter slammed for four, Grout fixed his captain with a look of disgust and reminded him of the financial interest he had in the game. It was then that Benaud suggested everything would be okay.

The 1961 Ashes was a five-Test, one-day series. To explain: the entire rubber came down to a famous day in the fourth Test at Manchester. The series was 1–1 at the time; Australia, thanks to a century from Bill Lawry and five-fors from Alan Davidson and 'Garth' McKenzie, won by five wickets at Lord's, and England squared the series with an eight-wicket win in the next Test at Headingley. Fred Trueman, on his home ground, bowled brilliantly to take match figures of 11 for 88. The performance was even more impressive than it seemed at the time: Trueman produced a spell of six for one in Australia's second innings, having spent the previous night sleeping in his car because of the breakdown of his marriage.

England dominated the fourth Test from the start, whipping Australia out for 190 and taking a first-innings lead of 177. Lawry's 102 kept Australia in the game – Davidson said he deserved the Military Cross for his innings – but when they lost three quick wickets on the final morning they were 334 for nine, and had an inadequate lead of 157. Davidson, a brilliant hitter down the order, and the No.11 McKenzie changed the mood with a last-wicket partnership of 98, in which Davidson smashed the dangerous off-spinner David Allen out of the attack. 'We'll do these jokers, Rich,' panted Davidson upon arriving back in the dressing-room.

At 150 for one, with Grout losing patience, England were cruising. Then Benaud duped Dexter with a top-spinner, and he was caught behind for a brilliant 76. Benaud flashed an I-told-you-so smile at Grout; it was the start of a legendary spell of five for 12 in 25 balls. He switched around the wicket, a very unusual tactic in those days, and bowled the England captain Peter May around his legs for a duck. The moment, and Benaud's joy, was captured in an iconic photograph (see page 139). After that, the house fell down: England lost their last nine wickets for 51 and Australia, having apparently lost the match on about eight different occasions, actually won it with twenty minutes to spare. It also meant they retained the Ashes with a game in hand. Benaud finished with six for 70, and the eternal love of all his team. 'I have never doubted the man since,' said Grout.

Benaud later said he was not nearly as confident about the outcome as he pretended to be. As a captain he was a class act and a class actor; he gave the illusion of control and certainty, even when Australia were under the pump. Comments like 'Stick with me, Wal, we're going to win this game' became self-fulfilling prophecies.

Wisden said Benaud was 'the most popular captain of any overseas team to come to Great Britain'. His leg-spin and breezy lower-order batting did not bloom as a cricketer until he became captain in his late twenties. His charismatic captaincy was one of the few reasons to watch Test cricket as it lurched towards inertia in the early 1960s.

Richie Benaud bowls Peter May around his legs, Old Trafford, 1961.

He introduced or developed a number of things we now take for granted, including the demonstrative celebration of wickets and inclusive captaincy. 'In public relations to benefit the game,' wrote Ray Robinson, 'Benaud was so far ahead of his predecessors that race-glasses would have been needed to see who was at the head of the others.' That included the most important public-relations tool of all: exciting, attacking cricket. Benaud and his West Indies counterpart, Frank Worrell, had resuscitated Test cricket with their approach during a wonderful 1960–61 series that included the first tied Test and was eventually won 2–1 by Australia.

'Captaincy is ninety per cent luck and ten per cent skill. . . but, for heaven's sake, don't try it without that little ten per cent,' said Benaud. 'As far as I know, there has never been a captain labelled as great who has not been lucky. It is the ten per cent skill which is brought in at that point. The captain who sees an opening and goes straight for the jugular is the one who is drinking champagne at the end of the day.'

Benaud was drinking champagne at the end of the day at Old Trafford. As he did so, Norman O'Neill filled the team bath. 'Go on Rich, dive in. With your luck you won't get wet.'

1962–63

'Whenever Ken walked to the wicket I thought a Union Jack was trailing behind him.'

[WALLY GROUT ON KENNY BARRINGTON, ENGLAND'S RUN-MACHINE OF THE 1960s]

SOME VERY FINE PLAYERS HAVE NEVER won an Ashes series. Well, okay, some very fine *English* players have never won an Ashes series: Mike Atherton, Graham Thorpe and Alec Stewart amongst others. But the finest of all was surely Kenny Barrington, England's banker during their 1960s drought. Barrington was proof that batsmen can change their spots. He began life as a dasher but, after being dropped early in his England career, morphed into a middle-order rock in his late twenties. Barrington was a force of nurture who ended with the formidable average of 58.67 from 82 Tests. He was also a very good advert for patriotism, as the Australian wicketkeeper Wally Grout recognised.

Barrington made over 500 runs in each of the 1962–63 and 1964 Ashes series. His 581 runs in the first of these were the most by an England batsman in Australia since Wally Hammond's famous run-glut of 1928–29 (see pages 59–60). The series had promised much, with the adventurous pair of Richie Benaud and Ted Dexter in charge of their teams, yet it was largely a disappointment.

England's eight-wicket victory in the second Test, built on eight wickets from Fred Trueman, was cancelled out a fortnight later in the third Test at Sydney. Alan Davidson, playing his final Ashes series, took nine wickets in the match, including five for 25 as England were demolished for 104. The England wicketkeeper John Murray, batting one-handed because of a shoulder injury, took eighty minutes to get off the mark.

The England team included the Reverend David Sheppard, who took a sabbatical from missionary work to help the cause of English cricket. When he dropped a sitter at extra cover to reprieve Neil Harvey – one of a number of costly dropped catches for England during the series which probably cost them victory – the exasperated bowler Fred Trueman said: 'Pretend it's Sunday, Reverend, and keep your hands together.'

Pretend it's Sunday, Reverend, and keep your hands together

The last two Tests of the 1962–63 rubber were a microcosm of Barrington's bittersweet Ashes experience. He made 63, 132 not out, 101 and 94, having been promoted to No.3 (see pages 112–113), but England could not force the victory they needed. In the fourth Test at Adelaide, Harvey made a dashing 154, in which he became the fourth man to pass 6000 Test runs after Hammond, Don Bradman and Len Hutton. Davidson bowed out with 24 wickets at 20 in the series and the England captain Dexter made 481 runs without a century, but these were not exactly career highlights.

The last two matches were largely forgettable draws, which meant Australia retained the urn. But it was a qualified triumph. When they declined to chase a target of 241 in four hours on the final day, they were booed and slow-handclapped by their own fans for their defensive cricket. England had been equally culpable throughout the series. It was the first ever drawn Ashes in Australia, and the start of the most forgettable period in cricket's greatest rivalry.

1964

'Declare, Simpson, you bastard!'

**[AN ENGLAND SPECTATOR TO THE
AUSTRALIAN BALCONY, FOURTH TEST,
OLD TRAFFORD, 25 JULY 1964]**

IT WAS ALMOST LUNCH ON THE THIRD DAY, and Australia were still batting. Their captain Bob Simpson was relaxing on the balcony, having just finished a monumental innings of 311 in almost 13 hours, when he heard his name being taken in vain by an England supporter who was tired of the recurring nightmare of forward defensives and thwarted hopes. The suggestion that Australia should declare did not impress everyone; the wicketkeeper Wally Grout took a demonstrative drag of his cigarette before replying: 'What about The Oval in 1938?'

That was a reference to the Test in which England scored 903 for seven (see page 95). Australia settled for a modest 658 for eight before declaring at Old Trafford. And the real villain of the piece was unquestionably the pitch: in all it produced 1271 runs for the loss of just 18 wickets. It was the nadir of a dull decade in which Ashes cricket was here for a long time, not a good time.

Imaginary studies show that, if a time machine existed, the 1960s would be the most popular destination of all. It was a time of unprecedented freedom in all kinds of areas: sex, fashion, sex, music, sex, drugs, sex. On the cricket field, England and Australia did not swing their way through the Sixties, they slow-danced like a pair of arthritic pensioners. Ray Davies was not thinking about Ashes cricket when he wrote 'You Really Got Me' in 1964.

There was a constant moral panic about boring play, and some even called for the Ashes to be abolished. One-day cricket began in

England with the Gillette Cup in 1963, a weird limited-overs world in which batsmen did such things as hit the ball hard.

How better to relay the sheer boredom of 1960s Ashes cricket than with some data. Fifteen of the twenty-five Tests were drawn, as were three of the five series – which is more than half the total of drawn Ashes series in the 133-year history of the contest.

That the 1964 Ashes did not end in a draw was down to one innings: Peter Burge's thrilling 160 in the third Test at Headingley. Australia were in trouble against the spin of Norman Gifford and Fred Titmus when Ted Dexter decided to take the new ball. At that stage Australia were 189 for seven, still 82 behind; they ended up with a match-winning lead of 121. Dexter was slaughtered in the press, though he found support from Denis Compton. 'I reckoned Dexter did the right thing in claiming the new ball,' he wrote. 'Dexter could not foresee how badly [Fred] Trueman was going to bowl.' Trueman was not the biggest fan of Dexter's captaincy. 'He had more theory than Darwin but little practical experience to back it up,' said Trueman, who had long since awarded himself a doctorate from the University of Life.

Australia knew a draw in the fourth Test at Old Trafford would ensure they retained the Ashes even if they lost the final Test. Simpson completed their mission with that 311. It was his maiden Test hundred at the fifty-second attempt. Not everyone was thrilled for him. In the *Daily Mail*, J. L. Manning called him 'the murderer of cricket'. John Woodcock was slightly more generous in the *Cricketer*. 'There was much to admire about his everlasting innings,' he said, '[but] as entertainment it ranked with chess by post.'

England scored 611 in reply, with Ted Dexter hitting 174 and Ken Barrington 256. The Western Australian seam bowler Graham McKenzie returned the unique and noble figures of 60-15-153-7 – his best, if most expensive, return of an excellent series in which he took 29 wickets – while the off-spinner Tom Veivers bowled 95.1 overs in England's innings. There probably was not much *joie de Veivers* after such a strenuous shift. He was not the only bowler who was bloody tired that summer.

1964

'Aye, but whoever beats it will be bloody tired.'

[FRED TRUEMAN ON HIS WORLD RECORD, FIFTH TEST, THE OVAL, 15 AUGUST 1964]

IT WAS A TEXTBOOK FRED TRUEMAN DELIVERY: quick, full and swinging away from the right-hander. Neil Hawke pushed at the ball, and then snapped his head back instinctively to follow its path as it flew off the outside edge. It went straight into the hands of Colin Cowdrey at second slip. 'That's it, he's out!' screamed the commentator Brian Johnston, his words barely audible above the shrieking of the Oval crowd. It was the kind of sound which, in those days, usually accompanied the sight of the Beatles emerging from a plane.

Trueman's arms, originally raised in appeal to the umpire, went limp and dangled by his side, as the top half of his body relaxed for just a second. His body language was that of a man who had been unto the breach a lot more than once, and an apt reflection of one of cricket's more laborious triumphs: after twelve years and almost 15,000 deliveries, Trueman had become the first man to take 300 Test wickets.

It was by some distance the most memorable moment of the 1964 Ashes, even though Australia got the draw they needed in that final Test at The Oval to ensure a 1–0 victory. Rain again played a part and England, 197 behind on first innings, might have lost but for a maiden Test century from the studious Yorkshireman Geoff Boycott.

Trueman almost reached 300 with a hat-trick; having dismissed Ian Redpath and 'Garth' McKenzie with consecutive deliveries, he was denied by Hawke. But Hawke obliged soon after, and shook Trueman's hand as he walked off.

Trueman's record looks small now, his 307 wickets a molehill next to the mountain that is Muttiah Muralitharan's 800, but the volume of international cricket has changed everything. At the time he suggested that anyone who beat his record would be 'bloody tired'. He was half right. In those days, the tiredness a bowler felt was as much because of first-class cricket as Test matches. Trueman ended his career with 2304 first-class wickets, Murali with just 1374.

The caricature of Trueman – offering earthy putdowns to batsmen about their mothers' failure to shut their legs, and, as a commentator, endlessly bemoaning the failings of his successors in the England team ('I just don't know what's going off out there') – is such that it sometimes obscures his sheer quality as a fast bowler. 'He had the most classical action of all time,' said Boycott. 'He was absolutely perfect.' And perhaps no bowler has ever had such an association with the outswinger, the ball that produced his defining moment.

Fred Trueman hugs Colin Cowdrey after taking his 300th Test wicket, The Oval, 1964. Captain Ted Dexter is staring at his boots, while Geoff Boycott hitches up his trousers. The Australian batsman is Tom Veivers.

1965–66

'What's the matter, Lawry? Have you taken the pill?'

[A BARRACKER ENQUIRES ABOUT THE AUSTRALIAN OPENER'S HEALTH, THIRD TEST, SYDNEY, 10 JANUARY 1966]

THE MAN SEEN AS EMBODYING ALL THAT was moribund and dull about the Ashes cricket of the 1960s was Bill Lawry, Australia's high-class defensive opener. The English writer Ian Wooldridge referred to him as 'a corpse with pads on'. Lawry was a target for Australian barrackers, too; when he hit a boundary in one game, a fan beseeched the heavens: 'Come on lightning, strike twice!' During one strokeless famine at Sydney in the third Test of the 1965–66 series, one barracker wondered whether Lawry was on medication that did not allow him to conceive anything other than a defensive stroke.

The contrast between Lawry and the England opener Bob Barber could barely have been more acute. Barber, a chirpy Lancastrian who wore life at a jaunty angle, prioritised fun over winning. He had a particular obsession with Sydney. 'What I really want to do is to play one innings as I think the game should be played,' said Barber early in the tour. 'And I want to play it at Sydney.'

He had the chance to do so in the third Test of that 1965–66 series. The first two at Brisbane and Melbourne were high-scoring draws, most notable for a thrilling debut century from the Australian teenager Doug Walters at the Gabba. Great as his innings was, it would be trumped by Barber's.

Attacking openers were the rarest of species in the 1960s. The other three openers in the 1965–66 series were Lawry, Bob Simpson and

Geoffrey Boycott: the 'corpse with pads on', the 'murderer of cricket' and a man who scored so slowly that, later in his career, when he was captain in a Test against New Zealand in 1977–78, his own England team-mates conspired to run him out. It wasn't hard for Barber to stand out in such company – but then his Sydney masterpiece would have stood out in any company.

For one day only, Barber entered the zone and touched greatness, clattering 185 from 255 balls in 296 minutes, full of crashing drives. Barber's father was sitting among the crowd when a local, not knowing who he was, asked him: 'Why can't we have a batsman like this Barber?' His approach was years ahead of its time. Maybe even decades: Barber's was the highest score by a batsman on the first day of a Test until Virender Sehwag slapped 195 against Australia in 2003–04. Boycott, his opening partner, called it 'one of the truly great displays of batting in Test cricket'. Those in the press box were equally charmed. 'Often in bleak moments do I cast back to Bob Barber's 185 in front of 40,000 on that sunny Friday in January '66,' wrote Jim Swanton.

Barber's innings was a rare sunlit interlude in another grey and monotonous series. England won the Sydney Test by an innings but then contrived to lose the next Test at Adelaide by a similar margin. The Australian captain Simpson constructed a slow-motion 225 and, in tandem with Bill Lawry, ensured that Australia passed England's first-innings score before they had lost a wicket. Simpson's innings took up 545 minutes; compared to Barber in the previous Test, he had taken an additional four hours over 40 runs.

The Victorian Bob Cowper settled in for an even longer haul in the final Test at Melbourne. His twelve-hour 307, the first Test match triple century to be scored in Australia, and still the most recent Ashes triple-hundred, ensured the Ashes were comfortably retained. The match produced over 1100 runs for the loss of only 20 wickets. Lawry played his part, supporting Cowper with a six-hour 108. Overall, including tour matches, he batted for forty-one-and-a-half hours against England during that tour. The cricket was already pretty dull, but Lawry managed to sex it down even further.

1968

'England carried Underwood, like an umbrella, in case of rain.'

[JOHN ARLOTT ON DEREK UNDERWOOD, DESTROYER OF AUSTRALIA IN THE FIFTH TEST AT THE OVAL, 27 AUGUST 1968]

'DEADLY' DEREK UNDERWOOD'S ENDURING reputation as a wet-wicket bogeyman was born at The Oval on the memorable final day of the 1968 Ashes. Until then the series had been relatively drab, following the pattern of the decade. Australia were unfancied before the tour and not particularly well regarded after it. They had struggled throughout the later 1960s to replace retired greats like Neil Harvey, Alan Davidson, Richie Benaud and Wally Grout. They thrashed India 4–0 at home during the previous Australian summer of 1967–68, but England – who sneaked an excellent 1–0 win in the Caribbean at the same time, and had discovered class acts like Alan Knott and John Snow – were fancied by many.

Australia's thumping 159-run victory in the first Test, in which Doug Walters lived up to his pre-tour hype with two 80-somethings in a low-scoring game, thus came as a wake-up call. England dominated rain-affected draws at Lord's, where Australia were skittled for 78 by David Brown and Barry Knight, and Edgbaston, before a marvellous fourth Test at Headingley was also drawn. England, who needed to chase 326 in 295 minutes to keep the Ashes alive, ended on 230 for four.

The last Test, like the second and third, had apparently been decided by the weather. Although England were in charge after big hundreds from John Edrich and Basil D'Oliveira, torrential rainfall seemed to have ensured a draw.

The notion of the crowd being a team's twelfth man has rarely felt as relevant as it did that day, when hundreds of supporters helped make the ground fit for play. England's main weapon was the twenty-three year-old left-armer Underwood, whose medium-paced spin bowling made him nigh-on unplayable on sticky wickets. Play resumed at 4.45pm, giving England 75 minutes to take the last five Australian wickets. They did not get the first until 5.24pm, and squeezed in three more in the next half hour. England rattled through their overs, bowling 20.3 in the last hour, with no delaying tactics by the Australians.

By the end, the captain Colin Cowdrey had set an unprecedented field, with everyone around the bat – an umbrella field for his umbrella bowler. There were five minutes remaining when the opener John Inverarity, having resisted so adeptly, offered no stroke to a ball from Underwood.

It produced one of English cricket's most famous photographs, an ostensibly generic scene, yet instantly recognisable (see pages 150–151). The bowler completing his appeal; the batsman looking towards backward point, unable to face his fate; nine fielders and the wicketkeeper, all around the bat, looking at the umpire, their faces at various points on a venn diagram that includes hope, need, desperation, conviction and fear. The umpire Arthur Fagg's right arm is not visible because of his head, but anyone who has seen a cricket match before instantly recognises what he is doing: giving the batsman out.

'He's out!' screamed Brian Johnston on the BBC. It is tempting to see this champagne moment as a sibling to Denis Compton's Ashes-winning boundary on the same ground fifteen years earlier. In fact it was more of a cousin, because although Underwood's wicket squared the series, it was Australia who retained the Ashes with a 1–1 draw.

Australia's Barry Jarman said that 'the crowds should have got a medal for winning the game'. Underwood finished with seven for 50 – and a new sobriquet or two. 'He has the face of a choirboy, the demeanour of a civil servant and the ruthlessness of a rat catcher,' said Geoff Boycott. 'On wet pitches, Deadly was his name.'

Derek Underwood snares John Inverarity lbw to secure a last-gasp England victory, The Oval 1968. The England players, left to right, are: Illingworth, Graveney, Edrich, Dexter, Cowdrey, Underwood, Knott, Snow, Brown, Milburn and D'Oliveira.

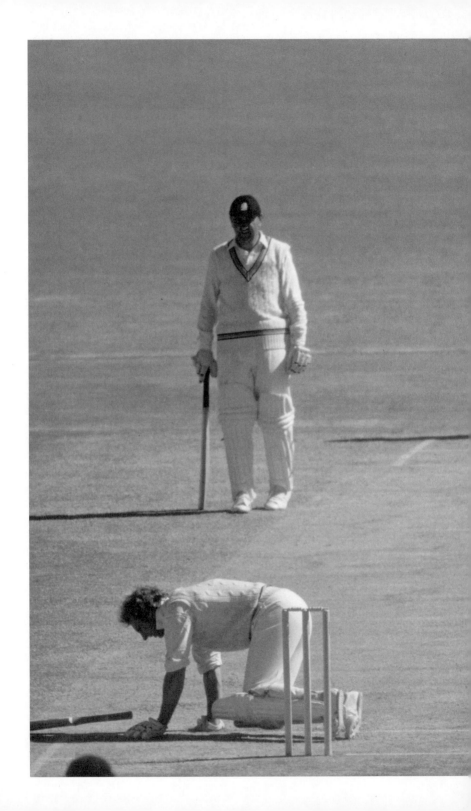

THE AGE OF
THE FAST MEN
1970–1989

1970–71

'I'm not afraid of leaving a trail of fractures among the opposition – a finger, a thumb, a whole right hand and one foot on the latest count. After all, that's what I'm there for.'

[ENGLAND FAST BOWLER JOHN SNOW REMINDS EVERYONE OF HIS ROLE IN THE SIDE, 1971]

THE BEST WAY FOR ENGLAND TO BEAT Australia in their own manor has invariably been to beat them in their own *manner* – with irresistible, aggressive fast bowling. England's three victories down under between 1932 and 1971 are each indelibly associated with a single fast bowler. England have caused Australia the most problems when they were able to fight fire with fire – or even with Snow. After Harold Larwood and Frank Tyson, John Snow would complete a legendary trinity of Ashes-winning fast bowlers.

Snow was the central figure of the 1970–71 Ashes, a series which heralded a new era of Anglo-Australian cricket: more colourful, more macho, more controversial – and at times downright nasty. At twenty-nine, Snow was one of the younger members of a hard-boiled England side. They weren't quite Dad's Army, but an average age of over thirty told a fair story; their captain Ray Illingworth was thirty-eight. Even two of the debutants, Brian Luckhurst and Peter Lever, were in their thirties, though there was also room for the twenty-one-year-old Surrey fast bowler Bob Willis, a replacement for the injured Alan Ward.

England had hosted the Rest of the World the previous summer – a series arranged hastily after South Africa's tour was cancelled – and did rather better than a 4–1 defeat suggests. By contrast, Australia were whitewashed 4–0 by South Africa in 1969–70, and the scoreline flattered them. They were searching for a new side, and would give nine debuts in the 1970–71 Ashes. Three of those new boys – Greg Chappell, Rodney Marsh and Dennis Lillee – went on to form Australia's heart and spine until they retired together in 1984.

They had mixed success at the start. Chappell made a debut century in the drawn second Test at Perth; Marsh, however, had such a poor debut in the first Test at Brisbane that he was soon christened 'Iron Gloves'. The contrast with his opposite number did not help; Alan Knott's gloves seemed to be made of velvet and velcro.

The series started as it meant to go on, with an umpiring controversy. On the first morning of the series at Brisbane, the opener Keith Stackpole was clearly run out by Geoff Boycott's throw when he was on 18. He was given not out and went on to make 207. Australia's collapse from 418 for three to 433 was an early indication of what Snow could do; he took the last four wickets in quick time to finish with figures of six for 114.

The game meandered to a draw, as did the second match. It was Perth's inaugural Test, though the pitch was not quite the trampoline it would become. England eventually set Australia 245 to win in 145 minutes; the captain Bill Lawry made his intentions abundantly clear by scoring six in the first 68 minutes. Lawry and Illingworth set the tone for a grizzled and attritional series in which any advantage was seriously hard-earned.

And so it was in the fourth Test at Sydney, when brilliant cricket from England's two awkward buggers, Geoff Boycott and Snow, blew the series open. The third at Melbourne had been abandoned, which led to the first ever one-day international being played and an extra Test being added to the schedule. At Sydney, Boycott batted as if he was in an ODI: his sparkling 77 on the first day was a rare attacking innings in a legendarily gritty career.

In the second innings, a more typical Boycott knock – 142 not out from 360 balls on a turning pitch – cemented England's advantage after they had taken a first-innings lead of 96. *Wisden* said Boycott 'put the seal of greatness on his batting' during the series. There were occasional accusations of selfishness, though he strongly rejects the story that he worked out how to read the mystery spinner John Gleeson but decided not to tell his team-mates. Despite missing the final Test he top scored with 657 runs, nine ahead of John Edrich.

Boycott's Sydney century gave Snow the opportunity to put England ahead. With Australia needing 416 to win, he managed to generate life from the Sydney track that was beyond all the other fast bowlers, and devastated Australia with career-best figures of seven for 40. He also accounted for 'Garth' McKenzie, who retired hurt after being hit in the face. It is often said that certain spinners can turn the ball square; Snow could make it lift almost vertically. The ball to McKenzie, in particular, exploded from a fullish length. England won the match by a whopping 299 runs, a victory that Basil D'Oliveira enjoyed more than anyone. 'I am surprised that Basil still has a forefinger on his right hand the number of times he stabbed it into the chest of complete strangers that night and told them, "We stuffed you,"' said Snow later.

> **He stalks through it all with an icy, menacing detachment**

For all D'Oliveira's overt aggression, it was Snow's inscrutable menace that really unnerved Australia. He took the abuse from the crowds and used it as fuel to raise his game. 'He stalks through it all with an icy, menacing detachment that turns to laughter when he is back in his hotel,' wrote the *Sun*'s Chris Taylor. He was utterly ruthless towards batsmen. 'I never let them forget the game is played with a very hard ball,' he said.

> **I never let them forget the game is played with a very hard ball**

It was hard for anyone to know what Snow was thinking, such was his singular nature. The son of a vicar, he would go on to write two volumes of poetry, and entitled his autobiography *Cricket Rebel*. 'Reading, music, painting, poetry are as necessary to him as food and fresh air,' said *Wisden*. He once replied to being told that the ultimate thing in life was to play for England by saying 'the ultimate thing in life is death'.

Illingworth knew Snow was special and treated him as such. He cut him far more slack than anyone else, and trusted Snow's word that he would deliver in the Test matches. He would have played more than 49 Tests but for a number of incidents; he was dropped by his county for not trying and by his country for barging India's Sunil Gavaskar in 1971. The establishment were allergic to Snow. 'Controversy, thy name was Snow, in the early 1970s,' said *Wisden*. Never more so than when he came into contact with the Australian umpire Lou Rowan.

1970–71

'Now *that's* a f****** bouncer.'

**[JOHN SNOW ATTEMPTS TO SETTLE
AN ARGUMENT OVER WHAT
CONSTITUTES A BOUNCER
WITH UMPIRE LOU ROWAN,
SECOND TEST, PERTH,
12 DECEMBER 1970]**

JOHN SNOW WAS PISSED OFF. BUT HE KNEW exactly how to unsettle his opponent. He landed a short ball just where he wanted it, so that it whistled fractionally over the batsman's head, and then aggressively pointed out that this is how one might define a bouncer. Except Snow was not trying to intimidate the batsman; he was talking to the umpire.

In the 1970–71 Ashes, England's toughest opponent was not Bill Lawry or Ian Chappell or a young Dennis Lillee. It was Lou Rowan. 'It was the only time I ever felt an umpire wasn't being completely honest,' said the captain Ray Illingworth. Snow would later say of Rowan: 'I have never come across another umpire so full of his own importance, so stubborn, lacking in humour, unreasonable.'

> **I have never come across another umpire so full of his own importance, so stubborn, lacking in humour, unreasonable**

Rowan managed to offend England in a million different ways. A recurring feature of the series was a semantic discussion between Snow and Rowan as to what constituted a bouncer. Snow was warned a number of times for intimidatory bowling, most notably in the second Test at Perth. He said he was bowling at rib or armpit height, rather than at the head, hence his and Illingworth's protestations. Rowan's interpretation was a little different. 'Well, someone's bowling bouncers from this end, and it's not me!' he said to Illingworth during one exchange.

Bouncers were not the only bone of contention during the series. England felt that Keith Stackpole in particular got away with a number of caught-behinds so obvious that even W. G. Grace might have

Well, someone's bowling bouncers from this end, and it's not me!

walked out of embarrassment. Illingworth recalled that Stackpole did start to walk on one occasion, only to realise he had been given not out and return to his crease.

Rowan was not the only umpire with whom England were dissatisfied. In the Melbourne Test, Snow remembered the debutant umpire Max O'Connell being so nervous that he called 'over', turned his back on the play and missed a clear edge from Stackpole. The Victorian opener ended up as Australia's top runscorer, though almost a third of those came in the first innings of the series: Stackpole stockpiled 207 but should have been given run out by Rowan when he made 18. Photographs proved that it was one of the more significant umpiring howlers of the decade.

Rowan also refused to allow England to use a roller before the second Test at Perth, contravening the laws of the game. It was in that match that he had his first major run-in with Snow. Snow was warned again in the fifth Test at Melbourne, this time by a different umpire, although England – and *Wisden* – felt that Australia's wrong-footed rookie fast bowler Alan 'Froggy' Thomson bowled far more bouncers without censure.

That match was another unyielding draw, in which Bill Lawry declared when Rod Marsh was eight runs away from scoring the first Test century by an Australian wicketkeeper. Earlier in the match Brian Luckhurst made his second century of his maiden series despite a fractured finger.

The inability of the umpires to lift a finger, and not just Rowan, had become a serious issue by then. England did not get a single lbw in the seven-Test series.* 'Under those circumstances it was little short of incredible that we bowled out the Aussies at all to win the series,' said Illingworth. The lbw law was slightly different in those days, with batsmen not out if they were playing a shot and the ball pitched outside off stump, yet it remains an eye-popping statistic.

Rowan was absent for the sixth Test at Adelaide, though the problems persisted. Boycott was disgusted when he was on the wrong end of a tight run-out call and threw his bat down. He stood his ground until a posse of Australian fielders, led by the Chappell brothers, offered him four-letter directions to the pavilion, with a bit of pushing and shoving to provide extra clarity. Despite a five-for from the impressive youngster Dennis Lillee, England controlled the match after Edrich's 130.

Boycott responded to the inevitable booing with another masterful second-innings century. Illingworth was heavily criticised for not enforcing the follow-on when Australia made precisely half of England's 470, though there were only two days between the fifth and sixth Tests and Snow and Peter Lever were shattered. The outcome of the match – Australia, set 469, ended on 328 for three – suggests the pitch would have won either way. England thus went into the seventh and final Test, the result of the washout at Melbourne in the third Test, needing a draw to regain the Ashes. Everybody thought it would be dramatic. They had no idea.

* Including tour matches, England did not get an lbw in the last 23 games and 102 days of their trip to Australia.

1970–71

'I've seen people hit by bottles and it makes a bloody mess of them.'

[ENGLAND CAPTAIN RAY ILLINGWORTH EXPLAINS WHY HE TOOK HIS TEAM OFF THE FIELD DURING THE SEVENTH TEST AT SYDNEY, 13 FEBRUARY 1971]

THE ASHES SERIES OF 1970–71 COULD only simmer for so long. There was an inevitability about it boiling over in the seventh and final Test, and an inevitability that it would start with a short ball from John Snow. That boiling point was duly reached shortly after Australia had taken a first-innings lead, when Terry Jenner, leg-spinning tail-ender and future mentor to Shane Warne, turned his back on a ball that followed him and clonked him on the head.

As Jenner was led from the field by a number of players, the umpire Lou Rowan warned Snow for intimidatory bowling – even though England claimed it was the first bouncer Snow had bowled, and it wasn't really a bouncer anyway because it would have hit Jenner in the chest had he stayed upright. Things were about to turn extremely nasty.

By now, Illingworth and Snow were up against a new captain, Ian Chappell. Bill Lawry was sacked and dropped after the sixth Test, a decision he first heard about on the radio. 'They gave him the selectorial axe right at the base of the skull, in one of the most unfeeling acts I have ever seen from any group of selectors,' said Richie Benaud later.

England, put in by Chappell, and without the injured Geoffrey Boycott, were bowled out for 184, though Illingworth thought they were allowed to get far too many and that England would have bowled Australia out for 50 on that pitch. The Jenner incident came with Australia on 195 for seven, just eleven runs ahead of England. As bowler, captain and umpire engaged in yet another discussion as to what constituted a bouncer, Illingworth wagged his finger at Rowan, which drew a rebuke from Benaud on television. 'I'm a backer of Illingworth, but in this case he's behaving not like an England captain but more like a prima donna of a South American football side arguing with the referee.'

The over ended soon after, whereupon Snow snatched his cap and walked into a wall of boos at fine leg, pointedly conducting the orchestra as he did so. As Snow waited by the rope for the next over, a drunken spectator grabbed his shirt and started to drag him towards the boundary board. Snow considered landing a pre-emptive right-hander but thought better of it, and the man was eventually pulled off by other spectators. 'He couldn't speak,' said Snow. 'He was stoned.'

As beer bottles and cans whistled past his head, Snow retreated to the middle, whereupon Illingworth decided to take his players off – a decision that was supported by Benaud and most others in the media. Illingworth said he would not return until the outfield was cleared and the players knew they would not be bottled. He was not at all enamoured when the team manager David Clark told the team to go straight back onto the field. Illingworth was bloody-minded, but he was not minded to see his players bloodied. He was warned by Rowan that he would forfeit the Test if he did not bring his team back onto the field, a step he was prepared to take. Eventually an agreement was made and the players returned.

At the close of play, Snow went into the Australian dressing-room to see Jenner. 'Let's have a look then,' he said. 'Oh, I only grazed you.' Jenner returned to the crease the next day, making a brave 30 to help Australia to a first-innings lead of 80.

England battled to 302 in a strong team performance, which left Australia needing 223 to win the match and retain the Ashes. There was a sense all series that Snow's pace might give someone a broken finger; in fact he broke his own digit against the wooden boundary fence as he tried to catch a hooked six from Stackpole. Australia started the final day on 123 for five, needing another 100. It was all over by lunch, with Basil D'Oliveira and Derek Underwood bagging two wickets apiece and Illingworth taking the crucial wicket of Greg Chappell.

The fact that England's triumph was ultimately achieved without Boycott and Snow, their best batsman and bowler, made it all the worthier. 'We didn't take any inviting for a drink that night,' said Illingworth. For all the controversy, England's 2–0 triumph brooked no argument. Or, as D'Oliveira put it straight after the game: 'We stuffed the bastards!'

Snow took 31 wickets at 22.83, the crowning achievement of a brilliant and controversial career. Nobody else on either side managed more than Underwood's 16. He made a bloody mess of Australia.

Terry Jenner is floored by John Snow, seventh Test, Sydney, 20 February 1971. Mayhem to follow.

1972

'"Australia take it lying down?" Pig's bloody arse they do!'

[AUSTRALIAN TEAM MANAGER RAY STEELE ATTEMPTS TO MOTIVATE HIS TEAM BEFORE THE SECOND TEST AT LORD'S, JUNE 1972]

RAY STEELE WAS FIFTY SHADES OF PURPLE. Australia were having a team meeting when their tour manager surveyed a headline in the *Sun* which reflected unfavourably on their defeat in the first Test. Steele narrowed his eyes, looked at the paper with contempt and slammed it down on the nearest table. It would be a long time before an emerging Australian side took anything lying down again.

At the start of the 1972 series, England's experienced side – the series began on their captain Ray Illingworth's fortieth birthday – were expected to be far too strong for Australia. They had only lost one of their last 27 Tests. As it turned out, England were on the way down, Australia were on the way up, and the teams met around halfway in a memorable low-scoring series in which neither side reached 400.

The fast bowlers John Snow and Dennis Lillee both took eight wickets in the first Test, which England won by 89 runs, although a thuggish 91 from Rodney Marsh gave them a scare. The bombastic South African-born all-rounder Tony Greig top-scored in both innings on his Test debut. It was after this match that Steele employed the age-old tactic of using negative publicity as a motivational tool, and it worked a treat.

The second Test at Lord's will be forever associated with an unassuming mutton-chopped swing bowler from Western Australia who had been rejected by Northants after a trial a couple of years earlier. At the home of cricket, Bob Massie enjoyed the sort of Test debut of which dreams are made. He started by bowling Geoff Boycott with a huge inswinger, and went on to take eight for 84 as England struggled their way to 272 in their first innings. He did even better second time round, bagging eight more for 53 to demolish England for 116 and deliver Australia a crushing eight-wicket victory. Massie's swing and unusual round-the-wicket angle were problems England could not solve.

Massie didn't just make the ball talk; he made it say supercalifragilisticexpialidocious. His new-ball partner and good friend Lillee thought that Massie's sixteen for 137 was the best performance he had seen, though others reckoned Lillee himself wasn't far behind. Illingworth said he bowled as well as Massie, yet he ended up with just four wickets. It may have been emphatically 'Massie's Match', but there was another vital factor in Australia's eight-wicket victory: an exceptional 131 from Greg Chappell which buttressed Australia's first-innings total of 308 in trying batting conditions.

If Massie was Australia's secret weapon, then England had an even more unlikely match winner in the form of a fungus called *fusarium*. After Australia had dominated the drawn third Test at Trent Bridge, they turned up to see a Headingley wicket perfect for Illingworth, and particularly Derek Underwood. Australia suspected foul play; England cited a freak storm the previous weekend and a fungus which left the pitch grassless.

Underwood, as unplayable as ever on a poor wicket, helped himself to ten for 82 and Australia were well beaten. England's victory gave them a 2–1 lead with one to play, and ensured they would retain the Ashes. 'We were dudded, we all know that, but we won't be whingeing about it to anyone, least of all the press,' said Steele to his team. The Australian batsman Ross Edwards bagged a pair to follow his 170 not out in the second innings of the previous Test.

Such a wild swing in personal fortunes had nothing on Massie's story. Nobody knew it at the time, but his Test career had already reached its halfway point – after his third match. Swing bowling is among the most precarious skills, its practitioners living in their

Greg Chappell cuts to the boundary.

own corridor of uncertainty: what happens if it stops swinging? It did for Massie during the 1972–73 tour of the West Indies, and his career never recovered. But he'll always have those five days at Lord's in the summer of '72. The Ashes may never have a greater one-hit wonder.

1972

'Australia, you f****** beauty!'

[RODNEY MARSH SINGS THE NEW
AUSTRALIAN TEAM SONG, FIFTH TEST,
THE OVAL, 16 AUGUST 1972]

EVERY TEST VICTORY IS SOMETHING TO CHERISH. Yet some are more special than others. Even though the Ashes had gone, Australia's win at the Oval in 1972 squared the series and signalled the emergence of a new side under the captaincy of Ian Chappell, who turned Test cricket into testosterone cricket. At that stage victory was a rare thing – this was only Australia's second in nearly four years – but they would become ever more regular over the next decade. And each time they would be accompanied by the new team song, 'Under the Southern Cross I Stand':

> *Under the Southern Cross I Stand*
> *A sprig of wattle in my hand*
> *A native of my native land*
> *Australia, you little beauty!*

Those are the official lyrics, though the players always replace the 'little' with something fruitier when they sing it together. There is some dispute as to when Rodney Marsh first belted out the song that would become almost as synonymous with the team as the Baggy Green cap. There is general agreement that it was sung at Sydney in 1974–75. Some say it was first sung at Brisbane, earlier in that series, but many, including Greg Chappell, recall singing it after the breakthrough victory at The Oval in 1972. It would be appropriate were that the case, because this was the game that symbolised the emergence of one of cricket's more famous sides.

The match was a triumph for the pillars of that new side. The Chappells, captain Ian and his brother Greg, both made centuries, while Dennis Lillee took five wickets in each innings to take his series tally to 31. There were a record 23 dismissals in the series for the wicketkeeper Marsh, too, and the joy of hitting the winning runs. When Australia began to struggle in pursuit of a target of 242, Marsh calmly took control with Paul Sheahan in an unbroken sixth-wicket partnership of 71. Marsh got so drunk after the game that he couldn't even remember drinking champagne. And that was at dinner time, before the night really got going.

Lillee, the Chappells and Marsh became symbols of a team that was bristling with 1970s machismo, a formidable brotherhood who overwhelmed opponents with their unique combination of sheer talent, hostility and hair. They were almost comically hirsute, with thick manes, shirts buttoned lower than Simon Cowell's to reveal clumps of chest hair, and the obligatory moustaches. Lillee's moustache was once quizzically observed by the comedian Eric Morecambe: 'Are you aware, sir, that the last time I saw anything like that on a top lip, the whole herd had to be destroyed?'

Even their appeals were magnificent. Lillee would spread his legs, arms and mouth wide, imploring the umpire to give a decision while simultaneously testing the fabric in the crotch area of his trousers. 'When appealing, the Australians make a statement,' said Vic Marks, the England off-spinner of the early 1980s. 'We ask a question.'

They were a team who didn't mind their Ps and Qs – even in front of Pommy Queens. A half-drunk Lillee greeted Her Majesty with a jaunty 'G'day!' when the team were invited to Buckingham Palace on the evening of their victory at Lord's in 1972. They were rough, tough and fiercely entertaining. Mike Brearley later said that 'Playing against a team with Ian Chappell as captain turns a cricket match into gang warfare.' Yet they had respect for their opponents. Well, some of them.

After the moribund last year of Lawry's captaincy, Australian cricket needed an injection of dash and charisma. Chappell had those qualities in spades, and so did his team. They also had the talent to dominate Test cricket for the next few years – and would have plenty of opportunities to try out the new team song.

1974–75

'I enjoy hitting a batsman more than getting him out. I like to see blood on the pitch. And I've been training on whisky.'

[AUSTRALIA'S RAW FAST BOWLER JEFF THOMSON LOOKS FORWARD TO HIS ASHES DEBUT, FIRST TEST, BRISBANE, NOVEMBER 1974]

DENNIS LILLEE WAS WALKING PAST the hotel bar when he spotted an increasingly familiar face. It was Jeff Thomson, who would be part of Australia's new pace attack when they started the Ashes series against England the following day. The team were going their separate ways after dinner and Lillee, noticing Thomson with a glass full of ice, remarked on the wisdom of Thomson's hydration priorities. 'Thommo' soon corrected Lillee, informing him that it was scotch, and that he'd be having a few of them. He was one of the few people in the world who wanted to feel rough when he went to work. 'When I go out to bowl I want a hangover from hell,' Thomson said. 'I bowl real well when I have a headache.'

Thomson had already revealed his preferred tipple in a newspaper interview. The England all-rounder Tony Greig later described how he strolled out to get the Sunday papers late on the Saturday night, and read all about his new opponent's taste for whisky – and claret on the pitch.

At that stage it seemed to many like token trash talk from a loser. 'He initially appeared more of a beach bum than a cricketer,' said the Essex batsman Keith Fletcher. 'We did not anticipate that he would have much of a role in the series.' Thomson had played one Test two years earlier, taking none for 110 against Pakistan, although nobody knew he had a broken foot at the time. There are conflicting stories as to whether England really saw their ordeal at the hands of Lillee and Thomson coming. Greig's story suggests they had an inkling of what was in store; others say their assault was as shockingly unexpected as Janet Leigh's bloody shower in Hitchcock's *Psycho*.

Many people thought Lillee would not be the same bowler after three stress fractures of the spine which even he thought would end his career. Lillee bowled medium pace in the Shield games before the Test series and was hit around the park. England came across Thomson when they played a warm-up match against Queensland. The story is told that he deliberately bowled within himself, having been told by his captain Greg Chappell to 'just f*** around. Don't show the English batsmen what you can do.'

If that was really the case it is indicative of Thomson's terrifying speed. While bowling within himself, he had the English papers referring to Bodyline, an Australian writer talking of 'bowling thuggery' and Fletcher saying he thought 'he'd knocked my arm off' when he was hit. Lillee describes Thomson as 'the easiest-going guy of all time', yet he had a combination of white-line fever

Stuff that stiff upper lip crap. Let's see how stiff it is when it's split

– as a teenager he received a life ban from playing football in New South Wales for punching a referee – and Pom fever. 'I thought, "Stuff that stiff upper lip crap. Let's see how stiff it is when it's split."'

England were an experienced side, with many of the players who had triumphed in 1970–71, though they had a new and not entirely popular captain in Mike Denness, who some felt was not good enough to earn his place as a batsman. They were without the stars of that triumphant tour, however: Geoff Boycott, originally named in the squad, pulled out for 'very good personal reasons' – the continuation of a two-and-a-half-year international exile – while England strangely omitted the ageing but still effective John Snow. They were nonetheless in decent health, having held their own in the Caribbean the previous winter before thrashing India at home and drawing 0–0 with a good Pakistan side.

Australia had run with the momentum from the 1972 series, winning impressively in the Caribbean and at home to Pakistan and New Zealand. Lillee and Thomson, however, had not played Test cricket for almost two years. In their absence, Max Walker had established himself as a trusty new-ball bowler. Or so he thought. Everything was about to change.

The unique slingshot action of the Australian fast bowler Jeff Thomson.

1974–75

'Ashes to Ashes, dust to dust, if Thomson don't get ya, Lillee must.'

[A SYDNEY *DAILY TELEGRAPH* CARTOON CAPTION PAYS TRIBUTE TO AUSTRALIA'S DEADLY PAIR OF FAST BOWLERS, 1975]

DENNIS LILLEE DIDN'T HAVE A FACE like thunder; he had a face like the apocalypse. Seconds earlier he had been on his backside on the Brisbane pitch, having lost both his wicket and his dignity when he fell over as he top-edged a Tony Greig bouncer. As Lillee started to stomp off, a picture of affronted pride, Greig reminded him where the facilities were and how appropriate a refreshing shower might be in the circumstances. Lillee looked at him and barked: 'Just remember who started this.'

For the next few minutes Lillee was like a stuck record. 'Just remember who started this,' he hissed repeatedly at his captain Ian Chappell, who had no idea what Lillee was talking about. It became clearer when Lillee announced: 'Just remember who started this: those bastards. But we'll finish it.'

Lillee has always been keen to point out that England started the bouncer war of 1974–75. 'It's like the song "We Didn't Start The Fire",' he said, continuing a long line of Billy Joel references in Ashes cricket. 'People often remember who did the damage not who started the fire.'

In the first Test of the series at Brisbane, more than half the Australian team were out hooking in the home side's first innings of 309, though it was Greig's decision to bounce Lillee, a lower-order batsman, that really stirred the hornets' nest. Lillee, who had clearly been intending to diligently bowl line and length until then, took the first ball of the England innings, and his run-up began from somewhere inside the sightscreen. 'Mate, it was full-on war,' said Jeff Thomson, 'and we gave it to them.'

The original plan was for Lillee to share the new ball with Max Walker, so that the tearaway Thomson could bowl with the wind after Lillee. But Chappell, sensing something in the air, decided at the last second to let Thomson share the new ball. 'For the next few overs,' said Chappell, 'I looked on in awe.' When the wicketkeeper Rodney Marsh leapt to claim a Thomson bouncer, he started wringing his hand in pain before realising the implications for England. 'Hell, that hurt,' he said to Chappell, 'but I love it.'

Hell, that hurt, but I love it

England were soon 57 for four and in trouble; the captain Mike Denness, upon being dismissed, took off his shirt and discovered that a bouncer had actually embedded his St Christopher medallion in his chest. Dennis Amiss had his thumb cracked by Thomson and John Edrich's hand was broken by Lillee.

As would happen in 2013–14 (see page 332), a group of experienced batsmen never recovered from the shock of being assaulted so savagely in the first innings of the series at Brisbane. Lillee and Thomson were also helped by the pitch. The groundsman, Clem Jones, was also the Lord Mayor of Brisbane; he sacked the curator ten days before the Test and appointed himself. The pitch he hastily prepared was grassy and uneven – not good when you were batting against Thomson, who was able to get dangerous lift from a fullish length on even the truest pitch. Dennis Amiss described it as Thomson's 'trapdoor ball', because it came out of nowhere.

England fought back for a time, thanks largely to an impudent and possibly insane century from Greig. Helmetless, as was the way of things then, he took on the fast bowling with crashing drives and deliberate uppercuts, and even started signalling his own boundaries and pretending to head bouncers as they passed him. Lillee did not like batsmen at the best of times – 'I treat them like faceless, meaningless thieves,' he said – but Greig's goading tipped him over the edge. Australia's bowling became ragged and Greig took advantage. 'We were trying to kill him,' said Thomson. The words sound unfortunate now, after Phil Hughes's death, but such hyperbolic language was common currency at the time.

Greig had the ability to take on the Aussies, and his 110 was one of the great counter-attacking innings in Ashes history, but his buccaneering arrogance was tantamount to a declaration of war. And this was a war that England could not win. 'Please don't make him mad,' said the tail-ender Derek Underwood to Greig during his century, as Lillee's face got redder and redder. It was certainly not apparent at the time, but ultimately there was respect for Greig's ability and attitude. 'He had the same attitude as me and after play we'd enjoy a few beers and laugh about it in the dressing-room,' said Lillee. 'I liked Tony Greig.'

Others could not cope. Keith Miller said England's top order were not batsmen but 'weak-kneed imposters'. Then again, Miller also said

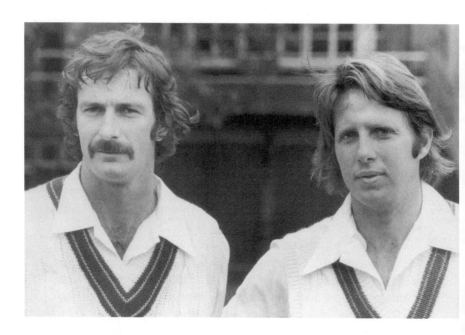

Lillee and Thomson, England's tormentors of 1974–75.

he was frightened of Thomson from 200 yards away in the press-box. In terms of the scale of the assault, this was Bodyline squared. Batting against Lillee and Thomson was like going to a backstreet dentist for a root canal armed only with a nip of whisky and a prayer. 'You had to be prepared to lose your front teeth,' said Denness.

Having bowled England out for 265, Australia made 288 for five in their second innings and then skittled England for 166 on the final day, winning by 166 runs with eighty minutes to spare. Thomson bowled the 6 feet 6 inch Greig with an awesome yorker – a 'sandshoe crusher' suggested by the wicketkeeper Marsh. For the next two years, until he sustained a serious shoulder injury, Thomson was like nothing cricket has ever seen.

Thommo didn't go to any Academy, he just grabbed the ball and wanted to kill some prick. . .

He had a unique roundarm action which meant the ball came at the batsmen as if fired from a slingshot. 'I just run up and go whang,' he said of his action. He rarely sledged batsmen, but had a habit of berating himself with 'You f****** slut!' if he bowled a poor ball.

'Thommo was by far the quickest bowler I've ever seen or opposed,' said his future team-mate Kim Hughes. 'Thommo didn't go to any Academy, he just grabbed the ball and wanted to kill some prick. . . he was as far ahead of any other bowler for sheer speed as [Don] Bradman was for runs.'

With his moustachioed fellow-assassin Lillee, Thommo simply brutalised England in 1974–75. 'Lillee and Thomson remain a combination to conjure with, as sinister in England as Burke and Hare, or Bismarck and Tirpitz,' wrote Gideon Haigh. They will always tell you they didn't start the fire, but they sure as hell poured industrial quantities of petrol onto it.

1974–75

'I don't think we have met – my name's Cowdrey.'

[COLIN COWDREY, AGED FORTY-ONE, GREETS FAST BOWLER JEFF THOMSON, SECOND TEST, PERTH, 13 DECEMBER 1974]

IT WAS LIKE SENDING YOUR GRANDAD out to deal with the burglars. When England needed to call for a replacement batsman in 1974–75 owing to injuries to Dennis Amiss and John Edrich, they eschewed a number of younger choices and selected Colin Cowdrey, who was about to turn forty-two and had not played Test cricket for three-and-a-half years.

It was almost Christmas, but Cowdrey had no hesitation about swapping the fireside for the hottest kitchen in sport, a glass of port for a game of bloodsport, and a dressing-gown for a suit of armour. He certainly came prepared. Tony Greig recalled the moment Cowdrey opened his cricket bag after arriving in Australia: 'Like bread rising in an oven, a mountain of foam rubber rose from the interior.'

Cowdrey took forty-seven hours get to Australia because of a flight delay, and then, after three days of constant nets, was pitched into the side to face Dennis Lillee and Jeff Thomson in the second Test. On the fast bowler's wet dream of a track that was Perth. On Friday the 13th. 'Cowdrey is going to cop it as quick as anyone,' warned Thomson.

He was at the crease soon enough, coming in at No.3 with England 44 for one, his padding making him look even plumper than usual, almost like the Michelin Man. 'His arrival,' wrote Christopher

Martin-Jenkins, 'was the signal for tears to prick the eyes of all but the stony-hearted.' Soon after arriving at the crease, Cowdrey introduced himself to a confused Thomson with old-world courtesy. 'I was revved up and just wanted to kill somebody and Kipper walked all the way up to me and said something like: "Mr Thomson, I believe. It's so good to meet you,"' said Thomson. 'And I said: "That's not going to help you, Fatso, now piss off."'

Thomson's taunts notwithstanding, Cowdrey already had the respect of the Australians,

Mr Thomson, it's so good to meet you. That's not going to help you, Fatso, now piss off

and he refreshed that by getting uncomplainingly into line to make 22 and 41 in the match. The scores may seem piddling, but Cowdrey batted for over four hours, took his hits and retained his good cheer. At one point, after an over in which he had been subjected to a grilling by Thomson, he said 'This is fun!' to his partner David Lloyd.

Australia routed England by nine wickets at Perth and proved that their triumph at Brisbane was not down to the uneven pitch. Yet England took significant pride in the performances of Cowdrey and the forty-two-year-old off-spinner Fred Titmus, who made 61 in the second innings, batting at No.8, in his first Test since 1968.

Australia were not just superior with the ball. Their slip and gully cordon were sensational, routinely snaring catches that might have required oven gloves; they took thirteen in the match, with Greg Chappell claiming seven of them to set a new Test record. There were also centuries from Ross Edwards and Doug Walters, who went into Ashes folklore in the final over of the second day.

Walters, who started the evening session on three not out, had raced to 97 as he prepared to face the last ball from Bob Willis. He needed four for a century and six to score 100 in the session. Walters belted Willis into the stands. For a true showman, there was only one option. Just as there had been only one option for a true cricket man like Cowdrey when he was asked to face Lillee and Thomson in the evening of his career.

'The injury did confirm my earlier comment that I could play Thommo with my cock.'

[DAVID LLOYD LAUGHS OFF BEING HIT IN THE GROIN BY JEFF THOMSON, SECOND TEST, PERTH, 15 DECEMBER 1974]

ONE DELIVERY SUMS UP THE 1974–75 Ashes. It did not take a wicket; it did not break a bone. It almost did something far worse. The footage is eye-watering even now. When England's left-handed opening batsman David Lloyd was hit amidships by a Jeff Thomson thunderbolt at the WACA, he toppled forward and went over like a folding deckchair (see pages 152–53).

Lloyd had top-scored in the first innings with an admirable 49, after which he cheerily informed his team-mates that he could play Thommo with his appendage. It seems nemesis cannot resist punishing even mock hubris, and Lloyd was duly felled in the second innings. The force of the blow was such that, in Lloyd's words, 'everything that should have been inside the box was outside'. He started thinking outside the box in a different sense, desperately wondering whether there was enough blood flowing to the parts that had been trapped in the little air holes by the force of the blow. 'I didn't need a doctor,' said Lloyd. 'I needed a welder.'

The story is a staple of the after-dinner circuit now, for both Lloyd and Thomson, though at the time Lloyd had the look of a man whose parental hopes were flashing before him. He now refers to it as 'a crisis in the Balkans'.

There was certainly a crisis down under for England. The extent of the physical and mental disintegration they suffered against Lillee and Thomson was unprecedented. So many batsmen were struck that it would have been quicker for England to install an X-ray machine in their dressing-room than to take trips to the hospital. But the most grievous damage inflicted was to England's spirit and self-belief.

The most extreme example of that came when the captain Mike Denness dropped himself for the fourth Test at Sydney. The third, at Melbourne, had ended in a classic draw – England 242 and 244, Australia 241 and 238 for eight, eight runs short of victory – but Denness had made just 65 runs in six innings. His decision brought mixed reviews: he was either courageous and selfless or a complete coward.

Denness was not the only batsman whose confidence was shattered. Dennis Amiss, who scored a vintage 90 in the first innings at Melbourne but managed just 85 in his eight others in the series, said facing Lillee and Thomson was 'like leaving the condemned chair. . . batting was a complete misery'.

Keith Fletcher, who provoked Lillee's ire by loudly displaying his approval when Greig hit the fast bowler on the elbow in the fourth Test, paid for his

Bloody hell! He's just knocked St George off his 'orse!

lack of judgement when Lillee – responding to the crowd's chants of 'Kill, kill' – smacked him on the head with a short one. 'Bloody hell!' shouted Geoff Arnold in the England dressing-room. 'He's just knocked St George off his 'orse!'

Fletcher escaped serious injury, though he was pinned on both the glove and the head by a similar delivery from Thomson in the second innings, with the ball rebounding almost to cover. Thomson does not keep much 'cricket shit' in his house, but he has an oil painting of Fletcher being hit on the head. 'Coming fresh into the series is like walking into a pitched battle between the mafia and the IRA,' wrote the *Daily Mail*'s Ian Wooldridge. 'You knew they'd been at each other's throats but you couldn't believe it was this uncompromising, this violent or this uncouth.'

John Edrich had a rib fractured, Bob Willis was hit by an accidental beamer, and a short ball from Lillee went between Arnold's gloves and face before clearing the wicketkeeper Rodney Marsh and battering into the sightscreen. 'Even I was relieved that one missed,' said Lillee.

Australia dismissed England for 228 to win by 171 runs and take an unassailable 3–0 lead with two to play. With hindsight, England's shock after Brisbane was so great that Australia effectively had an unassailable 1–0 lead with five to play. But this was confirmation of what everyone knew was going to happen: Australia had regained the Ashes.

Lillee beat England up again in the fifth Test, taking eight wickets in another big victory despite 11 wickets from Derek Underwood and a marvellous unbeaten century from Alan Knott, the wicketkeeper who had a touch of unorthodox genius with the bat. This time Lillee was without Thomson in the second innings, his fellow quick bowler having torn his right shoulder playing tennis on the rest day, and Australia were without both for most of the final Test at Melbourne when Lillee broke down after bowling six overs in England's first innings. In the absence of a new-ball pair who had shared 58 wickets in the series, England's batsmen were finally safe to come out from behind the sofa, or the square-leg umpire: Denness, back in the side, made 188 and Fletcher 146 in a consolation innings victory.

Max Walker, suddenly elevated to senior status, bowled beautifully and took eight for 143 in England's only innings. Walker was an entirely different type of bowler – a significant challenge, but one England could play with their bats, rather than their gloves, heads – or even their cocks.

1975

'Take a good look at this arse of mine, you'll see plenty of it this summer.'

[ENGLAND'S DEBUTANT DAVID STEELE INTRODUCES HIMSELF TO ROD MARSH, SECOND TEST, LORD'S, 31 JULY 1975]

DAVID STEELE WAS LATE FOR THE most important appointment of his working life. He was making his England debut in the second Test at Lord's in 1975, and received the usual gin-soaked encouragement as he made his way through the Long Room. Then, instead of walking out towards the middle, Steele went down a flight of stairs too many and ended up in a basement toilet.

It sounds like an appropriate location for a man about to face Dennis Lillee and Jeff Thomson after a career in the relative comfort of county cricket. In fact Steele was barely nervous at all; he was simply in such a Zen zone that he forgot where he was going. His form was not very good going into the Test, and he had a modest career record, but he was handpicked by the new England captain Tony Greig and experienced the happy coincidence of which all cricketers dream: a Test debut at a time of serenity and stratospheric confidence. 'That morning,' he said, 'was the best I ever felt in my career.'

When he finally arrived in the middle, his timekeeping added another layer to the abuse he copped from the Australians. Lillee and Thomson had spent most of the last nine months giving English batsmen grey hairs (when they weren't breaking their bones, that is), and now

England had resorted to a bespectacled thirty-three-year-old who *already* had grey hair – and whom they had never heard of. David and Goliath had nothing on David against Lillee and Thomson.

When Steele arrived, Thomson looked him up and down – or rather down and further down. 'Bloody hell,' he said, 'who have we got here, Groucho Marx?' Thomson is also supposed to have called Steele 'Father Bloody Christmas'. They didn't think much of his librarian

Bloody hell, who have we got here, Groucho Marx?

chic, but they might quietly have been impressed by his cheek. Steele cheerfully told Lillee and Thomson to 'bugger off and bowl', before informing the wicketkeeper Rodney Marsh that he would be seeing plenty of his backside this summer. He was true to his word.

Steele's selection is among the most inspired hunches in Test history. The *Sun*'s Clive Taylor christened him 'the bank clerk who went to war'. He was selected when Greig replaced Mike Denness after England were thrashed in the first Test. Denness sealed his own fate by becoming the first England captain to bowl first in a Test at Edgbaston. A young Essex batsman called Graham Gooch made a pair on debut;* Lillee, Thomson and Max Walker all took five-fors in Australia's innings victory.

The result meant that England were now 5–1 down in the back-to-back Ashes. The second of those was only a four-Test series, because of the inaugural World Cup earlier in the summer, but 4–0 looked a good bet at the time. England were still suffering residual shock from their battering in Australia the previous winter. As such, an eventual 1–0 series defeat was a minor triumph – especially as Australia then thrashed West Indies 5–1 in the Antipodean summer of 1975–76 before the Windies defeated England 3–0 in the heatwave summer of 1976.

Steele helped England draw each of the remaining Tests, his successive innings of 50, 45, 73, 92, 39 and 66 restoring pride to

---

* The story goes that, on arriving at the crease, Gooch said 'Good morning, Ian,' to the Australian captain Ian Chappell. 'What's so f****** good about it?' came the reply.

David Steele hits out, Headingley 1975.

English cricket. It's true that things were in his favour: the pitches were far slower than in Australia, so he could get onto the front foot, and Thomson was not quite as devastating as the previous winter. It was nonetheless a heartwarming and very English triumph, and not just because England actually lost the series. Steele was rewarded with two years' worth of lamb chops, having been sponsored by his local butcher's, and the BBC Sports Personality of the Year award.

Had there been a Sports Stud of the Year award, Thomson would have been the main contender. At one stage on the 1975 tour of England, it was neck and neck between maiden overs bowled and maidens bowled over until he slipped down six consecutive dot balls. 'I don't try to be Joe Blow the superstud,' said Thomson. 'It just happens.' Thomson was the subject of constant approaches during that tour, from women wanting something rather more than an autograph. 'All shapes and sizes with just one thing in common – they wanted my body.'

> **I don't try to be Joe Blow the superstud. It just happens**

The only thing that neutered Thomson was the English pitches. England had the better of the draws at Lord's – when John Edrich made 175 and the recalled John Snow ran through the Australian top order one last time – and Headingley, and might have won the latter but for a notorious protest against the imprisonment of a man named George Davis for armed robbery. The pitch was sabotaged with knives and oil and the final day could not be played; Australia would have resumed on 220 for three, needing 445 to win.

After Ian Chappell made 192 and Thomson bowled his hottest spell of the summer, Australia forced England to follow on in the final Test at The Oval. England batted two-and-a-half days in the second innings to save the game. Bob Woolmer made 149 in over eight hours. 'I was sick of the sight of his arse,' said Thomson. Woolmer's was not the only arse Australia were sick of that summer.

1977

Tony Greig: 'When are your balls going to drop, sonny?'
David Hookes: 'I don't know, but at least I'm playing cricket for my own country.'

[ON-FIELD EXCHANGE DURING THE CENTENARY TEST, MELBOURNE, 14 MARCH 1977]

TONY GREIG THOUGHT DAVID HOOKES was an easy target. Hookes was twenty-one, making his Test debut for Australia, and Greig, England's South African-born captain, decided to ram home the point that he was now at big school by questioning when he might experience puberty. Hookes's reply, pointing out that he would be undergoing puberty in the country of his birth, quickly silenced Greig. It was not the only time Hookes would shut Greig up during the Centenary Test of 1976–77.

The match was a feelgood celebration of 100 years of Anglo-Australian cricket, played precisely a century after the first – pre-Ashes – Test match, on the same Melbourne ground. The occasion was rich in echoes of the past, with 218 Ashes alumni present. The urn was not at stake, though as the match would prove, the concept of an uncompetitive match between Australia and England was an oxymoron.

Hookes, on his Test debut, and Derek Randall, in his first Test against Australia, overshadowed more decorated team-mates with their intrepid, impudent batsmanship. Not that the batsmen had much joy at the start of the match. England assumed control by dismissing Australia for 138. Dennis Lillee replied with six for 26, rolling England over for just 95. By now Lillee was almost the perfect fast bowler, an irresistible force of pace, craftsmanship and mongrel.

As the pitch flattened out, so the runs began to flow. Rod Marsh strong-armed the first Ashes hundred by an Australian wicketkeeper, and Hookes demonstrated his talent with a lovely 56, in which he belted Greig for five consecutive fours.* In the best traditions, Greig made a beeline for Hookes at the close of play, said 'well played' and asked him if he wanted to share a beer.

Australia reached 419 for nine declared in their second innings, in no small part because of a courageous 25 not out from Rick McCosker, who came out at No.10 looking like Boris Karloff in *The Mummy* after having his jaw broken earlier in the match by the increasingly potent Bob Willis. England, chasing an apparently impossible target of 463, got extremely close because of a thrilling innings from Randall, a jaunty, hyperactive soul who batted as if his underpants were made of 50 per cent cotton and 50 per cent ants. Observing the dotty-looking Nottinghamshire batsman from behind the stumps, Marsh remarked: 'Hey, Randall, your mother wanted a girl and your father wanted a boy. But they had you so they were both happy.'

When Lillee sat him on his backside with a bouncer, Randall doffed his cap; when Lillee hit him on the head, Randall pointed out the futility of such tactics. 'No point hitting me there,' he said, 'there's nothing to damage.' Randall's innings assumed epic proportions as England got closer to their target. He appeared to be caught behind on 161, only for Marsh to call him back because he was unsure whether the ball carried. 'Have you gone all religious?' said the Australian captain Greg Chappell.

Eventually Randall fell for 174, and Australia won by 45 runs – exactly the same margin of victory as in the first Test a century earlier. The Anti-Corruption Unit might have wanted a word with Dame Fortune.

---

* The vibrant brilliance of Hookes's debut has been imbued with enormous poignancy by subsequent events. He failed to fulfil his potential at Test level, averaging 34 in twenty-three Tests, and died in 2004 after a fracas with a bouncer outside a Melbourne bar.

'The only fellow I've met who fell
in love with himself at a young age
and has remained faithful
ever since.'

[DENNIS LILLEE ON GEOFF BOYCOTT,
WHO RETURNED TRIUMPHANTLY TO THE
ENGLAND SIDE IN THE SUMMER OF 1977]

GEOFFREY BOYCOTT WAS THE BATSMAN who gave selfishness an even worse name. Yet on this day all anybody wanted was for Boycott to think about himself. It was the fourth Test, on his home ground at Headingley, and he had the chance to become the first man to make his hundredth first-class hundred in a Test match. The entire country demanded a fairytale.

It was often said that Boycott would be the best man to bat for your life. Now he was batting for something far more important than your life – he was batting for *his* legacy.

The Ashes summer of 1977 belonged to two men: Boycott, who returned from a three-year exile in the most emphatic manner imaginable, and the media mogul Kerry Packer, whose imminent revolution cast a shadow over the traditional battle between England and Australia. When his attempt to buy the exclusive broadcasting rights for Australian cricket was blocked in the courts by cricket's establishment, he signed up many of the world's leading cricketers to play in his own breakaway competition – World Series Cricket – for rather larger sums of money than they were then receiving for playing Test cricket.

Geoff Boycott drives Greg Chappell for four to reach his hundredth hundred, Headingley, 1977.

Australia had not yet been seriously weakened by Packer; only Dennis Lillee was missing from the side that beat England in the Centenary Test. Tony Greig was sacked as England captain for his dealings with Packer, though he stayed in the side under his replacement Mike Brearley. England recovered to have the better of the drawn first Test, with Bob Willis's first-innings seven for 78 the start of a fine personal series. England won the second Test at Old Trafford despite a high-class 112 from Greg Chappell, which accounted for more than half of Australia's second-innings 218. It was one of only two centuries for the Australian batsmen in the series.

Boycott managed that on his own. His exile ended when he replaced Dennis Amiss for the third Test at Trent Bridge; he was joined in the team by the debutant all-rounder Ian Botham from Somerset. The twenty-one-year-old Botham took five for 74 in the first innings, including the grandest of first Test wickets: Chappell bowled, dragging on a loose delivery. A golden arm was born.

When England replied to Australia's 243, Boycott, not always the best judge of a run, ran out the local hero Derek Randall. The footage shows Boycott with his head in his hands after his act of folly. He was already under asphyxiating pressure because of the expectation surrounding his return. Given the circumstances, Boycott regards his 107 as his greatest innings. He added a match-turning 215 for the sixth wicket with Alan Knott, and saw England to a seven-wicket victory with 80 not out in the second innings.

After his best innings came his most famous, two weeks later at Headingley. Boycott knew there was a chance to play an innings that would define him. Rarely has a century felt as inevitable as it did that day. Dame Fortune was clearly on Boycott's side: he was dropped on 22 and survived a huge appeal for caught behind later in his innings. Just before the close on the first day, he on-drove Greg Chappell for four and raised his arms in triumph, prompting an eight-minute pitch invasion. It was his hundredth first-class hundred, on his home ground, in the Test when England regained the Ashes. 'It was like knowing the weather is hot without being aware of the temperature,' he said. 'It was all just noise. It was the most magical moment of my life.'

He went on to score 191, more than three times the next highest score in the match; it was a performance spread over more than ten hours. Boycott didn't so much book in for bed and breakfast as a John and Yoko bed-in. This time, however, nobody seemed to mind his snail-like progress. Botham made it two five-fors in his first two Tests as England trounced Australia by an innings.

The final Test was a rain-affected draw, in which Australia's Mick Malone became one of the more interesting one-cap wonders: he made 46, his highest first-class score, and bowled 47 out of 111.2 overs in England's first innings of 214. England's bowling hero was unquestionably Willis, who ended the series with 27 cheap wickets. Thomson, though not quite as terrifying as before his shoulder injury, picked up 23 scalps in the series despite not taking a five-for.

Given the choice between Raquel Welch and a hundred at Lord's, I'd take the hundred every time

Thomson and Australia had no real answer to Boycott, a man who lived for batting. 'Given the choice between Raquel Welch and a hundred at Lord's,' he said, 'I'd take the hundred every time.' In the second innings of the final Test, Boycott made 25 not out to end with a series average of 147.33. His greatest performance over a whole series surely came in 1970–71, but the heroics of 1977 sealed the Boycott legend.

'He's got a degree in people, hasn't he?'

ENGLAND'S BIGGEST ASHES TRIUMPH is one of their least memorable. They won 5–1 in Australia in 1978–79, yet their hosts lost so many players to Kerry Packer's World Series Cricket that it might have been flattering to describe them as a 2nd XI: for all their virtues at a lower level, players like Kevin Wright, Phil Carlson and Trevor Laughlin will not be entering any Halls of Fame in the near future.

England, by contrast, were at full strength. Ian Botham was emerging as a cartoon hero, and they had found a divine batting talent in the left-handed strokemaker David Gower. From the moment Australia slipped to 26 for six on the first morning of the series, Maurice Mentum was on England's side. The hosts never recovered.

Runs were at a premium throughout a series in which a score of over 200 was a significant milestone. Australia had the fast bowler Rodney Hogg to thank for their success with the ball. He excelled in his debut series, taking 41 wickets at 12.85, including a match haul of 10 for 66 in Australia's only win, the third Test at Melbourne.

Hogg also coined the phrase that would define the cerebral England captain Mike Brearley. No captain, English or Australian, has an Ashes record to match Brearley's: P15 W11 D3 L1, including three series victories. In every way, he was a profound influence on the battle for the urn at the end of the 1970s and the early 1980s.

Brearley was picked primarily for his captaincy, as his batting was not really up to Test standard – although he was a little better than an eventual Test average of 22.88 would suggest. His presence was an affront to some Australians. They saw him as effete, effeminate, and he wouldn't have earned a place under the Australian system, where the best XI is selected and a captain then chosen.

You have done for Australian cricket what the Boston Strangler did for door-to-door salesmen

They weren't always enamoured with his opening partner either. When Geoff Boycott batted all day for 63 in the second Test at Perth without hitting a single boundary, the Australian politician Jack Birney wrote him a note. 'You have done for Australian cricket what the Boston Strangler did for door-to-door salesmen.' At one stage on tour Boycott went 857 minutes without finding a boundary.

England's players loved playing under Brearley, and none more so than Botham. The most psychologically astute of captains, he still inspires reverence and awe in cricket fans of a certain age.

The contrast between the captains was painful, with Australia's Graham Yallop increasingly beleaguered. The home side did at least find a couple of gems in the feisty Hogg and the nuggety left-handed batsman Allan Border. Hogg could be thoroughly nasty when the mood took him. The great South African Allan Donald once said that all fast bowlers need 'a touch of the Rodney Hoggs'. He wasn't talking about the ability to maintain a disciplined line and length under pressure. Hogg did not always see eye to eye with his captain during the 1978–79 series. 'At one stage Hogg suggested we survey the back of the Adelaide Oval,' said Yallop, 'and I don't think he had tennis in mind.'

A year later England returned to face a full-strength Australia. With Test cricket still working out its place in a post-Packer world, Australia took part in overlapping series against the West Indies and England. The Test and County Cricket Board declined to put the Ashes at stake; either they knew England were certain to lose, or they knew England were certain to lose.

England lost all three Tests of the 1979–80 series through abysmal batting. Botham, in his bowling pomp, took 11 wickets in the first Test at Perth and scored his first hundred against Australia at Melbourne, but Australia's fast bowlers, especially Dennis Lillee, were too good for England. At Perth, Lillee tried to use an aluminium bat sold by a company owned by a friend of his. When Brearley complained, the umpires made Lillee use a wooden bat. It was a brief blast of heavy metal in cricket's rock'n'roll years.

Brearley grew a thick beard during the tour and was christened 'Ayatollah' by some Australian fans. A banner at the MCG paid tribute to him: 'Gold Medallion Award for Greatest Whinger Would Have To Be Won By J. M. Brearley, Classical Music Lover.' 'I was seen by the man in the Sydney street as the embodiment of all that's bad in the British,' said Brearley. 'I wore my sweater over my bottom for a start, and that proved I was a "poofter": you don't see Lillee or Thomson hiding the male hammer, do you?'

Six months later came another Centenary Test – this time at Lord's, to commemorate 100 years of England–Australia clashes in England. It was a forgettable draw for most, though fans of the Australian batsman Kim Hughes still talk about his two innings – 117 and 84 – in hushed tones, especially his astonishing straight six

I wore my sweater over my bottom for a start, and that proved I was a 'poofter': you don't see Lillee or Thomson hiding the male hammer, do you?

off Chris Old that came within a few metres of clearing the Lord's pavilion, a feat that was never achieved in the twentieth century. England would be far less kind to Hughes a year later.

'We were going to sack him anyway.'

AS IAN BOTHAM LOOKED UP, EVERYBODY else looked down. Botham, the England captain, was walking towards the Lord's pavilion after completing a pair in the second Test at Lord's when he encountered a humiliating wall of silence. The MCC members who had spluttered joyously into their G&Ts over his match-winning exploits since his debut in 1977 now treated him like a pariah.

'Not a single MCC member looked me in the eye,' he later wrote. 'They all just sat there dumbstruck. Some picked up their papers and hid behind them, others rummaged in their bags. Needless to say, I was fuming.' The implication was that Botham was finished. He thought, 'I'm twenty-four, you muppets,' but even that aggressive defiance could not disguise the hurt. It was a crushing, brutal ostracism.

Botham resigned the captaincy after the game, the inevitable conclusion of a year of misery in which England won none of his twelve Tests in charge. Before he took the captaincy, he averaged 40 with the bat and 19 with the ball in twenty-five Tests; as captain those averages yoyoed to 13 and 33.

Botham's fortunes in 1980 and 1981 were like the big dipper in reverse. After an astonishing one-man show in the Golden Jubilee Test in India – when he became the first man to take ten wickets and score a century in the same Test – he was an irresistible choice to succeed the retiring Mike Brearley as captain.

Even in his early twenties, Botham was already being hailed not just as England's greatest-ever all-rounder but as England's most gifted post-war cricketer – in short, a player of almost boundless potential. Then reality's incisors got to work. England failed to win a single Test home or away to the West Indies in 1980 and 1981 and came into the Ashes having won only one of their previous seventeen Tests. The man the Indians called 'Iron-Bottom' had been shown to have feet of clay.

Not a single MCC member looked me in the eye. They all just sat there dumbstruck. Some picked up their papers and hid behind them, others rummaged in their bags. Needless to say, I was fuming

Australia had an equally dodgy record overseas – one Test win in four years – and a young captain, the dreamily talented Kim Hughes; he replaced Greg Chappell, who had decided to take a rest from cricket. The only Chappell Australia still had was Trevor, the youngest and least gifted of the three brothers. Their squad included an uncapped twenty-four-year-old swing bowler called Terry Alderman.

Alderman and Dennis Lillee shared 17 wickets in a thrilling opening Test at Trent Bridge. It was the kind of match in which every run feels like a minor triumph; on a green wicket, with not a single over of spin bowled, only 621 runs were scored in the match and Australia sneaked home by four wickets. England had a comical stream of dropped catches to blame, three of them by Botham, whose playing contribution was just three wickets and 34 runs.

Matters came to a head in an otherwise forgettable draw at Lord's. Botham completed a pair when he was bowled round his legs by the left-arm spinner Ray Bright on the final day. It was actually an admirable golden duck, because he had sacrificed himself in pursuit of quick runs. But as he walked through the members he says he was 'made to feel like a villain'.

The cliché of taking it one game at a time is usually one of a sportsman's best friends, but it was the opposite for Botham in the summer of 1981. He was tired of being appointed as captain on a one-match basis, and the strain on his family was such that his wife Kathy lost a stone in a month.

On the final day of the Test, Botham decided to quit unless he was appointed as captain for the rest of the six-match series. The selectors, worried about his wretched form, had decided to move on anyway. The whole situation was handled grubbily, with Botham not having the chance to tell his wife or the team before it was announced. 'I quit for the sake of my wife. For the sake of the team. For my own peace of mind. In that order.'

I quit for the sake of my wife. For the sake of the team. For my own peace of mind. In that order

Bedser is usually criticised for a lack of basic humanity in telling the press that Botham was going to be sacked anyway. But this was not quite a case of Bedser callously trying to push Botham after he had jumped. Bedser, a man who believed in honesty above all else, was asked a question and replied that 'We had decided to make a change before Ian came to see us.' This was simply one part of a press conference in which he praised Botham's handling of the situation and suggested he could be captain again in the future.

But Botham would never get that chance. He has an intractable conviction that his poor form as captain was nothing more than 'pure coincidence', and that he was starting to feel far more comfortable in the job. Almost everybody would disagree with Botham, but it is a fascinating insight into a mindset that enabled him to do such astonishing things on a cricket field. The things he was about to start doing again.

1981

'Come on, let's give it some humpty.'

[IAN BOTHAM TO GRAHAM DILLEY,
THIRD TEST, HEADINGLEY,
20 JULY 1981]

IT WAS ONLY BECAUSE ENGLAND HAD lost the Headingley Test of 1981 that they were able to win it. They had given up, and with that came the blessed freedom of the damned. The miracle started not when Ian Botham came to the crease in the second innings, but when he was joined soon after by the startlingly blond Kent fast bowler Graham Dilley. On a wicket full of booby traps, England trailed Australia by 92 with three wickets remaining, having been forced to follow on. They had already booked out of the team hotel and Ladbrokes had offered 500/1 on an England victory.

With England already one down in the series, the noble thing might have been to knuckle down and lose with a bit of honour. That was also the boring option, and after the year he'd had, Botham was due a bit of fun. 'You don't fancy hanging around on this wicket for a day and a half, do you?' he said to Dilley, who concurred. 'Right. Come on, let's give it some humpty.'

Before the humpty had come the great fall, with Botham resigning as England captain after the second Test at Lord's. Mike Brearley came out of international retirement to become England's emergency captain. He found out that he had been chosen via a reverse-charge phonecall, because the chairman of selectors Alec Bedser had run out of coins. Botham, without the psychological backpack weighing him down, started to enjoy his cricket again. His relationship with Brearley certainly helped. If Brearley had a degree in people, then he had a PhD in Botham. 'He needs a father figure, and I need a younger brother,' said Brearley.

He asked Botham if he was in the right state of mind to play – knowing full well both what the reply and the tone of the reply would be – and gently ribbed Botham's bowling run-up, calling him the Sidestep Queen. Botham took six wickets in Australia's innings, but on a dodgy pitch their total of 401 for nine declared was, both captains agreed, 'worth a thousand'. Bob Willis laboured through 30 overs

He needs a father figure, and I need a younger brother

without taking a wicket. He had not been in the original squad because of doubts over his fitness and the consensus was that he was probably playing his last Test.

Although Botham struck an unfettered fifty, England were dismissed for 174 and forced to follow on. That evening, with the rest day to follow, Botham invited both sides to his house at Epworth, near Doncaster, for a barbecue. An epic night's drinking – led by Botham, whose form in this sphere never fluctuated – ended with the players of both sides having a rugby scrum on the lawn in the small hours.

When play resumed on the Monday, Australia looked set for a quick kill. England were 105 for five when Botham came to the wicket, and 135 for seven soon after. By then, Dennis Lillee and Rodney Marsh had famously bet against their own team, putting a small wager on England. 'Being a small-time punter, I had been unable to resist the juicy 500/1,' said Lillee. 'It was as simple as that. I have never had any qualms over the matter and I have never lost a moment's sleep because of it.'

He'll have lost plenty of sleep over what happened once England started to give it some humpty. 'I guess I never will come to terms with it,' said Lillee. It was Dilley who went on the attack first, launching a series of strokes so brilliant that Botham was compelled to try to better him. The Kent fast man, who bowled right arm but batted left-handed, did a passable imitation of Garfield Sobers to lash his first Test fifty, striking 56 in a partnership of 117 that took just 80 minutes.* Botham carried on merrily, mixing agricultural mows with classical batsmanship. At times he played in the V – the V between third man and fine leg, as the ball flew off the edge of another lusty yahoo. 'Bloody lucky innings,' sniffed Lillee. 'I expected to get him out virtually every ball.'

What started as a bit of fun for England imperceptibly morphed into something more serious as the day progressed, but by then Botham had no inclination or need to sober up his approach. He made a cathartic century, with vital support from Chris Old, and overall his 149 not out from 148 balls included 27 fours and one unforgettable six. As Botham charged Terry Alderman and smoked the ball back over his head, the camera lurched left and right like the viewpoint of a seasick drunk and the Yorkshire crowd roared with primal aggression. 'Don't bother looking for that, let alone chasing it,' said the BBC commentator Richie Benaud. 'That's gone straight into the confectionery stall and out again.'

Don't bother looking for that, let alone chasing it. That's gone straight into the confectionery stall and out again

Botham dragged England back into the game off his own bat – or rather Graham Gooch's. Botham had borrowed Gooch's bat on the spur of the moment, fancying a heavier weapon than usual. 'He hadn't used it much in the match, and I thought there were a few runs left in it.' With his borrowed bat, he hit the ball like he wanted to kill it.

In the final session on the fourth day England plundered 175 runs in 27 overs. At the close, the England wicketkeeper Bob Taylor went into the Australian dressing-room with some bats for them to sign, only to be told to 'F*** off with your f****** bats.'

---

* Dilley, a genuinely fast, but inconsistent, bowler, took 138 Test wickets at a respectable 29.76. The scorecard of his first Test match, at Perth in 1979–80, included the matchless dismissal: 'Lillee, caught Willey, bowled Dilley'. The likeable hero of Headingley, whose potential Ian Botham believed was blighted by coaches who insisted on line and length at the expense of pace, would die – penniless – of cancer at the age of only fifty-two.

Ian Botham hooks Geoff Lawson for four, Headingley, 1981.

Even with Botham's heroics, Australia needed only 130 to win and go 2–0 ahead with three to play. At 56 for one, they were cruising. Willis was preoccupied with no-balls – he had bowled 32 in the previous Test at Lord's – and did not enjoy bowling up the hill. Brearley allowed him to switch ends so that he was going downhill with the wind at his back. 'Let me worry about the no-balls,' he told Willis. 'Just run up and bowl fast and straight.'

Willis soon dismissed Trevor Chappell, caught behind fending off a throat ball. There was no celebration, just a quick turn and walk back to his mark. Even when he picked up Hughes and Graham Yallop for ducks in the same

> **I looked into his eyes and it was like there was nobody there**

over soon after, there was not a hint of joy. Every sportsman dreams of being in the zone; Willis was, but this was a different kind of zone. 'I looked into his eyes and it was like there was nobody there,' said Dilley.

Willis had the dual motivation of saving his career and, in all probability, saving an Ashes series. After lunch he continued to charge in – 'I don't go as far as that on my holidays,' said one former Test bowler of his run-up – and, before anybody knew what was happening, Australia were 75 for eight. Across the nation it had become an unofficial Bank Holiday. The Stock Exchange stopped, while the best vantage points outside Headingley were the ones by the windows of Radio Rentals stores, where groups of people watched the developing drama.

Lillee and Ray Bright fought against the rising tide with a quick-witted partnership of 35 in four overs. Australia were 110 for eight, 20 from victory, when Lillee mishit Willis towards mid-on. Mike Gatting, not necessarily the man you would want in such circumstances, ran in and took a fine low catch. In the next over, from Botham, Old dropped two sharp chances at slip. It did not matter: Willis pegged back Alderman's middle stump to complete the most famous victory in Ashes history. He finished with figures of eight for 43.

Finally there was a celebration, as Willis thrust his hands in the air, but even then it was more a kind of dead-eyed relief than an expression of joy. He turned on his heels to run back to his mark, realised there was no more work to do and ran in a circle before haring for the pavilion.

Later that day Brearley received a telegram from the comedian Spike Milligan. 'Marvellous – have my ticket for the wedding,' it read, in reference to the marriage of Charles and Diana a week later. The match was later voted Britain's favourite sporting moment. England, 500/1 at one stage, had won by 18 runs. They had not just come back from the dead; they had come back from a cremation.

Bob Willis, accompanied by Gooch, Gatting and Willey, runs off after taking eight for 43, Headingley, 21 July 1981.

1981

'He didn't want to bowl, you know.'

[MIKE BREARLEY ON IAN BOTHAM'S RELUCTANCE TO TAKE THE BALL DURING THE FOURTH TEST, EDGBASTON, 2 AUGUST 1981]

WITH THE FOURTH ASHES TEST AT Edgbaston slipping away, a fortnight after Headingley, England needed another miracle. Mike Brearley and Ian Botham were in no doubt as to who might provide it. But it wasn't Botham. With the Edgbaston pitch turning, John Emburey was England's main hope of another Australian collapse. Botham did not even want to bowl; he thought Brearley should use the part-time spin of Peter Willey at the other end. Then Allan Border, Australia's middle-order rock, was dismissed by Emburey, and both Brearley and Botham sensed a change of mood.

Australia had recovered remarkably well from the trauma of losing at Headingley. For the first three days of the Edgbaston Test they were in control of a match in which nobody scored a half-century. Brearley top-scored with 48, one of his best innings for England, but Australia's first-innings lead of 69 looked more than enough when England were 167 for eight second time around. Emburey's 37 not out inched them to 219, meaning Australia needed 151 to win. With Border in over-my-dead-body mode, batting 175 balls for 40, they were in control at 105 for four.

Botham had had a quiet match, with one wicket and scores of 26 and three, and was almost absent-minded as England drifted towards defeat on the Sunday afternoon. Then Emburey got one to spit at

Border, who was caught by Mike Gatting. Botham no longer needed any persuading to bowl. 'I don't think Mike could have got the ball off me if he tried.'

He had no reason to try. Botham struck early, when Rodney Marsh was bowled, and Ray Bright was trapped lbw next ball. Botham flexed the muscles on both arms in a primeval celebration. That, you suspect, is the precise moment when the whole of Australia realised: it is happening again.

Botham, bowling fast, full and straight, rampaged through the Australian lower order, taking the last three wickets to complete a spell of five for one in 28 balls. Australia collapsed from 105 for four to 121 all out and lost by 29 runs. It was only the second time Test cricket had been played on the sabbath in England, and Beefy had Australia for Sunday lunch. Australia, who should have been 3–0 up in the series, were now 2–1 down.

Marsh proved that tough guys do cry when he broke down after the game. Hughes ended the night dancing on a table at a benefit function for Bob Willis. A conversation with his opposite number Brearley revealed how he was really feeling. 'I suppose my Mum'll speak to me,' he said. 'Reckon my Dad will too. And my wife. But who else?'

Edgbaston was the moment Botham took out a lease on the Australian psyche that would last over a decade. 'There was a mission in life for Ian Botham,' said David Gower. 'It was Aussie-bashing.' After this match, the name Botham would have the same impact on Australians as the word 'Macbeth' on a gaggle of thespians. For 99 per cent of the game at Edgbaston Botham had been an irrelevance, yet he was the Man of the Match. 'The greatest matchwinner the game has ever known,' said Brearley, and he wasn't talking about John Emburey.

> **There was a mission in life for Ian Botham. It was Aussie-bashing**

Ian Botham shakes hands with Mike Brearley after bowling England to
victory in the fourth Test at Edgbaston, 2 August 1981.

1981

'WAS BOTHAM'S INNINGS THE GREATEST EVER?'

[HEADLINE ON THE FRONT PAGE OF *THE TIMES* DURING THE FIFTH TEST AT OLD TRAFFORD, 17 AUGUST 1981]

IT WAS THE PERFECT BOUNCER FROM Dennis Lillee. Fast, straight at the head, giving the batsman no room to free his arms. Ian Botham, batting without a helmet, launched instinctively into a hook shot, but the ball was on him faster than he expected. It looked like it was about to do serious damage to Botham. A moment later it was sailing into the crowd.

Botham's innings in the fifth Test at Old Trafford was a perfect companion piece to his Headingley century; the first was a beery slog, the second a calculated demolition. After another Australian batting collapse – this time in the first innings, when they were bowled out for 130, precisely the total they needed to win at Headingley – Botham arrived in the second innings with England on 104 for five, a lead of 205. Batting was particularly hard going on this third day: in 34 overs, England had scored 34 runs for the loss of four wickets.

Unlike at Headingley, Botham took a long time to play himself in: he had three from 30 balls, and 28 from 53 when the second new ball was taken. It was the cue for a bit of Tarzan cricket, as Botham emphatically bested Lillee and Terry Alderman in a battle of machismo, and then tucked into the spinner Ray Bright for afters, perhaps with that Lord's humiliation in mind (see page 194). Botham reached his hundred by scoring 72 off his first 33 balls with the second new ball. There were six sixes, an Ashes record at the time, including two blind hooks off Lillee. Twice Botham did not look at the ball as he launched into the shot; twice it sailed into the crowd. Look, no eyes!

On its front page, *The Times* wondered whether it was the finest innings ever played. This, remember, was long before the age of clickbait; besides, a writer like John Woodcock, whose article it was, did not do hyperbole. 'I refuse to believe that a cricket ball has ever been hit with greater power or rarer splendour,' he wrote. Nor was this a giddy, instant reaction to Botham's brilliance; the article appeared on the Monday, thirty-six hours after Botham's innings.

It was the completion of a unique Ashes trilogy. Technically this was by far the most impressive of the lot. Botham did not rely on force of personality but force of sheer talent. There was barely a false stroke in the entire innings. He ended with 118 from 102 balls.

By now the country had been officially diagnosed with Ashes fever, and the sheer joy in England's comic-book comeback was another reminder of the healing power of sport. At the start of the summer England had been depressed, with riots and rebellion against the Thatcher government. By the end, thanks to Botham and the wedding of Charles and Diana, it was a happy place.

Botham regularly highlights the support he received from Chris Tavaré during his innings. Tavaré, a man next to whom Geoff Boycott was a Caribbean dasher, batted almost twelve hours in the match for scores of 69 and 78, and some cheery tailend hitting enabled England to set Australia a ridiculous target of 506 to keep the series alive. They failed nobly, with Graham Yallop and Allan Border making centuries in a 103-run defeat.

The series was over by the time of the sixth Test at The Oval, though there was a chance for Botham to demonstrate a different type of heroism. With Bob Willis injuring himself mid-match, a half-fit Botham bowled 89 overs in the Test and took ten wickets. At the end of the series he slept for almost two days solid. He ended with 399 runs at 36.27 and 34 wickets at 20.58; not bad for a man who was hurtling towards rock bottom at the start of the summer. The series will forever be 'Botham's Ashes'.

'They just tore each other's clothes off.'

THERE ARE TWO SIDES TO EVERY GLORY. In England the story of the 1981 Ashes is all about Ian Botham, Bob Willis, Ian Botham, Mike Brearley, Ian Botham and Graham Dilley. In Australia, it is as much if not more about the civil war that raged within the team.

When Greg Chappell pulled out of the tour, the cartel of senior players, primarily Rodney Marsh and Dennis Lillee, all thought Marsh should have been made skipper. The captaincy went instead to Kim Hughes, the teacher's pet of Australian cricket. Hughes was blessed and cursed by his talent; throughout his career he had to cope with older people who disliked him before they had even met him because they had heard so much about his talent.

Now he had to cope with being undermined by Lillee and Marsh, two of the most intimidating and powerful men the game has known. In Christian Ryan's biography of Hughes, *Golden Boy*, a number of players talk of Lillee suddenly lengthening his run – and shortening his length – every time Hughes came to bat in the nets. On one occasion, as a ball whistled just past Hughes's head, Lillee said, 'Sorry.' 'Oh, that's okay,' replied Hughes. 'Sorry I didn't f*****' hit ya,' said Lillee.

On pure talent, Hughes should have been a great. 'You're the Fred Astaire of cricket,' said the fast bowler Len Pascoe to him on one occasion. He charged fast bowlers, decades before it was in vogue, and played one of the finest Test innings of all time when he made an unbeaten century in an Australian total of 198 against West Indies' four horsemen of the apocalypse in the Melbourne Test of 1981–82. His two innings in the Centenary Test of 1980 at Lord's are still discussed with reverence. Yet he is primarily associated with two failures: the Ashes of 1981, and his tearful resignation speech three years later.

It could all have been so different. 'But for a bloke called Botham who walked on water for three matches we could have won that series 4–0,' he said. Instead they were christened Kim's Kamikaze Kids. One

Australian captain Kim Hughes and fast bowler Mike Whitney ponder a problem called Botham, Old Trafford, 15 August 1981.

They showed about as much character as a melting chocolate ice cream

reporter said, 'They showed about as much character as a melting chocolate ice cream.' There were individual successes for Australia on that tour. Allan Border, quietly, was the only man to pass even 400 runs, ending with 533. Terry Alderman took a staggering, Australian-record 42 wickets in his debut series, while Lillee, on his final tour to England, picked up 39. But these are almost footnotes in the story of *(Kim vs Rod + Dennis) vs Botham.*

Hughes was not a great captain, yet there was not much he or anyone could have done against the rising tide of Botham in 1981. What he did demonstrate was rare dignity, both at the time and subsequently. 'I don't say this about a lot of blokes, but I love Kim Hughes,' said Greg Chappell, another who sometimes made life difficult for Hughes during his playing career. 'I admire what he's been through because my life's been very easy compared with Kim Hughes's life, and I think most of us could say that.' When he did crack, it was in bizarre circumstances at the end of the tour. After a few drinks and a full and frank exchange of views, he and Lillee started grappling each other in front of a packed bar.

It's fair to say this was not homoerotic wrestling, or banter in physical form. Yet they didn't hit each other; they merely kept wrestling until the strange event ran its course, and they then walked off half naked. Lillee was probably sorry that he didn't effing hit him. Maybe Hughes was too.

1982–83

'I went into the England dressing-room and lost it. I gave them a real mouthful and told them they were going to pay for it at Sydney. I bet they all thought "what a dickhead".'

[JEFF THOMSON ON HIS REACTION TO LOSING THE FOURTH TEST, MELBOURNE, 30 DECEMBER 1982]

JEFF THOMSON HAD TWO CHOICES. He could take it out on himself, or he could take it out on the Poms. Thomson was bristling with rage after Australia lost the fourth Test at Melbourne by three runs. They lost because he got out. But the fact they even got close to victory was down to the incompetence of the Poms, and he decided to let them know what he thought of them. This was a case of attack as the best form of defence mechanism, because Thomson did not want to dwell what had just happened. 'I could not talk about it for years,' he said of the game. 'It was one of the all-time low moments of my life.'

Thomson had not been part of the 1981 Ashes, which provided a number of all-time low moments for the whole Australian team. Both sides had changed captains in the eighteen months since. Greg Chappell was back in the Australian team, with Bob Willis leading England. 'Well, Bob, this must be the worst English team ever to reach these shores' was the first comment he received at a press conference after England's arrival. Chappell was without Dennis Lillee for all bar one Test, though Thomson was fit to play most of the series and stuck it up the Poms for one last time on home soil.

We must be the only working-class family who have gone ex-directory

Australia lost both Lillee and Terry Alderman during the drawn first Test in Perth. Lillee was injured, while Alderman dislocated a shoulder rugby-tackling a pitch invader who had punched him in the back of the head. 'We must be the only working-class family who have gone ex-directory,' said Bill Donnison, whose son, Gary, was brought down by Alderman.

Those on the pitch were celebrating England reaching 400 after what felt like an eternity. Chris Tavaré had set the agenda, scoring 89 from 337 balls. Roget may disagree, but the word Tavaré is the antonym of Australian, and he became a source of fascination throughout the series with his dead bat, 1940s-detective face and inscrutable demeanour. His batting was so ugly that you couldn't take your eyes off it – except on the first day of the fourth Test at Melbourne, when he made a carefree 89 and took on the off-spinner Bruce Yardley. It was as surprising as seeing Mother Teresa in a boob tube.

Tavaré was decades before his time. Not in his style of batting, clearly, but because he would have been a star in this age of irony. Had cricket hipsters existed in 1982, Tavaré would have been their God. He was the ultimate alternative hero.

Without Alderman and Lillee, Australia found an authentic hero in Geoff Lawson. He took 20 wickets in the second and third Tests, which Australia won, and ended the series with 34 in five Tests. England's Hercules, Ian Botham, returned temporarily to the ranks of the mortals: in 10 innings his top score was 58, and he claimed 18 wickets at an average of 41. He was not entirely without influence, however; one of those wickets decided the fourth Test, and gave England a chance of retaining the Ashes.

It was a spandex-tight Test. England made 284 and 294; Australia, having made 287 in the first innings, needed 292 to win. They seemed finished at 218 for nine, but Allan Border and Thomson got them within a handful of runs of victory. Willis chose to give Border singles to get Thomson on strike, a tactic for which he was heavily criticised, and which may have wound Thomson up further.

With Thomson playing sensibly, Australia were on the brink of an unlikely victory.

Then Thomson edged Botham towards the slips. Tavaré dropped a simple chance, and time stood still before Geoff Miller claimed the rebound. An otherwise ordinary series had produced one of the great Ashes Tests, with England winning by three runs. Some of the Australians – whose part in the match was over – polished off eight cans of beer in the 90 minutes it took to decide the match in the final morning. Thomson, drunk on adrenaline and rage, went into the England dressing-room and informed them what would happen at Sydney.

He did not quite live up to his promise, but Australia kept England at arm's length throughout the fifth Test and got the draw they needed to regain the Ashes. Hughes ended a redemptive series, in which he was the highest scorer on either side, with a sparkling 137 in the second innings. England's first-innings collapse from 146 for three to 237 all out ended their hopes of squaring the series, though they at least drew the game thanks to 95 from the nightwatchman Eddie Hemmings.*

Australia's victory was far more emphatic than the 2–1 scoreline suggested. Indeed, they should probably have won the series 3–0. But don't mention that to Thommo.

---

* During the accompanying one-day series, Australian fans released a piglet onto the field in Brisbane as a tribute to England's larger players. It had 'Eddie' daubed on one side, in reference to Hemmings, and 'Botham' on the other.

1985

'It's hard work making batting look effortless.'

[DAVID GOWER, ENGLAND CAPTAIN AND STAR OF THE 1985 ASHES, ON HIS BATTING APPROACH]

CHANCE CAN BE THE FINEST THING. The happiest, most run-filled summer of David Gower's life started in an office at Grace Road, the home of his county Leicestershire. He was talking about bats with Mike Turner Junior, a club player and son of the Leicestershire chief executive, when Turner produced his new willow. Gower idly bounced a ball off it, felt the rare sensation of leather on sweet spot, and instantly thought: 'This bat's too good for you, sunshine!' Gower persuaded Turner to give him the bat, covered it in the stickers of his sponsor Gray-Nicolls and got to work.

Gower's style was so captivating that it was easy to lose sight of the substance behind it. The touch of his bat on the ball may have seemed gossamer-light, but it brought him a weighty haul of Test match runs. Only Jack Hobbs has scored more Ashes runs for England than Gower's 3037. He got almost a quarter of those in one run-soaked series. There have been more spectacular individual Ashes performances, yet none quite as dreamy, charming and idyllic as Gower's in 1985. 'Gower might have been more at home in the 1920s or 1930s, cracking a dashing hundred for MCC, the darling of the crowds, before speeding away in a Bugatti and cravat for a night on the town,' wrote Scyld Berry in 1984. A year later, he was English cricket's perfect romantic lead. With his curly blond hair and languid manner, he even looked the part. The flat pitches limited the need for a helmet. 'I remember spending a lot of time batting in my white floppy hat,' he said.

It's easy to forget how much pressure he was under at the start. He had not made a century in over a year since succeeding Bob Willis as England captain, and there were inevitable post-Botham concerns that leadership had compromised his rare talent. He was described as 'dispirited and close to the plughole'.

Although England had been blackwashed the previous summer by the West Indies, they came into the Ashes in positive mood after a stirring 2–1 victory in India. Australia, at the same time, were being thrashed 3–1 by the West Indies, during which their captain Kim Hughes resigned in tears. He was replaced by Allan Border, whose Ashes squad was without Terry Alderman and Rodney Hogg, banned because of their part in a South African rebel tour. England's rebels were available again, most notably Graham Gooch.

Gooch and all the other batsmen enjoyed a summer of plenty against two relatively weak bowling attacks. Apart from Ian Botham, who would take 31 wickets and bowl genuinely fast for the last time in his career, the raw young Queenslander Craig McDermott and the late arriving Kent swinger Richard Ellison, the bowlers had little impact. It was the summer of what Gooch calls the 'daddy hundred'.

The first came from his new opening partner. Nottinghamshire's Tim Robinson won an excellent first Test at Headingley for England with a mighty 175. Border went even better in the next Test at Lord's, where Australia squared the series, with 196 and 41 not out in a nervy run chase. In the first innings he was infamously dropped at short leg by Mike Gatting, who instinctively threw the ball up in celebration and then failed to grab the rebound.

After two high-scoring draws, the series was nip and tuck. Then Gower went into overdrive, enjoying the three happiest weeks of his career as England thrashed Australia by an innings at Edgbaston and The Oval to win the series 3–1. In the fifth Test at Edgbaston, Gower's beautiful 215, along with centuries from Robinson and Gatting, put England in total control. A new-look Botham, sporting a mane of hair with blond highlights, gleefully kicked Australia while they were down: with England pursuing a declaration, he smeared 18 from seven balls, including monstrous straight drives for six off McDermott from his first and third balls. Australia were in such disarray during his short innings that, when he caught Botham in the deep, Jeff Thomson instantly turned to the crowd flicking V signs. It was the kind of exhilarating cameo that only Botham could provide. He says that innings is the first time he was actually conscious of his celebrated ability to clear bars; in the distance he could see spectators streaming into their seats.

'Ian represents everything that's the best in Britain,' said the crackpot former DJ-turned-publicist 'Lord' Tim Hudson, who had a short spell as Botham's manager in 1985. 'He's Biggles, the VC, El Alamein, the tank commander. He's everything. I mean how could a schoolboy not want to be like Ian Botham?'

A bedraggled Australia were reduced to 36 for five on that fourth evening by Ellison, the mop-haired swing bowler who had been recalled for the match after spending the summer on the sidelines. His 10-wicket haul in the match included a gorgeous inswinger to bowl Border on that fourth evening, part of a game-breaking spell of four for one.

Australia battled hard for survival on the fifth day until the game turned on the controversial dismissal of Wayne Phillips. He cut Phil Edmonds hard onto the boot of the short leg Allan Lamb, from where the ball looped into the hands of Gower. Phillips was given out, even though Australia were convinced it was a bump ball.

England needed only a draw in the final Test at The Oval to regain the Ashes. They all but secured it on the first day, which they finished on 376 for three after a partnership of 351 between Gooch (who made 196, his first Test century against Australia), and Gower (157). Nobody else made more than 16 in the innings. Gower was out just before the close, having batted nigh-on flawlessly. 'That was the apogee,' he later said. There were seven more wickets for Ellison, and England won easily with a day to spare.

As his curly locks were drowned in champagne by Botham on the balcony, Gower jokingly told the world that 'the West Indies will be quaking in their boots'. England inevitably lost 5–0 the following winter, and Gower lost his job as captain at the start of the 1986 summer, yet nobody could take the perfect summer of 1985 away

David Gower square-drives, Lord's, August 1985.

from him. He made 732 runs – still a record for an England batsman in a home Ashes series – and regained the Ashes as captain. At twenty-eight, he had fulfilled his talent in precisely the manner he had always wanted. He had also worked bloody hard to do so, but you wouldn't have known it from watching him.

1986–87

'For heaven's sake, let's not panic. England have only three major problems. They can't bat, they can't bowl and they can't field.'

[THE *INDEPENDENT*'S MARTIN JOHNSON PREVIEWS THE FIRST TEST, BRISBANE, NOVEMBER 1986]

NEVER MIND THE COVER; SOMETIMES you shouldn't judge a book by its first chapter. England's all-conquering trip down under in 1986–87 – in which they won two one-day trophies as well as the Ashes – started in the most ignominious fashion possible. With their batsmen dealing in binary, they were thrashed by Queensland and would have lost heavily to Western Australia but for the weather. Their chances were dismissed by almost everyone, and most famously by the *Independent*'s Martin Johnson.

What few people in England realised at the time was that Australia were not much better. They had not won in ten Tests, England in eleven. Promising newcomers such as Steve Waugh, Dean Jones, Bruce Reid and Merv Hughes were a long way from fulfilment, and the captain Allan Border was still carrying an indecent load. His opposite number was now Mike Gatting, who had replaced David Gower during the previous English summer. Although Graham Gooch was unavailable, Gatting had an experienced core that included Gower, Ian Botham, Allan Lamb and John Emburey. The performances in the earlier tour matches did not bother them too much. 'The senior players were adjusting to the wine and the socialising,' said the opener Chris Broad.

At a team meeting the night before the series, Botham announced that it was time for England to apply their gameface. As ever, he backed up word with deed. After a tense first day, Botham wrenched the initiative with a violent hundred that included a famous assault on Hughes. In the battle of the mullets, Botham won emphatically, pillaging 22 from one over. 'Jeez, Merv, that one went so far it should have qualified for frequent flyer points,' said Jones after one six. At the other end, Gower was a happy onlooker. 'I should be telling you to calm down,' he said to Botham, 'but I'm having too much fun.'

> **Jeez, Merv, that one went so far it should have qualified for frequent flyer points**

Tone-setting performances are invaluable at the best of times but, given the fragility of both teams, this was a masterpiece of the genre. Amid the fear and loathing, there was significant respect. 'Ian Botham would make a great Aussie,' said Jeff Thomson, instantly challenging historians to find if he had ever previously said anything vaguely complimentary about England and the English. Botham and Thomson had an unspoken larrikinship.

It was Botham's last great Ashes performance. He took an important five-for later in the series at Melbourne, though that was mainly with long hops and aura. In a sense Botham took those wickets during his Brisbane innings, because the performance was so dominating and emphatic it further strengthened the psychological hold he had on the Aussies. Five-fors from Graham Dilley and John Emburey helped England complete an excellent and unexpected eight-wicket victory, despite a century from the opener Geoff Marsh when Australia were forced to follow on. It's a reflection of England's 1980s woes that this was one of only two Tests in his forty-one-match career in which Dilley was on the winning side, the other being Headingley 1981.

The emphatic manner of England's win made Johnson's 'can't bat, can't bowl, can't field' comment look a little silly, though he produced a decent rejoinder to any suggestion he should eat his words: 'Right line, wrong team.'

1986–87

'Hobbs, Hammond and Broad: it doesn't quite ring true, does it?'

[CHRIS BROAD REFLECTS ON HIS RECORD-EQUALLING THIRD ASHES HUNDRED OF THE SERIES, FOURTH TEST, MELBOURNE, 27 DECEMBER 1986]

CHRIS BROAD FELT MORE SECURE WHEN he was away from home. That paradox stemmed from the unique impatience of England's selectors in the 1980s. During home series, when they had the pick of the entire country, they were liable to drop players after one failure; overseas, those who started the series in the team had a far better chance of ending it there. That was one of the main reasons why Broad excelled overseas, where he scored all six of his Test hundreds. He particularly liked life in Australia. Of the 500-plus batsmen to have played at least 10 Test innings down under, only Sir Donald Bradman has a higher average.

> **I waddled in off a few paces and the Australian batsmen obliged**

Broad, a bolshie Nottinghamshire left-hander with a jutting-arsed stance, made centuries in three consecutive Tests in 1986–87 as England retained the Ashes with a match to spare. Only Jack Hobbs, Wally Hammond and Broad have scored hundreds for England in three consecutive Ashes matches. Broad had not even played for over two years when he was recalled to the squad to form a short-lived but triumphant opening partnership with Bill Athey. They added 223 on the first day of the drawn second Test at Perth, Broad going on to make 162. 'I've never hit the ball in the middle of the bat as often as I did today,' he said. There were also centuries for David Gower, Allan Border and an improbable 133 from the England wicketkeeper Jack Richards, playing only his second Test.

Border, Broad, David Boon and Mike Gatting made hundreds in the next Test, another high-scoring draw at Adelaide. On the final day, a lady produced a board and started doing her ironing, inviting jokes about the shirtfront of a pitch that had produced a bore draw.

The series was decided on the first day of the Boxing Day Test at Melbourne, when Ian Botham and Gladstone Small took five wickets apiece to bowl Australia out before tea for just 141. England ended the day in complete control at 95 for one. Both were unlikely heroes; Botham was barely fit, Small was mixing the drinks on the morning of the match when he was told he had to play because of an injury to Graham Dilley. Botham says he was '50–60 per cent fit. . . I waddled in off a few paces and the Australian batsmen obliged.'

Broad made his third hundred in consecutive Tests. England won the match by an innings, with Small taking the Ashes-winning catch off the bowling of the left-arm spinner Phil Edmonds. Not bad for a man who had spent Christmas Day, the day before the match, getting progressively drunk. His seasonal carousing captured the spirit of England's last rock'n'roll Ashes tour. Elton John was around the England team so often that he might have been the team mascot, while Phil Collins and George

We didn't hold back on having a few drinks on the tour. We partied like it was our last bloody tour

Michael also put in appearances in the England dressing-room. 'We didn't hold back on having a few drinks on the tour. We partied like it was our last bloody tour.' One night before a tour game, Botham, usually impervious to alcohol, lost a battle with a bottle of brandy and was in such a state the following day that he walked out to the middle without his bat.

England partied hard, but then they had plenty of reason to do so. This was an era in which players congratulated themselves on their professionalism if they turned down the offer of a tenth pint. England could eat, drink, be merry and win the Ashes. The young all-rounder

Phil DeFreitas shared a room with Botham and, on his first night, was handed a bottle of scotch with the simple instructions: 'You're on tour, pour.'

On the final day of the Melbourne Test, Australia had a drunken session of their own, though this was a wake rather than a party. They had even been criticised by the prime minister on TV, and Border had had enough. 'After a thousand beers,' said Border, 'we made a pact that it wouldn't ever be that bad again.'

> **After a thousand beers, we made a pact that it wouldn't ever be that bad again**

Border and the coach Bob Simpson chose to invest in young players of talent and character, and stick with them even if they failed at first. Yet it was a thirty-year-old stopgap who first changed the mood of Australian cricket. When Australia called up a man called Taylor,

Phillip DeFreitas, Phil Edmonds and Allan Lamb with a champagne-splashed Elton John after England's victory in the fourth Test at Melbourne, 28 December 1986.

everybody assumed it was the New South Wales opener Mark. A lady from Channel 9's *Today* programme broke the good news, only to then call him back and query whether there was another Taylor in Australian cricket.

It transpired Australia had picked *Peter* Taylor, Mark's off-spinning fellow New South Welshman who was not even in his state team at the time. *'Peter who?'* screamed the tabloids. Dean Jones made a thrilling 184 not out in a total of just 343, and then Taylor took six for 78 in the first innings to secure a lead of 68. Another slow bowler, the twenty-nine-year-old leggie Peter Sleep, took five for 72 in the second innings as Australia won an excellent match by 55 runs. It was only a consolation victory, yet it offered a hint of hope for a bright future. Nobody, not even the most optimistic Australian, had a clue how bright it would be.

AUSTRALIA
ASCENDANT
1989–2003

1989

'In my day fifty-eight beers between London and Sydney would have virtually classified you as a teetotaller.'

[FORMER AUSTRALIAN CAPTAIN IAN CHAPPELL IS UNIMPRESSED WITH STORIES OF DAVID BOON'S DRINKING BEFORE THE 1989 SERIES]

THERE WAS AN ABNORMAL AMOUNT OF TRAVEL sickness on the Qantas flight to London, and approximately 99.94 per cent of it was self-inflicted. As it descended towards Heathrow airport, the plane's captain addressed his passengers in the usual style. 'Ladies and gentlemen, welcome to London where it is six degrees outside,' he said. 'I want to wish the Australian team all the best. I know they'll do very well because David Boon has just broken the record, fifty-two cans from Sydney to London.'

Boon has always denied the story – 'If people haven't got something else to talk about they have led a f****** boring life,' he said in 2006 – but there are enough witnesses, one or two of them sober, to suggest that it happened. The teetotal Geoff Lawson, who kept score on the back of some sick bags, wished he had kept what would have been the ultimate in alternative Ashes memorabilia. Some were not worth keeping. 'The very instant we pulled up at our allotted gate,' recalled Steve Waugh, 'Tim Zoehrer lurched forward and filled up the sick bag to christen our tour.'

Boon was aiming to beat the record of forty-five cans, established by Rodney Marsh on the way to the World Cup in 1983. He didn't just take the record; he obliterated it. And he obliterated himself. The middle-order batsman Dean Jones acted as pace-setter for much of the twenty-four-hour flight. His father had told him to spend the journey picking the brain of somebody who had already played in England. The only thing Jones soaked up were about twenty-five cans on the way to the first stop-off in Singapore. At that point he was helped into an impromptu bed, 'pissed as a fart'. With Jones out of action, a number of other players took turns to sit alongside Boon and sink a few to help him on his way. It was a very early example of squad rotation.

When Australia landed, Merv Hughes gave a radio interview back home and jauntily informed everyone of what had occurred. 'The big news is that Boonie's cracked the first fifty of the tour!' This did not please the coach Bob Simpson, who had hoped that what happened on the plane would stay on the plane. 'I got in more trouble than the protagonist,' Hughes said. 'I was shitting myself that I'd be sent home.'

The big news is that Boonie's cracked the first fifty of the tour!

Boon, who became known as the 'Keg on Legs', was fined $5,000 – a lot for an international cricketer in 1989 – and put on probation. Simpson was not the only Australian who was unimpressed. Ian Chappell had been informed that Boon had drunk fifty-eight cans, rather than fifty-two, yet even that was not enough. 'What is the world going to think? That Australia has become a namby-pamby nation which doesn't know how to drink? For God's sake, in my day fifty-eight beers between Sydney and London would virtually have classified you as a teetotaller.'

Throughout the 1989 tour of England, Australia were emphatic proof that there are no team-bonding agents as powerful as alcohol and victory. A number of the players get almost misty-eyed when they talk about 1989. 'The spirit in the team was as good as anything I've ever been involved in,' said Ian Healy.

It needed to be. They were famously described as 'the worst team ever to leave Australia' by Tony Greig, among others. Collectively and individually, they were not so much written off as never written on in the first place. 'I am ready to bet Merv all the XXXXs he can drink that he doesn't bag 18 wickets in the series,' said Jeff Thomson. 'I reckon the English batsman could play him with a walking stick.' Graham Gooch says Australia were 'absurdly undervalued', yet himself admits he had 'never even heard of Mark Taylor before he arrived in England'.

In England, the re-appointment of David Gower as captain sparked abnormal optimism given the side he was taking over had won only two Tests in nearly four years. But then Australia's record was no better. They had won only one Test series in almost five years under Border, and even that was because of a diabolical umpiring decision, while losing seven series. But the cricket world was about to change forever.

Australia toast victory, Headingley, 1989. Captain Allan Border is on the far right; David Boon, moustachioed and beer-flecked, is third from the left, seated on Dean Jones's knee.

1989

'What do you think this is, a f****** tea party? No you can't have a f****** glass of water! You can wait like the rest of us!'

[ALLAN BORDER TO ROBIN SMITH, FIFTH TEST, TRENT BRIDGE, 12 AUGUST 1989]

NEVER ASK YOUR HEROES FOR A GLASS of water. Robin Smith did, during the fifth Test at Trent Bridge in 1989, and the response from the Australian captain Allan Border was not exactly dripping with period-drama politeness. The hard-hitting Smith had played in South Africa's Currie Cup, which did not have a vibe of goodwill to all men, yet even he was taken aback by Australia's verbal aggression throughout the series.

Border's rant at Smith symbolises the hardass approach he brought to the entire tour. He had been on the losing side in England in 1985, when he was chummy with his old mate and opposite number David Gower, and was in no mood for a similar experience. A chat with Ian Chappell hardened his heart. 'I can handle you losing to the West Indies, India and Pakistan,' said Chappell, 'but for God's sake don't lose to the Poms!'

Border was almost snarling as he got off the plane. 'I made a personal choice to have a harder edge as captain, be more stand-offish towards them. . . It was a hard thing to do and they all got the shits, but it was all part and parcel of what I wanted to achieve.'

The overwhelming harshness of the Aussies' approach shocked many England players. 'The Aussies went out of their way to be unsociable,' said Gower, 'and the atmosphere on the field was as unpleasant as many of our players could recall.' Smith wasn't the only one to experience Border's hard-faced wisdom. 'I've faced bigger, uglier bowlers than you mate,' was his generous compliment to Angus Fraser. 'Now f*** off and bowl the next one.' 'He was so famously bloody-minded to everyone on that tour,' wrote Gideon Haigh, 'that the Queen was lucky not to get an earful about the fall of Singapore.'

He was so famously bloody-minded to everyone on that tour, that the Queen was lucky not to get an earful about the fall of Singapore

Border's Australia introduced sledging to a new generation. They also gave it a name: mental disintegration. The phrase was coined by the fast bowler Carl Rackemann in the dressing-room during the final Test at The Oval, as Australia considered a delayed declaration. Rackemann suggested that to do so would achieve 'full mental and physical disintegration' by allowing England more time to consider the utter futility of their position – or, as Mitchell Johnson would put it in 2013–14, to 'cook 'em a bit longer'.

Australia started the tour in extremely cautious, even nervous, mood. Before the series, the opener Mark Taylor confided to team-mates that he did not think he was good enough to get runs at Test level. He would score 839 in that English summer – only Don Bradman and Wally Hammond have scored more in an Ashes series – and 7525 in his career. Steve Waugh, who began the series with no centuries from 26 Tests, edged his first ball of the first Test a fraction short of slip. He went on to make 177 not out and scored 393 runs before England finally dismissed him, on the twelfth day of the series. In doing so he created an aura that would endure for the rest of his career.

England blew the first Test before a ball was bowled. With the weather forecast dubious, and Headingley renowned for sideways movement and short matches in the 1980s, the chairman of selectors Ted Dexter started to talk in terms of a three-and-a-half-day game, of picking four seamers and bowling first. Gower says the idea gathered momentum on the morning of the game, and he allowed himself to be talked round. 'It galls me to think even now that the game was partially lost on placing undue reliance on Michael Fish's isobar chart on Breakfast TV.' England omitted the spinner John Emburey and bowled first on a belter. Australia made 601 for seven declared, and won the match when England's batting fell apart on the final day. It was the kind of pitch on which you could book in for bed and breakfast; England got drunk, lost their keys and ended up waking up on a park bench in a pool of their own drool.

Even victory at Headingley didn't completely relax Australia. At Lord's, where they went 2–0 up with a six-wicket win after another huge, unbeaten century from Waugh, they were so nervous during their run-chase that they banished Border to the shower for superstitious reasons and wouldn't let him back into the dressing-room until they had won.

The contrast between the captains was becoming acute. After a miserable third day's play at Lord's, an increasingly beleaguered Gower walked out of his press conference. He was asked what he would say to those who had tickets for the fourth day's play. 'We'll be trying our bollocks off. If that's what you want me to say, I'll say it.' When his old team-mate Phil Edmonds asked him why he had bowled everyone from the wrong end, he'd had enough. Gower 'swept out of the tent with as much dignity as I could muster' and straight into a taxi to see a performance of *Anything Goes*. Gower made a fiercely determined hundred on the Monday, the fourth day, but England lost regardless. It was time for Australia to have another party. And it certainly wasn't a tea party.

We'll be trying our bollocks off. If that's what you want me to say, I'll say it

1989

'Who can forget Malcolm Devon?'

[CHAIRMAN OF SELECTORS TED DEXTER
ON HIS NEW FAST BOWLER, DEVON
MALCOLM, FIFTH TEST, TRENT
BRIDGE, 14 AUGUST 1989]

THE CLICHÉ OF TAKING THE POSITIVES from a miserable defeat is not entirely new. When England went 4–0 down in the 1989 Ashes, losing the fifth Test at Trent Bridge by an innings and 180 runs having failed to take a single wicket on the first day, their increasingly beleaguered chairman of selectors Ted Dexter was asked if anything good had come from the game. 'Who,' said Dexter, 'can forget Malcolm Devon?'

Who indeed. Dexter is often ridiculed for the comment, but technically speaking he was correct. Nobody had forgotten Malcolm Devon; it's just that they hadn't heard of him in the first place. The man who made his debut in that Test was of course Devon Malcolm, Derbyshire's wild, woolly and in those days bespectacled fast bowler. And although Malcolm showed promise, figures of one for 166 in his only innings did not exactly ooze positivity. 'It was not quite clear whether he was referring to Malcolm, who took one wicket, or Devon, who conceded 166 runs,' wrote Martin Johnson.

> **It was not quite clear whether he was referring to Malcolm, who took one wicket, or Devon, who conceded 166 runs**

In Dexter's defence, naming all the England players that summer required the memory of an expert Simon Says player. There were twenty-nine of them in six Tests, partly because of injury and the rebel tour of South Africa, but mainly because of desperation. It was a summer in which even the most mediocre county player's heart skipped a beat if the phone rang on a Sunday morning, just before the squad announcement. It has become a popular pub game of cricket tragics up and down the land. What better way to fill those increasingly awkward silences than by attempting to name the twenty-nine players England picked for the 1989 Ashes?* Only two men – the captain David Gower and wicketkeeper Jack Russell – played all six Tests. Merv Hughes's 19 wickets in the series included seventeen different batsmen.

When Kent's Alan Igglesden became yet another debutant for the final Test at The Oval, the England coach Micky Stewart told the press he was their seventeenth-choice seamer, settling once and for all the debate over whether honesty is always the best policy. The total of twenty-nine players used is the highest in a Test series since 1921, and the announcement of the rebel tour after the fourth Test compounded an already desperate situation. England's apparent indifference was in total contrast to the overt and motivating patriotism exhibited by Australia. When Mike Atherton made his debut in the fifth Test, a senior player told him: 'You play your first for love and the rest for money.'

One man who always played for love was Ian Botham, yet even the bogeyman couldn't stop Australia when he was recalled after injury for the drawn third Test with England 2–0 down. Botham top-scored on his comeback with 46, but it soon became apparent that his superpowers had waned. In the fourth Test at Old Trafford, which England had to at least draw to keep the Ashes alive, Botham was bowled for 0 when he charged down the wicket, attempted to deposit the leg-spinner Trevor Hohns over the Pennines and missed completely. The shot was so bad that he could have been charged with bringing the game into disrepute.

On the same day Robin Smith hammered a majestic first Test century. He was a source of pride for England fans throughout the series, not

---

* Mike Atherton, Kim Barnett, Ian Botham, Chris Broad, David Capel, Nick Cook, Tim Curtis, Phil DeFreitas, Graham Dilley, John Emburey, Neil Foster, Angus Fraser, Mike Gatting, Graham Gooch, David Gower, Eddie Hemmings, Alan Igglesden, Paul Jarvis, Allan Lamb, Devon Malcolm, Martyn Moxon, Phil Newport, Derek Pringle, Tim Robinson, Jack Russell, Gladstone Small, Robin Smith, John Stephenson and Chris Tavaré.

least during an extended battle of machismo with Merv Hughes that became must-see TV. 'You can't f****** bat!' opined Hughes when Smith played and missed on one occasion. The next ball was short, wide and scorched to the fence. 'Hey Merv, we make a good pair,' said Smith. 'I can't f****** bat and you can't f****** bowl.'

Hey Merv, we make a good pair. I can't f****** bat and you can't f****** bowl

England's other big plus was Russell, who also made his maiden Test hundred at Old Trafford, this time in the second innings. But Australia cruised to victory again, to regain the Ashes with two matches to spare. It was among the more miserable days in English cricket history; that morning, the rebel tour to South Africa was announced, with the squad list including a number of the players in the Test side.

David Boon, who hit the winning runs, began the Australian celebrations at Old Trafford, singing 'Under the Southern Cross' on a table wearing just a jumper, jockstrap and – of course – his Baggy Green cap. The celebrations, which Boon described as 'strenuous', went on for most of the night, with Ian Healy and Steve Waugh breaking off at around 4am to give an interview to a Melbourne radio station.

Dexter later rounded off his work for the 1989 Ashes with a majestic *coup de grâce*, insisting with a straight face that 'I am not aware of any errors I have made this summer.' Poor Gower had an even worse summer. In press conferences his increasingly exasperated responses to questions came across as flippant and disdainful; during the third Test he even resorted to banging his head on the table like Basil Fawlty. The tabloids were merciless: 'Gower is the most disastrous leader since Ethelred the Unready,' said the *Sun*. 'Beyond question he should now stand down in favour of Ken Dodd.'

Gower's form held up reasonably well, with only Smith scoring more runs for England. By the end of the summer, Gower had taken to amusing himself. In the fifth Test at Trent Bridge, the openers Geoff Marsh and Mark Taylor batted throughout the entirety of the first day. At lunch on the second day, with Australia 398 for one, Gower cracked open the champagne 'to celebrate the first Australian wicket for a day and a half'.*

After losing the toss on an Oval belter, Gower told a TV interviewer that England had won the toss and would bat. Word spread around the ground, to such an extent that the debutant opener John Stephenson was padded up and ready to go. The crowd also thought England were batting. Instead they got to see Australia's openers three hours earlier than expected.

Gower's career low was Border's career high. Mark Taylor, Steve Waugh and Terry Alderman topped the averages but, more than anyone, the series belonged to Border. He had suffered extreme Ashes misery on a number of occasions but now was his moment. Only when the Ashes were won did he have a drink with his friend Gower. 'David, the last time I came here, I was a nice guy who came last,' he said. 'I was prepared to be as ruthless as it takes to stuff you.' He came, he swore, he conquered.

> **David, the last time I came here, I was a nice guy who came last. I was prepared to be as ruthless as it takes to stuff you**

Boon describes the tour as 'the best team performance by an Australian team that I was part of' – ahead of the famous 2–1 win in the Caribbean in 1994–95, when they ended West Indies' fifteen-year reign as unofficial world champions. After they went 2–0 up at Lord's, Australia's collective subconscious accepted they had England's number, and the series would unquestionably have ended 6–0 but for heavy rain in the third and sixth Tests. Session by session, the extent of Australia's dominance was mind-blowing. Just about the only game they lost was in the number of players picked: England 29 Australia 12. Or 30–12 if you include Malcolm Devon.

---

* Australia averaged 57.86 runs per wicket in the series, an Ashes record.

1989

'Thatcher Out! lbw b Alderman'

[GRAFFITI SEEN ON A TOILET WALL DURING THE SUMMER OF 1989]

THE WALLS OF A URINAL ARE A GOOD place to find brevity, if not necessarily the soul of wit. There are exceptions, mind, and one was found in 1989. It was not a good time for the Conservative Party, and Margaret Thatcher was the least popular person in the country, with the possible exception of the chairman of selectors Ted Dexter. Whether in pubs or on toilet walls, 'Thatcher Out!' was a familiar refrain up and down the land, and one wag – a word which in those days referred to a drily humorous person rather than a wife or girlfriend – made the obvious connection with Terry Alderman's wicket-taking exploits.

Alderman's apparently endless capacity to dismiss England batsmen lbw was one of the defining features of the 1989 Ashes. He came into the series having played only two Tests in four and a half years, primarily because of his involvement in the rebel tours of South Africa between 1985 and 1987. But he was the perfect horse for the English course: he had picked up 42 wickets in the 1981 Ashes, his debut Test series, and took 249 first-class wickets in just three seasons of county cricket for Kent and Gloucestershire.

'He was a very, very good impressionist,' said David Boon, 'who had developed a "deadly" reputation as as swing bowler.' Although Alderman did swing the ball, he didn't do so nearly as prodigiously as England thought – not least because the Duke ball was used ahead of the Reader for most of the series. England drove themselves round the bend with demons that didn't exist, and as such exposed themselves to a far greater, real-life demon: lbw Alderman.

Alderman did all sorts of damage with his wicket-to-wicket – or rather wicket-to-front-pad – bowling. In expecting outswing, England ended up planting their front leg and playing across the line. Either that or they offered no stroke; a number of England players were lbw shouldering arms in embarrassing circumstances. Most of the decisions were so obvious that Alderman's tour diary could have been called 'Plumb and Plumber'. This is not to belittle Alderman, who at the age of thirty-three was a master craftsman. In six Tests, he helped himself to 41 wickets at 17.36 – 19 of them lbw. The experience was even more disconcerting for batsman because of the fixed grin on Alderman's face as he ran in to bowl. It's easy to imagine a batsman thinking: 'What are you so effing pleased about?' a split-second before the ball began to home inexorably in on their front pad.

Alderman's ten-year Test career is essentially a story of two Ashes tours. In 1981 and 1989 he took 83 wickets in twelve Tests at an average of 19.33. In his other twenty-nine Tests he took 87 wickets at 34.60. His highest-profile victim in 1989, by some distance, was Graham Gooch, who had an *Ashes horribilis*. He was one of England's bankers, and had stood up proudly to West Indies' four horsemen of the apocalypse the previous summer. Yet he had no answer to Australia's murderous medium-pacer. 'Terry Alderman

Terry Alderman bowled the sort of leisurely swing usually associated with hammocks or palm trees, or the hips of Brazilian girls

bowled the sort of leisurely swing usually associated with hammocks or palm trees, or the hips of Brazilian girls,' wrote Harry Pearson. 'It was more of a sway, really.'

But it was Gooch who was really swaying. He kept falling over to the off side and missing straight ones, disorientated by Allan Border's clever decision to place one or two short midwickets to cut off Gooch's favourite hustling shot. Alderman was widely perceived as his nemesis, yet his front pad didn't discriminate: he had almost as much trouble with Geoff Lawson.

Gooch called it 'the lbw saga' and, despite an impromptu coaching session with Geoff Boycott in the Edwardian players' bathrooms at Lord's after the second Test, things got steadily worse. Until he asked to be dropped for the fifth Test. Gooch had just turned thirty-six and his game was a mess. 'I seriously wondered if I had come to the end of the road as far as Test cricket was concerned.' In fact he had come to a fork in the road; after missing that fifth Test, Gooch's international career entered a long, run-soaked final act in which he scored another 4186 Test runs at an average of 50.

Sorry, I'm out. Probably lbw Alderman

His golden period did not get off to the greatest start, however. When Gooch came back for the final Test after a three-week break in which he scored runs for Essex, he was ready for a fresh start. First innings: lbw b Alderman 0. Gooch's inner wag could see the funny side at least. The story goes that he changed his answerphone message to: 'Sorry, I'm out. Probably lbw Alderman.'

Gooch lbw b Alderman, Headingley, 1989.

'Count 'em yourself, you Pommie c***!'

[AUSTRALIAN UMPIRE PETER McCONNELL RESPONDS TO PHIL TUFNELL'S QUESTION ABOUT HOW MANY BALLS REMAINED IN THE OVER, SECOND TEST, MELBOURNE, 30 DECEMBER 1990]

PHIL TUFNELL HAD ASKED THE SAME question hundreds of times in his fledgling career. 'How many balls left, ump?' The answer was ordinarily between one and five. This time the response had him counting to ten, after Peter McConnell showed that, in Australia, the roles of umpire and barracker were not mutually exclusive. Even Tufnell, who was fully acquainted with the wilder shores of the English vernacular, was taken aback.

It was the second Test at Melbourne, and England were about to go 2–0 down in the series. It takes a very special series of cock-ups to lose matches by ten wickets and eight wickets after taking first-innings leads in both; in 1990–91, England managed precisely that. McConnell's abuse of Tufnell added insult to self-inflicted injury.

England had gone into the tour in pretty confident mood after an excellent twelve months under their new captain Graham Gooch. Their side had settled down after the fiasco of 1989; Australia's was largely the same, save for the return of their injury-prone beanpole of a left-arm seamer Bruce Reid – a man whose whirling action was once described as being 'all arms and legs, like a porn movie without the sex'.

England's batting had the feelgood factor of a snuff movie. It was a series in which, however secure they seemed, they were always able to snatch defeat from the jaws of dignity. The first Test at Brisbane was done inside three days; the highest score in the match was England's 194 on the first day of the series. A spectacular fielding performance gave them a lead of 42, but then their old nemesis Terry Alderman whipped them out for 114. Australia knocked off the necessary 157 without losing a wicket.

All arms and legs, like a porn movie without the sex

The press focused on the decision of David Gower and the stand-in captain Allan Lamb – Graham Gooch had a poisoned finger – to go to Kerry Packer's casino on the second night of the match. Especially since it was Lamb's dismissal, in the first over of the third day's play, which sparked England's decisive collapse. 'If we had been drunk,' said Lamb, 'we might have done a bit better.' The black comedy continued when the in-form Lamb pulled a hamstring running back to the team hotel during the tour match against Victoria, and missed the next two Tests.

Tufnell had a stormer on his first day of the Boxing Day Test at Melbourne – a storming hangover, that is. He had spent Christmas Day getting progressively hammered, as was the norm in those days, and was relieved when England won the toss and batted. A fine hundred from Gower – 'A DULL DAY AT THE CRICKET: ENGLAND FAIL TO COLLAPSE' was the *Melbourne Age* headline – took England to 352, and when Angus Fraser's forensic six for 82 restricted Australia's first innings to 306, England had control of the Test at the end of the third day.

But that was to reckon without England's penchant for self-destruction. Their collapses in the first Test were bad enough – eight for 77 and nine for 72 in each innings – but their disintegration in the Boxing Day Test was one for the connoisseur. At one stage they were 103 for one, a lead of 149. Then they were 147 for four. An hour later they were 150 all out. Reid took seven for 51 to complete match figures of 13 for 148 – the high point of a career ruined by injury. 'My biggest "if only" is Bruce Reid,' said Bobby Simpson, Australia's coach. 'He was a great bowler, one of the finest I have ever seen.'

Geoff Marsh and David Boon ground Australia to an eight-wicket victory with an unbroken five-hour partnership of 187. It was during their stand that Tufnell asked how many balls were remaining, and received an unexpected response. He was almost as shocked when Gooch came over and told McConnell he couldn't talk to Tufnell like that. 'You could have tied my tits together with candyfloss,' said Tufnell. 'Bugger me if the old sod wasn't standing up for me.'

Shortly after, Boon clearly nicked Tufnell behind, only for McConnell to give him not out. 'You f****** bastard,' said Tufnell. 'Now,' replied McConnell, '*you* can't talk to *me* like that.'

The way Tufnell describes their relationship – 'brief but intense, based on mutual contempt' – makes it almost sound like a fling in a Mike Leigh film. They resumed hostilities in the third Test at Sydney. Gower dropped Steve Waugh when Tufnell was on a hat-trick in the second innings. Australia held on for a draw, thanks mainly to an exasperating innings from the tailender Carl Rackemann, who took 76 balls to get off the mark and survived 102 balls for his nine runs to ensure Australia's survival. Tufnell was convinced he had him lbw on a number of occasions; McConnell disagreed. England promoted Gower – who made a wondrous hundred in the first innings and shared a 139-run partnership with Mike Atherton,* who made a rather slower century – to open, but a target of 255 in 25 overs in a Test is unrealistic now, never mind then.

It was clear that the chase was over when England sent Atherton in at No.7. He survived a big caught-behind appeal, and was called a 'f****** cheat' for not walking by the Australian wicketkeeper Ian Healy. 'When in Rome, dear boy. . .' replied Atherton, a delicious response that even has its own T-shirt. But the last laugh was emphatically Australia's; they regained the Ashes with two matches to spare.

---

* At the start of the tour, Atherton's batting was described by one Australian writer as having all the style 'of a tired and overworked gravedigger'.

'A fart competing with thunder.'

THE TRAP COULD BARELY HAVE BEEN more obvious if it had been shoved under a hotel door the night before. It was the last over before lunch in the fourth Test at Adelaide, and Australia had pointedly put Merv Hughes out at deep backward square leg for David Gower. Craig McDermott slipped one down the leg side; Gower flicked it for four. McDermott slipped another one down the leg side; Gower helped it into the wide open spaces at square leg for a couple. Mystic Meg's services were not required at this juncture. McDermott slipped a third delivery down the leg side; Gower flicked it elegantly, gracefully, poetically into the hands of Hughes.

Graham Gooch, Gower's captain and batting partner, stomped off furiously. 'It wasn't the look on his face that bothered me so much as the sounds of huffing and puffing, and the steam coming from his ears,' said Gower. When Gooch arrived in the dressing-room he said: 'What's he on?' It was the moment the mounting differences between the two finest England batsmen of their generation became irreconcilable.

Gower was by far England's best batsman in the first three Tests of the series, making two fine centuries, and took the tour match against Queensland at Carrara off. It was there that he and John Morris – both born on 1 April – decided to celebrate Robin Smith's century by flying a Tiger Moth over the ground. Most regarded it as a harmless prank; the England management were not among their number. That evening Gower went out to dinner, and returned to a series of notes pushed under his door by the England manager Peter

Lush. 'I could see the mounting fury in his handwriting.' Lush had unwittingly financed the trip; Gower had asked to borrow A$240, not specifying its purpose, before hiring the plane and the pilot.

The incident shared the front page of many English newspapers with the Gulf War. Originally, Gower and Morris were to be sent home until the vice-captain Allan Lamb persuaded Gooch, Micky Stewart and Lush to merely fine them.

The incident, and the response to it, reflected the difference between the philosophies of Gooch and Stewart, who prioritised fitness and discipline, and Gower's. 'If he could, he would mark man-for-man,' wrote Peter Roebuck of Stewart. What started as a schism was fast becoming a chasm; at times it seemed like England wanted to send Gower for languor management.

Many, including Gower and Mike Atherton, say the mood on the tour was far too serious. 'The atmosphere filtering through from the top was one of mild panic,' said Gower. 'There was a lot of technical bullshit flying about.' And that was before the series had even started. When Gower suggested an aggressive approach during the Sydney Test, Gooch shot back: 'I'm the captain here, so shut up and listen.' The management seemed to be frustrated with almost everyone. At one stage Stewart told Lamb he was drinking too much and should pace himself; he also said that 'Sometimes it takes Devon Malcolm a fortnight to put on his socks.'

Sometimes it takes Devon Malcolm a fortnight to put on his socks

Gooch later described Gower as 'my greatest failure of man-management'. The Adelaide Test, in which their relationship finally collapsed, came a week after the Tiger Moth incident. Gower's frustration was compounded by the fact that his form, so good before the incident, was dreadful thereafter. England at least drew that fourth Test, thanks to a defiant second-innings rearguard led by Gooch. Apart from Gower's dismissal, the match is best recalled for an innings that Gower or any of cricket's great aesthetes would have been privileged to play: with Australia in trouble on the first day, Mark Waugh made a divine debut century. He'd been called up to replace his brother Steve, whose form had declined after his marvellous Ashes in 1989. 'I told you so,' said Waugh to his captain Allan Border. 'You should have picked me earlier!'

The capacity for collapse that had decided the series at the start recurred in the final match at Perth. England slipped from 191 for two to 244 all out on the first day and were eventually thrashed by nine wickets. McDermott took eight first-innings wickets and then, when he batted, was given a send-off by Phil Tufnell. 'You've got to bat on this in a minute,' said McDermott. 'Hospital food suit you?'

At the start of the tour, a report said England's top three had 'all the never-say-die qualities of a kamikaze pilot'. By the end the bottom eight was the problem, with some spectacular collapses. Gooch looked a broken man at the end of the series. 'Our fielding has been the worst I have ever seen in all forms of cricket', he said, though he didn't specify whether that included Essex under-5s. Gooch, who always had a nice line in earthy lyricism, then highlighted the mismatch that is fart vs thunder, though some reports suggest he was referring to his attempts to make the team more disciplined rather than take on Australia. Either way, Gooch had a face like thunder the day Gower fell straight into Australia's trap.

**David Gower and John Morris in their Tiger Moth biplane,
Queensland, January 1991.**

'If it had been a cheese roll, it would never have got past him.'

SHANE WARNE IS THE ONLY MAN to take 195 Test wickets with one ball. His first delivery in Ashes cricket had such a resounding impact that it played a part in each of the other 194 wickets he took against England over the next fourteen years. Warne's first ball came with England 80 for one in reply to Australia's 289 in the first Test at Old Trafford. It curved sharply outside leg stump and then, as Mike Gatting pushed forward, hissed viciously across his body to hit the off stump. Scarcely anybody knew what had happened. Gatting ooohed, thinking he had been beaten; on *Test Match Special*, the commentator Jonathan Agnew said, 'Gatting is taken on the pad – he's bowled!' Adrian Murrell's picture captures the scene perfectly: Ian Healy, the wicketkeeper, whoops with delight while Gatting is a picture of befuddlement (see page 246).

Two days later it was christened the 'Ball of the Century' by Robin Marlar in *The Sunday Times*. 'Was The Ball the first in history to actually travel round corners?' he wrote. 'This is the stuff to bring back interest in cricket.' And leg-spin. 'Warne was the hero who rescued the goddess of wrist-spin, delivered her the kiss of life and gave her chest a quick feel while he was down there,' wrote the *Wisden Cricketer*'s Simon Lister. The ball to Gatting was the start of fourteen years of unapologetic Pom-bashing. It is usually the case that an aura takes years to build and weeks to destroy; Warne's aura took a minute to build and will last forever.

Australia's wicketkeeper Ian Healy exults as Mike Gatting is comprehensively bamboozled by Shane's Warne's 'Ball of the Century', Old Trafford, 1993.

England were not unduly worried about him before the series. They should have been. After a poor start to his Test career, in which his bowling average peaked at 335, he had impressed against Sri Lanka, the West Indies and especially New Zealand. Australia came into the series in good heart, having come within a whisker of dethroning the unofficial world champions the West Indies in an epic series.

England had endured a run of five consecutive Test defeats, including a humiliating and often farcical 3–0 defeat in India the previous winter. 'England are so decrepit, so old and doddery like Dad's Army, the Aussies will shove it right up them this summer,' said Jeff

England are so decrepit, so old and doddery like Dad's Army, the Aussies will shove it right up them this summer

Thomson before the series. 'Your bowling doesn't even rank as high as ordinary. They couldn't harry a granny.' The Australian captain Allan Border sounded as though he intended to carry on where he had left off in 1989: 'I'm having nothing to do with the British media,' he announced. 'You're all pricks.'

Warne's wonder ball came on the second afternoon of the series at Old Trafford. Gatting's size – not to mention his status as one of England's best players of spin bowling – made it even more startling. 'How anyone can spin a ball the width of Gatting boggles the mind,' said Martin Johnson in the *Independent*. The England captain Graham Gooch also made play of Gatting's girth with reference to a cheese roll. Warne was not exactly pencil-thin either; 'Shane Warne's idea of a balanced diet,' said Healy, 'is a cheeseburger in each hand.'

After a chipper maiden Test century from Healy, who was fast becoming a significant pain in England's behind, Australia went on to win the match by 179 runs on the final day, when Gooch's proud rearguard century ended in strange circumstances when he was out handled the ball. There were eight wickets apiece for Merv Hughes, who would carry the seam attack, and Warne.

'Warne is a good bowler, but we are not particularly worried about him,' said the England coach Keith Fletcher on the evening of the

Gatting dismissal. 'He will not turn it as much elsewhere.' Fletcher was both right and wrong. Warne turned very few deliveries that far again – but he turned them even further in the heads of England's batsmen. The Gatting ball became as powerful as a judicial precedent: *Warne v Gatting (1993)*, the case summary held that an English batsman should never be truly comfortable at the crease when Shane Warne is bowling.

England got a long and painful introduction to Warne in 1993. He bowled 2639 balls, a record for any Test series. Warne had not exactly planned the first of those deliveries – he called it a 'pure fluke' – but there is a compelling case for the often facile observation that he made his own luck. His natural talent allowed him to get such decisive drift and spin; more importantly, his courage and mental strength allowed him to give it a rip first up, risking a long hop but chasing a wicket. 'I see myself as a strike bowler, selling my soul and anything else to get a wicket,' he said ahead of the series.

He got into England's collective head so much with that one ball that he could play mind games without realising. And when he wanted to play mind games, there was nobody better. Warne became England's rogue psychiatrist, driving them round the bend with demons both real and imaginary. Towards the end of his career, he would talk about a new delivery before each Ashes series: the zooter; the gazunder; the one that tells you the time in five continents. There was no such thing, but with Warne you could never be sure. He was deliciously untrustworthy, a kind of confidence trickster – except he didn't gain confidence, he took it away.

At times it was hard to know what did more talking: Warne or the ball. He was somehow both insidious and in-your-face. And if cricket had its own IQ Test, Warne would be off the scale. Against England, Warne gobbled up records like they were cheeseburgers. Two in particular stand out: most Test wickets against one country (195), and the only man to take 100 wickets in another country (129 of Warne's 195 came in England). One ball made it all possible.

1993

'He offended me in a former life.'

[AUSTRALIAN FAST BOWLER MERV HUGHES
TO UMPIRE DICKIE BIRD WHEN ASKED
WHY HE WAS SLEDGING GRAEME HICK,
SECOND TEST, LORD'S, 19 JUNE 1993]

MERV HUGHES' SEND-OFFS WERE OFTEN more memorable than the wickets that preceded them. His best came against Pakistan; Hughes was called a 'fat bus conductor' by Javed Miandad and, upon dismissing Miandad shortly after, shouted 'tickets please'. The most heartfelt, however, came against England. Hughes took over a third of his 212 Test wickets against the Poms, and every one was greeted like his first.

He came into his own during the 1993 Ashes. With his new-ball partner Craig McDermott suffering appendicitis during the second Test at Lord's, and Australia using two spinners in a four-man attack for all bar one of the six Tests, Hughes bowled himself to the door of the knacker's yard for the cause.

In the second Test at Lord's, with McDermott incapacitated during Australia's first innings, Hughes was the only seamer in the side, save for a few overs of support from the Waugh brothers. At least he had plenty of runs to work with. Australia pummelled 632 for four declared. There were centuries from Michael Slater, Mark Taylor and David Boon. Had Mark Waugh not been bowled by Phil Tufnell for 99, the top four would have scored centuries in a Test innings for the first time. Slater, chirpy and effervescent, had added some botox to a wrinkled top order.

Hughes broke the back of England's first innings, including

dismissing his new favourite victim Graeme Hick for the third consecutive innings, and they followed on 427 runs behind. It was during a particularly splenetic burst of sledging at Hick that Hughes was asked by the umpire Dickie Bird why he had it in for Hick. 'He offended me in a former life,' replied Hughes.

Australia, and Hughes in particular, were seriously affronted when Hick was compared to Sir Donald Bradman before he had even played a Test match, and decided to do something about it. But they also recognised how dangerous Hick could be if he settled at international level. Hughes' relentless abuse was a very, very, very, very, very backhanded compliment.

Although he was wicketless in the second innings at Lord's, with Shane Warne and Tim May completing an innings victory, Hughes was involved in the most important wicket. He was the boundary fielder when Mike Atherton, one of the few reasons for England fans to be hopeful during the series, was desperately run out for 99 after slipping in the middle of the pitch. It is a defining image of England's despondency that summer.

England's misery was also reflected by the mercurial all-rounder Chris Lewis. He was on a pair, with England trying to save the game, when he danced down the wicket to May, got caught in four minds, ended up playing no stroke at all and was stumped. Like Hick, Lewis seemed to have cracked Test cricket when he made his maiden century the previous winter; like Hick, he was dropped just two Tests into the summer as England decided to have an enigma clearout.

I'll bowl you a f****** piano, you Pommie poof – let's see if you can play that

With Hick gone, Hughes turned his attention elsewhere. There was plenty of abuse to go round. He says he did not bowl to batsmen, he bowled at them. 'He was all bristle and bullshit,' said Atherton, 'and I couldn't make out what he was saying, except that every sledge ended with "arsewipe".' Hughes had a peerless strike-rate of around nine expletives every ten words. Just as a bowler needs his stock ball, so a sledger needs his stock lines, and Hughes had those: 'I'll bowl you a f****** piano, you

Merv Hughes dismisses Graeme Hick with a – four-letter – flea in his ear, Old Trafford, June 1993.

Pommie poof – let's see if you can play that', or 'Does your husband play cricket as well?'

In England in the summer of 1993, Hughes became a kind of cult villain. 'He swings it both ways through the air (and that's just his stomach),' wrote Martin Johnson in the *Independent*. 'The mincing run-up resembles someone in high heels and a panty girdle chasing after a bus; his coiffeur appears to have been entrusted to an inebriated sheep shearer somewhere in the outback, and from beneath the koala bear attached to the underside of his nose, pour forth words of such eloquence ("eff off, yer Pommie bastard, the pavilion's that way. . .") that you wonder why he is not Australia's poet laureate.'

The mincing run-up resembles someone in high heels and a panty girdle chasing after a bus

When Steve Waugh was once asked to name his favourite animal, he replied, 'Merv Hughes'. Hughes is a far gentler soul than many realised at the time, and was simply getting in character when he went on the field. The 1993 Ashes were the finest of his career, statistically and actually: at the age of thirty-one he gave so much to Australia – his 296 overs in the series were 143 more than any other seamer on either side – that his career was never quite the same again. But he did take 31 wickets in six Tests. And that meant 31 extra-special Merv send-offs.

1993

'McCague will go down in
Test cricket history as the rat
who joined the sinking ship.'

[A LINE FROM AN ARTICLE IN THE
AUSTRALIAN NEWSPAPER THE *DAILY
TELEGRAPH-MIRROR* AHEAD OF THE THIRD
TEST, TRENT BRIDGE, 1 JULY 1993]

TED DEXTER WAS QUITE CLEAR IN HIS MIND. After the farce of the previous home Ashes, when England used twenty-nine players, there was an obvious need for stability. 'We don't envisage chopping and changing,' he said to the press before the series. But they didn't envisage being 2–0 down after two Tests. As the series become progressively more miserable, England looked to all points of the compass for answers. In all, they used twenty-four players in six Tests.

For the third Test at Trent Bridge, England made five changes. Their team included four new caps – Mark Lathwell, Graham Thorpe, Mark Ilott and Martin McCague – as well as Nasser Hussain, who had not played for three and a half years. McCague, born in Northern Ireland but raised in Australia, was the subject of a memorable put-down before he had even bowled a ball.

It's often forgotten that the Test was a largely successful one for McCague and England. Not only did they avoid defeat to end a run of seven in a row, their young side dominated the match and seemed set for victory before the seventh-wicket pair of Steve Waugh and Brendon Julian calmly batted out the final session. Thorpe, after a limp first-innings failure, made a splendid debut century, while McCague roughed Australia's batsmen up far more emphatically than figures of four for 121 would suggest. 'We will hear a lot more from Mr McCague before the series is out,' said Bob Willis.

In fact, we didn't. He went wicketless in the next Test at Headingley, when Australia – as at Lord's – batted until the third day and scored over 600 for the loss of four wickets. Border, in his final Ashes series, coldly applied his boot to the English throat one last time with 200 not out. They won the match, effectively by an innings and a half, just as they had two Tests earlier, and in doing so retained the Ashes with two games to spare. Graham Gooch resigned as captain, allowing Mike Atherton to fulfil his apparent destiny at the age of twenty-five. 'If I look more miserable than normal, it's because I am,' said Gooch.

Atherton's debut as captain ended in an eight-wicket defeat at Edgbaston. The spinners Shane Warne and Tim May shared all ten second-innings wickets. Warne's fifth was that of Graham Thorpe, suckered in a manner that accelerated his Test-match education. England were eight down, with Thorpe on 60, when the wicket-keeper Ian Healy loudly announced that Thorpe was batting for a not-out to improve his average. 'F*** it,' thought Thorpe. 'I'm not playing for myself. I'll show you.' He charged down the wicket and was stumped by a mile.

Although Australia had won the previous two Ashes by a combined score of 7–0, 1993 was the series in which they truly developed the aura that would define the next decade of England–Australia contests. England, particularly once Atherton took over, were keen to build a young team for the future – copying the precise template that Australia had used in the mid-1980s and which was now bearing fruit. A proud victory in the final Test at The Oval, when Devon Malcolm arguably bowled even faster than during his legendary destruction of South Africa a year later, and Angus Fraser returned splendidly after more than two years out with injury, was seen as the start of a different Ashes tale.

It was, but only in the sense that England would continue to win meaningless matches for the next decade. Long before the Decision Review System, a different kind of DRS – Dead Rubber Syndrome – was a feature of the Ashes. Another feature of modern contests, the symbolic opening delivery, was about to be introduced.

1994–95

'Man for man, on paper,
the Australian side stand out
like dogs' balls.'

[GREG CHAPPELL PREVIEWS
THE 1994–95 ASHES]

THIS TIME, FINALLY, IT WAS GOING TO be different. For the first time in almost a decade, England were ready to compete with Australia. They had drawn 1–1 at home to South Africa, who had drawn 1–1 home and away to Australia. They had a powerful batting line-up and a bowling pool full of dangerously loose cannons. Thousands stayed up in England to watch the start of the series. Phil DeFreitas ran in to bowl the first ball. It was short, wide, and Michael Slater blazed it for four.

There were thousands of balls bowled in the 1994–95 series, but none resonated like the first. The legend has it that Australia won the Ashes after one ball, so decisively did Slater's boundary set the tone. He hit another four in DeFreitas's first over, and then Martin McCague took the second over. . .

By the end of the first day, Australia were 326 for four, with Slater making a raucous 176 before he fell to the oldest trick in the book: c Gatting b Gooch. Those two had a combined age of seventy-eight. Four years earlier, as captain, Gooch said England were 'a fart competing with thunder'. This time, old farts were the problem for the England captain. Mike Atherton wanted a younger, more vibrant side, particularly because of the fielding demands on the big Australian grounds. Gooch and Gatting both had largely unproductive series and retired from international cricket at the end.

Gatting, never athletic at the best of times, had got even rounder with age. When he came up against Dennis Lillee, who came out of retirement aged forty-five for the traditional tour opener at Lilac Hill, Lillee said: 'Move out the way, Gatt – I can't see the stumps!'

At times during the tour it seemed like the England bowlers couldn't see the stumps, so errant was their line. Ray Illingworth, England's new chairman of selectors, promised to fight fire with fire and controversially selected McCague ahead of Angus Fraser in the tour squad. 'We are getting near the pace of Lillee and Thomson,' said the coach Keith Fletcher,

The Poms are on a rollercoaster ride to the shitheap

whose body was briefly inhabited by Don King. 'A heap of shit,' was Lillee's assessment of Fletcher's claim. It was a metaphor that he and his old bowling partner seemed to like; the *Guardian*'s Mike Selvey recalls Jeff Thomson, during one Ashes tour in the 1990s, cheerily informing the press box that 'The Poms are on a rollercoaster ride to the shitheap.'

What Illingworth and his other selectors did not fully process is that England did not just need express pace; they needed premium pace. There were no latter-day John Snows in his squad. McCague had a miserable time in the opening Test at the Gabba, and never played for England again. Devon Malcolm was potentially devastating but inconsistent, and DeFreitas, excellent in English conditions, was never the same overseas. Indeed, DeFreitas and McCague were later described as 'probably the weakest new-ball pair in the history of the Ashes'. And that was by their coach, Fletcher. Only Darren Gough, a revelation on his first England tour, was consistently impressive. Australian judges, the harshest judges around, instantly took to Gough's combination of heart, positivity and talent. He was, as a *Guardian* sub-heading put it, 'The lad wi' nowt taken out'.

Shane Warne took eight for 71 in the second innings to beat England handsomely in the first Test at Brisbane, and added a hat-trick in another huge victory at Melbourne. Craig McDermott, at his ferocious peak, took five for 42 as England were bowled out for 92 in their second innings.

As in 1993, England had much the better of a drawn third Test. Gough changed the mood of the series with a violent half-century and followed it up with an exhilarating six-for as Australia were ransacked for 116. With so much time in the match, England were able to declare the second innings as and when they pleased. Atherton infamously called time with Graeme Hick dawdling on 98 not out. Hick, scorer of 136 first-class hundreds, never did make an Ashes century. But it would not be fair to blame Atherton for his ultimate failure at Test level. This was the first innings of 1995, and Hick went on to have by far his best year as a Test player, averaging 58. He would surely have failed as an England player regardless.

The short-term damage was undeniable, however. 'It created a bad atmosphere in the dressing-room,' said Hick. 'It went very quiet. And even when we took the field, it was very flat.' Australia's openers added 208, which ultimately saved the game. Fraser, called up because of a grotesque series of injuries, bowled superbly on a juiced-up wicket to take five for 73 as Australia reached 344 for seven. There have been few more lovable grumps than Fraser, who usually looked shattered by 11.02am but would still be England's most reliable bowler at 5.58pm. 'Fraser's approach to the wicket,' wrote Martin Johnson, 'resembles someone who has his braces caught in the sightscreen.'

Fraser's approach to the wicket resembles someone who has his braces caught in the sightscreen

The injuries mounted up to such an extent* that England had only twelve fit men for the fourth Test at Adelaide, and had to bat the wicketkeeper Steve Rhodes – who was averaging 4.75 in the series – at No.6. With the Ashes gone, England won thrillingly. Gatting ground out an ugly, six-and-a-half hour 117 and, although Greg Blewett provided the antonym with the most beautiful debut hundred seen at Adelaide for, ooh, at least four years (see page 244), some fearless counter-attacking from the brilliant Thorpe kept England in the game.

---

* Six of England's original sixteen-man squad went home with injury – as did Neil Fairbrother, one of the replacements. Even the physio, Dave 'Rooster' Roberts, broke a finger at one stage.

He was one of the few Englishmen, along with Gough and Atherton in particular, to stand up to the Australians; in one Test Thorpe offered to meet Steve Waugh round the back of the stand so that they could settle their differences in the traditional style.

After Thorpe's innings, DeFreitas savaged McDermott in the course of an outrageous 88 from 95 balls. To describe DeFreitas as an all-rounder, as many did, was like describing Dame Edna Everage as a man: you kind of knew it was true but it was rarely evident. On this day it was gloriously so. He hit 22 from one McDermott over with a series of legside swishes that seemed to travel ever further as the over progressed. Some seriously fast bowling from Malcolm wrecked Australia's top order, and England clinched a memorable victory with 35 balls remaining.

England might even have squared the series in the final Test at Perth had they not dropped a preposterous 10 catches. One of them so infuriated Thorpe that he instinctively volleyed the ball in frustration, giving Australia two overthrows, or rather overkicks. Australia imperceptibly crushed England, as they had in the second Test, and it ended as a rout, with 329 runs between the sides. Blewett made another gorgeous hundred and Steve Waugh – who had recovered from his mid-career slump to become the world's best batsman – was left stranded on 99 not out when his brother Mark, acting as a runner, was run out.

On the fourth evening, with England in a mess, Fraser came out as nightwatchman only to realise he had forgotten his box. For the next few overs he and Mike Atherton had to swap each time the strike was rotated. It rather summed up the tour.

'Tufnell, can I borrow your brain? I'm building an idiot.'

FOR MUCH OF THE 1994-95 ASHES, Australian triumphalism was infused with laughter. There was even a hint of pity, the ultimate indication of a non-contest. From Martin McCague, the rat who joined the sinking ship and was then thrown off it for not being good enough, to Phil Tufnell, Australia took enormous pleasure from England's woes.

Tufnell was the man Australia loved to slate. He was the subject of what he described as 'good-natured, relentless abuse. . . My general tactic when I was down at third man was to give a bit back and hope that no one punched me, and I just about got away with it.'

Tufnell took a sensational running catch to dismiss Michael Slater, a key moment in England's victory in the fourth Test at Adelaide. If that was one of his Ashes highlights, then the moment he was asked to donate his brain for the purposes of building an idiot was up there too: he describes it as his favourite bit of crowd sledging.

In reality, Tufnell was a very smart spin bowler, with the temperament of a quick bowler – 'You can't bowl fast and smoke 20 fags a day,' he said – but the contrast with his opposite number, the smartest of them all, did him no favours. 'I'm not going to tolerate a situation where we get some hang-up about Warne,' said the captain Mike Atherton, yet there was no choice – especially for Tufnell. 'That bloke's making me look ordinary,' he lamented.

Phil Tufnell, Australia's favourite idiot.

In the second Test at Melbourne, Tufnell prepared to walk to the crease and considered his situation. He had made nought in the first innings, and a split-second earlier Warne had completed the first Ashes hat-trick in ninety years. 'F*** me, Fletch,' said Tufnell to his coach Keith Fletcher, 'I'm on a pair and a quadruple here.'

His first tour, four years earlier, had been a pretty harsh introduction to Australian life – especially when he was called a 'Pommie c***' by an umpire (see page 239). It did not turn out quite as it had been in the brochure in his head. 'Sun, beaches, barbecues and crumpet. . . that was what was going through my mind, not whether the Sydney pitch would turn. . . I felt like I was about to go on the best holiday ever, and my cricket heroes were coming with me.'

In one of English cricket's more bone-headed administrative decisions, someone judged that the hard-living Wayne Larkins and the volatile Tufnell would make perfect room-mates. Tufnell sensed which way the wind was blowing on the flight over, when Larkins revealed a one-word vocabulary: Chablis. Tufnell himself had a fair crack at David Boon's record of fifty-two in-flight tinnies, and vaguely recalled getting into the late thirties. 'As I was wobbling through the concourse, a passer-by caught my bleary eye and hailed me with a cheery: "G'day, you Pommie bastard."'

As I was wobbling through the concourse, a passer-by caught my bleary eye and hailed me with a cheery: 'G'day you Pommie bastard'

A bowler of unfulfilled talent, Tufnell would never win the Ashes, home or away. Thirteen years after his Test debut, however, 'the Cat' would triumph at last on Australian soil. In 2003, he won the reality TV show *I'm A Celebrity, Get Me Out Of Here* at Murwillumbah in New South Wales. Not bad for a Pommie bastard.

'Mark Taylor, the Australian captain? Ah, but for how long?'

AUSTRALIA ARRIVED FOR THE 1997 ASHES tour as indisputably the best team in the world, and with their captain fighting for his life. That unusual situation was easily explained: they had won their last six Test series, but Mark Taylor had not made a half-century in his previous twenty Test innings. Taylor's form was such a story before Australia arrived that he couldn't even hand over his passport at the immigration desk without being reminded of his predicament.

The situation got worse before it got better. England thrashed Australia 3–0 in the ODI series that preceded the Tests, and Taylor dropped himself for the last of those games. The series was a triumph for the Hollioake brothers: Adam hit the winning runs in all three matches, while Ben, aged nineteen, stroked 63 from 48 balls on his international debut at Lord's. The way in which he took Glenn McGrath and Shane Warne to the cleaners suggested the discovery of a rare talent and captured the blissful early-summer mood of innocence and hope. It did not pan out that way; Hollioake was in and out of the one-day side before he died in a car crash at the age of twenty-four. His career and life were indelibly associated with that perfect day at Lord's.

At that stage the Hollioakes could not get into a settled Test side, which had recovered from the embarrassment of drawing 0–0 in Zimbabwe to gain an excellent 2–0 win in New Zealand. Australia were also settled, the Taylor issue notwithstanding; in May 1995 they became unofficial world champions after ending West Indies' fifteen-year unbeaten run in a Test series. They confirmed their position at the top of the new world order in 1996–97 by beating West Indies again, and triumphing away to their new biggest rivals South Africa. McGrath had ascended to the cusp of greatness, while Matthew Elliott was an excellent addition to a batting line-up so strong that the much-hyped Ricky Ponting could not get back into the side after being dropped.

The one-day series, and the giddy mood around England, ensured Australia knew they were in for a battle when the Test series began at Edgbaston. They had no idea how big a battle. Before lunch they were reeling at 54 for eight. When Darren Gough bowled Greg Blewett off a no-ball, he said, 'Don't worry, I'll get him out next ball instead' – and did just that. By the end of the day, England were 200 for three in reply to Australia's 118. 'If anyone slags us off after that, they need beheading,' said Gough. Geoff Marsh, Australia's coach, wanted to empty his head. 'Where's the nearest classical record shop?' he said. 'I need some soothing music.'

A mighty 207 from Nasser Hussain, the innings of his life, and a rollicking century from Graham Thorpe gave England a huge first-innings lead of 360. During his innings, Hussain responded to some sledging from the substitute fielder Justin Langer with a memorable put-down: 'I don't mind this lot chirping at me, but you're just the f****** bus driver.'

I don't mind this lot chirping at me, but you're just the f**** bus driver**

In fact Langer had also acted as counsellor to Taylor at Derbyshire a couple of weeks earlier. It was there that the *Mirror* asked Taylor to pose with a bat a metre wide. He said no, whereupon the man from the *Mirror* jumped in front of Taylor to ensure they got their picture. During the same game, after being dropped in the field, Taylor's tether reached its end. 'That's bloody it, mate,' he said to his batting partner Langer. 'I just can't f****** play!' Langer told him that was 'rubbish'. 'Watch the bloody ball really close, stick in here – and it will come.'

It came on the third day of the Edgbaston Test, when Taylor made one of the great career-saving centuries. It was not a great century in the truest sense – England bowled poorly, feeding his leg-side strength – but it was as admirable as it was well-received. The following morning, when his parents came down for breakfast at the B&B in Birmingham, they received a standing ovation. 'I still have the butterflies,' said Taylor, 'but now they are flying in formation.' Few knew at the time that the selection committee had agreed that Taylor would stand down if he failed in that Test.

I still have the butterflies, but now they are flying in formation

Despite Taylor's century, England won the Test at a canter, romping to their target of 119 in just 21.3 overs on a giddy Sunday evening in Birmingham. It was the first time any of the players had won a live Ashes Test,* and the nation celebrated regaining the Ashes for the first time since 1986–87. The crowd chanted 'Ashes Coming Home', a variation on the words of 'Three Lions', the official song of the 1996 European football championship.

The problem was there were five Tests remaining, and Australia had woken up with a start. 'We got rid of our biggest problem – me,' said Taylor. He got just four runs in his next four innings, but nobody noticed. Taylor was no longer the issue. Besides, his team were busy staging a fearsome comeback.

---

* It was also the only live Ashes Test England won against a side containing both McGrath and Warne.

264   GENTLEMEN AND SLEDGERS

'That Glenn McGrath, what a bastard.'

[MICK JAGGER ON GLENN McGRATH,
WHO TOOK EIGHT FOR 38 IN THE
SECOND TEST AT LORD'S,
21 JUNE 1997]

UNLIKE SHANE WARNE, GLENN McGRATH did not make much of a first impression on England. He was dropped after his first Ashes Test, when he took none for 101 at Brisbane in 1994–95. He fared little better in the opening Test of the 1997 series as England won by nine wickets. At that stage, McGrath had eight wickets at 47 from three Ashes Tests, and the talk of world cricket's next great fast bowler looked like bunkum. The Lord's Test rather changed English perceptions.

The match was a rain-affected draw, allowing England to preserve their cherished 1–0 lead, but McGrath emphatically changed the mood of the series by demolishing England for just 77 in the first innings. He took eight for 38, the start of a love affair with the Lord's slope. 'The national spirit of self-confidence which followed victory at Edgbaston had been both drenched and deflated,' said *Wisden*.

McGrath went on to take 36 wickets in the 1997 series, and 157 Ashes wickets at an average of 20.92 overall. He was a miracle of patience and repetition, so accurate that journalists were almost contractually obliged to describe him as 'metronomic'. His was a form of Chinese torture. Drip drip drip. Dot dot dot. 'I just try to bore the batsmen out,' he said. 'It's pretty simple stuff, but the complicated thing is to keep it simple.'

McGrath had a sharp bouncer, sparingly used, and in 1997 he was genuinely quick. It was then that he started to prey upon the England captain. By the time Mike Atherton retired in 2001, he had fallen a world-record nineteen times to his nemesis. Although McGrath was a fast bowler who prioritised accuracy over hostility, he shared one thing with the West Indies' formidable pace attacks of the 1980s: the desire to undermine the rest of the opposition by claiming a symbolic scalp. For the West Indies it was the captain, for McGrath it was the best player – who in the case of Atherton doubled up as captain. Whether it was Atherton, Brian Lara, Jacques Kallis or Sachin Tendulkar, McGrath aimed to remove the head with surgical precision.

Australia admired Atherton's toughness and recognised his importance. 'They say he's like a cockroach you can't kill,' said Adam Hollioake in 1997. 'You stamp on him but he keeps coming back.' Atherton never quite recovered the same authority once McGrath got to work on him during the 1997 series. McGrath nagged at his off stump and his self-doubt, and

They say he's like a cockroach you can't kill. You stamp on him but he keeps coming back

eventually overwhelmed him psychologically to the point where Atherton was playing the bowler, not the ball. 'If McGrath bowled to Michael Atherton,' said Ricky Ponting, 'you just knew Atherton would be absolutely shitting himself.' Shaun Pollock, a similar bowler in many ways, caused Atherton nothing like the same trouble. Atherton was already being worn down by his back problems, and his team's lack of spine; McGrath was the last thing he and England needed.

Michael Atherton falls – yet again – to Glenn McGrath.

'Oh, I get it.
Nobody's talking to Steve.
Okay! I'll talk to my f****** self.'

[STEVE WAUGH REALISES THAT
ENGLAND HAVE DECIDED NOT
TO SLEDGE HIM, THIRD TEST,
OLD TRAFFORD, 3 JULY 1997]

STEVE WAUGH WAS TALKING TO HIMSELF. It was the first sign of a different kind of madness. When he came to the crease on the first day of the third Test at Old Trafford, Australia were in serious trouble at 42 for three and in danger of going 2–0 down in an Ashes series. It was a scenario Waugh would not countenance. England, theorising that sledging Waugh made him more determined, went to the other extreme, which made him more determined still. He survived a huge lbw appeal first ball after missing a full toss from Andy Caddick, a sliding door in Ashes history, and then got to work on reasserting the natural order of Ashes cricket.

History may be written by the victors, but that forgets how hard they sometimes must work to earn the right to write that history. Australia, 1–0 down, were tottering at 160 for seven on that first day at Old Trafford. England might just have been dreaming about going 2–0 up, about winning the Ashes, but Waugh was still at the crease. Finding important support from Paul Reiffel, he made 108 in a total of 235. Then, after Shane Warne's six for 48 gave Australia a first-innings lead of 73, Waugh rammed home the advantage with a painstaking 116.

Pain was the operative word: by now his right hand was badly bruised, and he winced after almost every delivery. But if such injury might prompt most to try and get the job done as quickly as possible, Waugh went the other way: this innings was 97 balls and 142 minutes longer than the first. It was a wonderfully deliberate performance, as if he wanted to give England more time in the field to realise the extent to which the momentum had now shifted. If you didn't know better, you'd think he was actually enjoying the pain. He certainly enjoyed inflicting it on England.

Australia have given England a few bogeymen, but none quite like Stephen Rodger Waugh, the Baggy Green made flesh. He was the only man who played in every series from 1989 to 2002–03, and took sadistic, and in this case masochistic, pleasure from hurting the Poms. He made all manner of Ashes centuries – a personal milestone in 1989, on one leg in 2001, to save his career in 2002–03 – but his best, in terms of combining will and skill, surely came at Old Trafford in 1997. And so did his second-best. It's just hard to know which is which.

Australia completed a statement victory by 268 runs. It was a triumph, too, for their captain Mark Taylor, who decided to bat first on a very lively pitch because he wanted Warne to bowl last. The decision worked perfectly.

Don't worry, Thorpey, you've just dropped the Ashes

After such a crushing defeat, England began to panic. In the fourth Test they dropped Andy Caddick and replaced him with Mike Smith, Gloucestershire's in-form swing bowler. But the ball did not swing, and Smith took no wickets in his only Test appearance. He should have had one, but Matthew Elliott was dropped by Graham Thorpe at slip. 'Don't worry, Thorpey,' said his captain Mike Atherton, 'you've just dropped the Ashes.'

At that stage Australia were 50 for three in reply to England's 172, in which Jason Gillespie had bowled riotously to take seven for 37. Steve Waugh was out the ball after Elliott was dropped, so Australia might feasibly have been 50 for five, yet talk of dropping the Ashes feels like a red herring. Australia were simply too good. Elliott made

199, with the recalled Ricky Ponting hammering a century in his first Ashes Test. Reiffel, Gillespie and Glenn McGrath did the rest, dismissing England for 268 to triumph by an innings and 61 runs.

Let's have you right under Nasser's nose

England turned to their lucky charm, the Hollioakes, for the fifth Test, but the die was cast and Australia won by 264 runs. 'Back to the nets, idiot,' crowed the wicket-keeper Ian Healy after Ben Hollioake failed with the bat. Healy's soundtrack from behind the stumps was a regular feature from 1989 to 1999; once, when the long-nosed Nasser Hussain was batting, Healy pointed to a fielder and said, 'Let's have you right under Nasser's nose,' before placing him yards from the bat.

A thrilling dead-rubber victory at The Oval persuaded Mike Atherton to postpone his plan to resign as captain. Phil Tufnell, in his first Test of the summer, took 11 wickets in the match, and England defended a target of just 124 to win by 19 runs. The ghosts of recent Ashes past, chasing low scores and losing in dead rubbers, converged on Australia.

When the pressure point comes, English cricketers crumble

The 3–2 scoreline failed to reflect Australia's clear superiority. England topped and tailed the series with memorable victories, but at the key point of the series it was all Australia. 'When the pressure point comes,' said Warne, 'English cricketers crumble.' The pressure was never greater than in that third Test at Old Trafford, when Waugh talked the talk to himself and then emphatically walked the walk.

1998–99

'No, but I'd have Darren Gough as twelfth man.'

[AUSTRALIAN CAPTAIN MARK TAYLOR,
WHEN ASKED IF HE'D HAVE ANY
ENGLAND PLAYERS IN HIS TEAM,
FIFTH TEST, SYDNEY,
6 JANUARY 1999]

EVERYBODY KNEW IT WAS OUT. Michael Slater, turning for a second run, was a fraction short when Dean Headley's superb throw from long on hit the stumps direct. As the players waited for the third umpire, Slater took his gloves off in anticipation of a walk to the dressing-room. 'That's out,' said both Ian Botham and Bill Lawry in the commentary box. The players waited for the red light to come up and indicate the end of Slater's innings. Instead it was the green light. Slater, a batsman who mostly batted in fifth gear, did not need asking twice to speed off into the distance.

The 1998–99 series was a familiar story with a twist. England struggled against a crafty leg-spinner – but his name was not Shane Warne. Stuart MacGill, standing in for the injured Warne, quickly proved that he was good enough to have earned 100 caps in any other era.

Warne's shoulder injury gave England considerable hope when they flew to Australia in October 1998. Although Australia were still the world's best side, they had been hammered in India earlier in the year. England had just won their first five-Test series since 1986–87, beating South Africa 2–1 in a spiteful contest, and were turning into a hard, competitive side under their new captain Alec Stewart.

They competed well for much of the first Test, in which Steve Waugh, Ian Healy and Mark Butcher all made fine centuries, although it took a stunning electrical storm on the final afternoon to save them after MacGill knifed through the middle order. The next Test, on the Perth trampoline, was over almost before it started; England were spreadeagled for 112 in just 39 overs on the first day. Despite a highly promising debut from Alex Tudor, which included the wickets of both Waugh brothers, Australia won easily by seven wickets. The match lasted barely two and a half days.

For the third consecutive Australian tour, England's hopes of regaining the Ashes officially ended at the earliest opportunity, in the third Test. Australia won by 205 runs in Adelaide – 179 of which came during a masterful unbeaten century from Justin Langer in the first innings. Although England's bowlers toiled heroically in forty-degree heat on the first day, a wearily familiar batting collapse was the abiding memory of the contest: England slipped from 187 for three to 227 all out on a perfect pitch for batting.

The most frustrating thing about England in the 1990s was not how bad they often were, but how good they could occasionally be. Like at Melbourne after Christmas when they won a wonderful fourth Test by 12 runs.*

At almost four hours, the final session of the fourth day was the longest in Test history, a consequence of a slow over-rate earlier in the day, a washout on the first day which meant subsequent days were extended, and the extra half-hour being taken with a result in sight. Australia needed just 175 to win, but a spectacular catch from Mark Ramprakash to dismiss Langer sparked a steady collapse from 103 for two. 'They obviously thought they'd piss the game,' said Headley. 'But the next person came in, nicked off. Next person came in, nicked off. . .'

---

* England went into the match at rock bottom. Four days earlier they had been humiliated when an Australia XI chased a target of 376 in just 55.2 overs to win by nine wickets. Angus Fraser took nought for 72 from 11 overs. After the game, Darren Gough, who missed the match, turned up dressed as Father Christmas and said he had a present for Fraser: new bowling figures. Fraser did not see the funny side and the two almost came to blows.

Headley redefined indefatigability, taking six for 60 before Darren Gough blew the tail away in a burst of yorkers. He did it again at Sydney a few days later, taking England's first Ashes hat-trick of the twentieth century. Australia took to Gough on his first tour four years earlier, and his performances in 1998–99 confirmed their perception that he was a Cobber in Pom's clothing.

Although the fit again Warne dismissed a mesmerised Butcher in his first over back in Test cricket, England were well set in the fifth Test when Slater was controversially reprieved by the third umpire Simon Taufel. At that stage Slater had 36. He went on to make an awesome 123, his third second-innings hundred of the series, in a total of 184. England lost by 98 runs. MacGill outbowled Warne – as was usually the case when the two played together – and ended with twelve for 107, the best figures in an Ashes Test by a spinner since Jim Laker's 19 for 90 in 1956 (see page 129).

Whereas Warne's weakness was for women and cheese sandwiches, MacGill's was for fine wines and the arts scene

MacGill and Warne were chalk and cheese. 'Whereas Warne's weakness was for women and cheese sandwiches,' wrote the Guardian's Tanya Aldred, 'MacGill's was for fine wines and the arts scene. He once read forty-two novels on a tour of Pakistan.' Warne, by contrast, once boasted that he had never read a book from cover to cover, even though he has 'written' three.

MacGill and the constantly excellent McGrath shared 51 wickets in the series. Gough and Headley excelled for England, though they did not do enough to get in the Australian captain Mark Taylor's composite XI at the end of the series. Gough, said Taylor, would have been twelfth man because of his personality and dressing-room influence. England would tell you the umpire Taufel was their twelfth man at Sydney.

Soon after the series, Taylor retired from cricket and was replaced as captain by Steve Waugh. It seemed impossible, but Australia were about to get even better.

2001

'Adam Gilchrist: ????'

[ENGLAND COACH DUNCAN FLETCHER'S SHEET OF BOWLING PLANS BETRAYS THE LACK OF IDEAS FOR CURBING AUSTRALIA'S REVOLUTIONARY WICKETKEEPER, AUGUST 2001]

IT WOULD ONLY BE A SMALL VICTORY, BUT Andy Caddick was happy to take it after the day he'd had. Adam Gilchrist was on 99 in the first Test at Edgbaston and about to face the final ball of Caddick's over. Caddick wanted to keep Gilchrist on strike so that England could have a go at the No.11, Glenn McGrath; he was going to bang the ball in so short that it would pass comfortably over Gilchrist's head. That's what Caddick did – but in a split-second Gilchrist improvised and played a deliberate periscope shot over the wicketkeeper Alec Stewart's head for four (see page 275). England's plan had failed and Gilchrist had a century in his first Ashes innings.

That bespoke plan was about the only one they had for Gilchrist, as evidenced later in the series when Mike Atherton took a look at the coach Duncan Fletcher's sheet of bowling plans and noticed a series of question-marks next to Gilchrist's name.

When Gilchrist arrived at the turn of the century, he made a great team into an all-time great team. He also revolutionised the role of wicketkeeper-batsman by scoring runs in a quantity and manner that no wicketkeeper had ever done before. He did not care for the coaching manual, as his periscope shot showed, or for the norms and mores of Test match batting: Gilchrist scored at almost unprecedented speed. After reaching his century at Edgbaston, he cut loose and smashed his way to 152 from 143 balls.

Gilchrist was not the only addition to the Australian side for the first Ashes series of the twenty-first century. They had finally found room for the sledgehammer and silk of Matthew Hayden and Damien Martyn, hitherto unfulfilled batting talents, while the blistering pace of Brett Lee completed one of the great bowling attacks with McGrath, Jason Gillespie and Shane Warne.

Perhaps most importantly, their captain Steve Waugh had decided to revolutionise Test-match batting. He instructed his team to attempt to score a minimum of 300 runs per day, a task they approached with relish. Throughout the 2001 series they scored their runs at an Ashes record 4.26 per over – or 383 in a full day of 90 overs. It was among

**Adam Gilchrist reaches his century on his
Ashes debut, Edgbaston, 2001.**

the most fundamental changes in the history of Test cricket, later copied by all the other Test nations.

Between 1999 and 2001 they won a record sixteen consecutive Tests before the run ended during a classic series in India, which they lost 2–1. For all Australia's improvement, England went into the summer of 2001 in optimistic mood. After becoming the worst team in the world when they slipped to the bottom of the world rankings in 1999, they had improved markedly under Fletcher and the captaincy of Nasser Hussain. They won four series in a row, including outstanding victories in Pakistan and Sri Lanka, before drawing at home to Pakistan just before the Ashes. Graham Thorpe and Gough were world-class, while Michael Vaughan had emerged as a classical young batsman with an immaculate defence.

England's plans started to unravel before the series, however, with a series of injuries and embarrassments in the one-day series that preceded the Tests. The first day of the first Test at Edgbaston did not live up the hype; it exceeded it. There were 427 runs and 12 wickets. After England slipped to 191 for nine, the last pair of Alec Stewart and Caddick smashed 103 in 13 overs of delirious cricket. As Gough, at the pinnacle of his career, ran in to bowl the first over of Australia's innings, the Edgbaston crowd could barely have been in more raucous mood. A few minutes later, Gough's first over had been smashed for 18 by Michael Slater, and the whole of England started to deflate.

However much they grate on you, however much you want to kick sand in their cocky, craggy faces, something special happens the moment they pull on the Baggy Green cap

Gilchrist announced himself to English fans on the third day. He had made only two runs in his previous four Test innings, and had dropped two catches in England's innings, but played with the same freedom as usual. In all he hit 20 fours and five sixes in his 152. From the last 12 deliveries of his innings he smashed 37. He added 63 for the last wicket with McGrath, who made one.

A hotchpotch England batting line-up, without the injured Thorpe and Vaughan, collapsed from 142 for two to 164 all out in the second innings, and Australia won by an innings with a day to spare. They spent that unexpected day off watching their compatriot Pat Rafter lose to Goran Ivanisevic in the delayed Wimbledon men's final. Steve Waugh even wore his Baggy Green cap; Atherton said it was 'enough to make you puke'.

'However much they grate on you, however much you want to kick sand in their cocky, craggy faces, something special happens the moment they pull on the Baggy Green cap,' wrote Tanya Aldred in the *Guardian*. 'To see them in action is to observe an incomparable force of nature.'

Gilchrist's innings at Edgbaston gave him an instant aura, evident when England dropped him four times in the first innings at Lord's. At least two were sitters, the kind of chances England had routinely taken in the previous twelve months. Despite a smooth 108 from Mark Waugh, England were still in the game when Gilchrist came to the crease; by the time he had departed for 90, they were 214 behind on first

Mate, you're slow, is that the best you can do?

innings and their morale had been crushed. McGrath and Gillespie shared 15 wickets in an eventual eight-wicket victory. Lee only took two wickets and had a generally disappointing series, but he put Thorpe out of the rest of the series during a fiery-second innings spell by breaking his hand before dismissing him. 'Mate, you're slow, is that the best you can do?' was Thorpe's unwise provocation. The sight of Australia's least effective bowler trouncing England's best batsman in a head-to-head contest summed up the chasm between the sides.

After the game, there was much talk about how to stop Gilchrist. England had no idea. Gilchrist's swashbuckling counter-attacking – the last thing weary bowlers needed after chiselling out the first five wickets – made him a master of mental disintegration even without saying a word. Warne, as he was about to remind us, went about that particular tactic rather differently.

2001

'Come on, Ramps, you know you want to.'

[SHANE WARNE TRIES TO TEMPT
MARK RAMPRAKASH INTO CHARGING
DOWN THE WICKET, THIRD TEST,
TRENT BRIDGE, 3 AUGUST 2001]

DEEP DOWN, MARK RAMPRAKASH KNEW it was the wrong thing to do. But he was going to bloody do it anyway. Hitting Shane Warne back over his head was the only way to shut him and his mates up. He was a good player of Warne, and had nothing to worry about. Ramprakash waited a few balls. Then Warne tossed one up, and Ramprakash danced down the wicket. A second later it was all over.

Ramprakash had been recalled to the England side for the second Test because of an increasingly grotesque number of injuries: of the five Ashes Tests that summer, Graham Thorpe missed four, Michael Vaughan five and Nasser Hussain two, which meant a reluctant Mike Atherton had to stand in as captain at Lord's and Trent Bridge. A decent second-innings 40 in that second Test at Lord's was more than enough for Ramprakash to retain his place.

England – as was invariably the case in the third Test between 1989 and 2002–03 – had to win the Test to keep their token chances of retaining the Ashes alive. That seemed unlikely when Glenn McGrath took his usual five-for to induce a collapse from 142 for four to 185 all out. Then Alex Tudor, who had not played a Test since scoring 99 not out as a nightwatchman against New Zealand two years earlier, took an even cheaper five-for as Australia were bowled out for 190. They only got that many because of a ninth-wicket partnership of 66 between Adam Gilchrist and Brett Lee.

Although 17 wickets fell on the first day, a tense Test was effectively decided on the second evening. England were 115 for two, a lead of 110, with the stand-in captain Mike Atherton and Ramprakash playing well. Then Atherton was wrongly given out caught behind, and Alec Stewart was bowled for nought in Warne's next over.

Ramprakash was now the senior player, and the pressure of the situation and Warne's sledging started to asphyxiate him. Atherton recalled Warne goading Ramprakash before he departed: 'Come on, Ramps, you know you want to.' Ramps didn't want to at all, until Warne opened his mouth. Soon after Atherton's dismissal, Ramprakash charged down the wicket and almost knocked himself off his feet with almighty yahoo. He looked like Leatherface swinging his chainsaw in *The Texas Chainsaw Massacre*. He missed completely and was stumped by Gilchrist.

It was the key moment of yet another absurd collapse. The last eight wickets went down for 47, with Warne taking six for 33. Australia stormed to their target of 158 in just 29.2 overs to win by seven wickets and retain the Ashes inside eleven days' playing time. The only English joy was thoroughly misplaced; during that run-chase, Steve Waugh was stretchered off after tearing a calf. The goading and cheering of the England fans, as well as being a little pathetic given the series scoreline, was a *schadenfreudian* slip. Waugh was usually the Michael Corleone of cricket: it's nothing personal; it's strictly business. But the England fans made it personal, and ensured Waugh was doubly determined to take revenge.

2001

Mark Waugh: 'Mate, what the f*** are you doing here? There's no way you're good enough to play for England.'
James Ormond: 'At least I'm the best player in my family.'

[ON-FIELD EXCHANGE DURING THE
FIFTH TEST AT THE OVAL,
25 AUGUST 2001]

FOR A MAN WHO PLAYED ONLY TWO TESTS, James Ormond made a lasting impression. When Ormond walked out to bat on his Test debut at The Oval in 2001, he was given the usual Australian encouragement. 'Look who it is,' said Mark Waugh at second slip, before launching into an appraisal of whether Ormond had any right to be playing Test cricket. Ormond's pithy response had the rest of the Australian slip cordon collapsing in guilty laughter.

Mark had long since been nicknamed 'Afghan', because he was the forgotten Waugh.* His brother Steve missed the previous Test at Headingley, which meant Adam Gilchrist captained the side. Australia took control as usual in a rain-affected match, with Glenn McGrath taking seven for 76 in the first innings and Ricky Ponting hitting a storming 144, the start of a six-year purple patch in which he averaged over 70 in Test cricket. Eventually, late on the

---

* A reference to the Soviet–Afghan war of 1979–89.

fourth evening, Gilchrist set England a target of 315. With the ball misbehaving so much on the fifth morning that it needed an ASBO, that looked impossible.

Then Mark Butcher started to middle his cover drives, and the demons in the pitch suddenly disappeared. Butcher went on to make a match-winning 173 not out, with 23 fours and a six. It was a perfect example of a good player who was touched by greatness for one beautiful day. 'It's like everything is in slow motion,' he remembered. 'Everything coming down the pitch exactly where I want it to be – it was like you had enough time to make a decision twice.' England won by six wickets with time to spare.

Although the Ashes were lost, a feelgood mood enveloped England for the few days between the fourth and fifth Tests. Then Steve Waugh came into bat, towards the end of the first day's play at The Oval, with Australia the small matter of 292 for two. Waugh had no business being anywhere near a cricket field, only nineteen days after suffering a bad calf injury at Trent Bridge – the original prognosis was that he would be out for three to six months – but the laughter of the England fans motivated him to go above and beyond the call of duty.

He could barely run, yet he willed his way to an inevitable century. Waugh moved from 99 to 100 with a quick single, and almost tried to swim the last few yards: he ended up on his chest on the floor, his bat raised in triumph. Even England fans had to concede it was magnificent stuff. It contrasted starkly with the behaviour of Usman Afzaal, who celebrated a decent fifty at The Oval as if he had just cured baldness, and was out a few balls later. He never played for England again.

Waugh's unbeaten 157 helped Australia to 641 for four, with Phil Tufnell (one for 174) marmalised in his last Test. Mark Ramprakash's second and final Test century of an underachieving career saw England to 432 (Warne seven for 165), but Australia imposed the follow-on and Warne and McGrath did the rest. They also found a new opening partnership in that Test: Justin Langer was used out of position as an opener when Australia decided to drop Michael Slater. 'You can all go and get f*****!' said Slater when informed of the

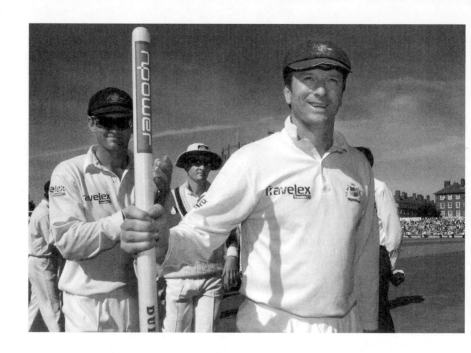

Steve Waugh leads his victorious side off the field at The Oval, 2001. Gilchrist and the younger Waugh twin, Mark, follow in their captain's wake.

decision. Langer and his new partner Matthew Hayden added 158 and went on to become the most productive opening partnership Australia have ever had. England needed a new opening partnership when Atherton retired after the match. His last dismissal was appropriate enough: c Warne b McGrath. It was the nineteenth time he had fallen to McGrath, a new Test record. The two shared 18 wickets in the match and 63 in the series.

Australia celebrated their 4–1 victory with a mammoth drinking session in the Oval dressing-room, and a nude lap of the ground later that evening. This was the greatest of all the Australian sides to terrorise England in modern times, and the one Ashes series in which they had Steve Waugh, Gilchrist, McGrath and Warne, not to mention other greats like Hayden, Ponting and Jason Gillespie – plus the second-best player in the Waugh family.

'IS THERE ANYONE IN ENGLAND WHO CAN PLAY CRICKET?'

[SYDNEY *DAILY TELEGRAPH* HEADLINE
DURING THE FIRST TEST, BRISBANE,
8 NOVEMBER 2002]

ENGLAND'S 2002–03 ASHES TOUR TURNED into a farce before a ball was bowled in the Test series. There were the hopelessly botched rehabilitations of Darren Gough and Andrew Flintoff, who were picked in the original squad despite knee and hernia injuries but ended up flying home without playing a single Test, and then Nasser Hussain inexplicably decided to bowl first on a Brisbane shirtfront after winning the toss.

When Australia ended the first day on 364 for two, with England's young fast bowler Simon Jones in hospital after suffering a sickening injury and a number of embarrassing dropped catches as the day progressed, there were no silver linings to be found. 'Get up, you weak Pommie bastard!' was one comment that stayed with Jones, and drove him on in 2005.

After one day of the series, England were being ridiculed again, no more so than in the Sydney *Daily Telegraph*'s famous headline. *The Melbourne Age* got stuck in too. 'These tourists seem a pale imitation of the bulldog brigade seen in previous decades. They must prove they belong to the tradition of Ken Barrington and Herbert Sutcliffe or else this must be the last time their country is invited to play a five-match series, a custom that insults other countries and flatters their own.'

In the eighteen months since winning 4–1 in England, Australia had confirmed their place as the best team in the world, and one of the greatest of all time, by trouncing their closest rivals South Africa home and away. England muddled along, getting reasonable results as a new, young side began to emerge under the tough captaincy of Nasser Hussain. 'What you get from Nasser is honesty,' said Gough. 'There aren't many captains who look you in the eye and tell you you're a tosser.'

What you get from Nasser is honesty, There aren't many captains who look you in the eye and tell you you're a tosser

He might have looked in the mirror and called himself a tosser after his Brisbane decision to bowl first. 'The biggest drought Australia's ever witnessed and I found some moisture and bowled first,' he said later. Matthew Hayden pummelled 197 and added another second-innings century to make it precisely 300 runs in the match. Hayden, who was in the wilderness for so much of the 1990s, had developed into the biggest bully in world cricket. He was a fast batsman – not just in the sense that he scored his runs quickly, but that he inverted the traditional relationship between new-ball bowler and batsman. Even if it was the first over of the day, Hayden would be happy to clump a bowler straight back over his head for four.

In the second innings at Brisbane he outscored the entire England team; they were bowled out for just 79 and lost by 384 runs. Australia won by an innings in the second Test at Adelaide despite a magnificent 177 from Michael Vaughan on the first day. Ricky Ponting, who was establishing himself as the world's greatest batsman, made 154. The match was best summed up by 11.2 overs of mayhem on the third evening. Waugh declared at 552 for nine because he wanted a wicket before the close; he got three, with the captain Hussain bowled off the final ball by a storming leg-cutter from Andy Bichel.

Australia completed the inevitable retention of the urn in a record 11 days, finishing England off in brutal fashion with another innings victory at Perth. On a bouncy pitch, Brett Lee came into his own. He only took five wickets in the match, but he scared England witless even before he forced Alex Tudor to retire hurt when he ducked into a bouncer. At one stage Tudor thought he had lost an eye. Lee almost vomited on the pitch, and felt even worse because of what he had said to the non-striker Alec Stewart moments earlier: 'Tell him to tread on his stumps, otherwise I'm going to kill him!'

Lee was the subject of no-ball calls from the Barmy Army during the fourth Test at Melbourne, which brought out the headmaster in Justin Langer. 'These people stand behind a fence drinking beer, most of them 50 kilos overweight, making ridiculous comments.'

Langer's unsung 250 – still the highest Ashes score since 1965–66 – was the decisive innings of the match, and Australia won by five wickets despite another swaggering hundred from Vaughan. The first Ashes whitewash since 1920–21 seemed inevitable – but then both Glenn McGrath and Shane Warne had to pull out of the final Test. In their absence, and with the aid of an important toss, England won crushingly by 225 runs. In what became a one-innings shootout, an imperious 183 from the inevitable Vaughan was the difference, and Andrew Caddick helped himself to seven second-innings wickets in what turned out to be his final Test.

Even in defeat, there was a triumph for Australia: the captain Steve Waugh, who was under enormous pressure after a poor year, saved his career with a legendary first-innings century, when he hit the last ball of the second day for four to reach three figures. Waugh had been so out of form that, during the fourth Test at Melbourne, Hussain gave Langer free singles to get Waugh on strike. 'You smartarse prick!' was Waugh's response to Hussain. It was a rare chance for Hussain to get one back. For most of his career, he had heard Waugh deliver the same line. 'Enjoy it, Nasser. This is your last Test. We will never see you again.'

Waugh was Australia's talisman, the only man who played in each of Australia's eight consecutive Ashes series wins between 1989 and 2002–03, and his century seemed to encapsulate the sheer indomitability of the team. But Australia were becoming desperate for a real contest when they played the Poms. They were about to get that, and then some.

2002–03

'This will sound arrogant, but I really fancied facing McGrath. . . I found him quite juicy.'

[MICHAEL VAUGHAN REFLECTS ON HIS BRILLIANT 2002-03 SERIES]

THE BALL FROM GLENN McGRATH WAS infinitesimally short of a length, if that. It demanded respect, and it got none. Michael Vaughan rocked back and launched it through midwicket for four.

It was only the third ball Vaughan had faced from McGrath in Test cricket. He went on to take 12 from the over and hit McGrath for 25 in 19 balls before McGrath had him caught behind. Overall Vaughan made 33 from 36 balls in his first innings of the 2002–03 Ashes series; it seems a nothing score, but there have been few more important cameos ever played by an England batsman because it confirmed Vaughan's instinct that Australia could be attacked just like any other team.

Vaughan's performance took exceptional talent as well as nerve, because McGrath had publicly targeted him before the series. The individual contest between McGrath and Vaughan was hyped like a boxing match. Vaughan, who had scored three centuries in four Tests against India in England's most recent series, was determined to take the Aussies on. Before the series, he got fed up with team-mates telling him you couldn't do that; it only furthered his resolve to do so. 'This will sound arrogant, but I really quite fancied facing McGrath,' he said. 'If the ball was seaming he was a bit of a nightmare, but if it was swinging I found him quite juicy.'

Though England lost 4–1, Vaughan's batting in the 2002–03 series is among the finest by an England batsman since the war. He only passed 50 on three occasions – but each time he went huge, making 177, 145 and 183. As he promised, he took on McGrath, and Shane Warne too. McGrath dismissed Vaughan twice in the first Test at Brisbane, and caught him spectacularly off the bowling of Warne in the second at Adelaide, but Vaughan would not change his approach.

Vaughan had no psychological scarring, having missed the 2001 Ashes through injury. He was not intimidated by the Australians. When he drove Andy Bichel to cover on the first day at Adelaide, and seemed to be caught low down by Justin Langer, Vaughan stood his ground. He was reprieved by the third umpire and, despite constant abuse from Langer in particular, made a further 158 runs.

Vaughan did not just make runs; he made them with the most beautiful batting England fans had seen since David Gower. Two shots stood out: the silky-smooth cover drive and swivel pull. It was only three years since Vaughan had been seen as an heir to Mike Atherton, such was his defensive excellence, but he had become a thrilling attacking opener.

Michael Vaughan takes on Glenn McGrath, second Test, Adelaide, November 2002.

He ended the series as the world's No.1 batsman in the ICC rankings. He was never the same with the bat once he became England captain a few months later, though there were sporadic reminders of his silky majesty. England lost a great batsman and gained something even rarer; a great captain. One who was not afraid of Australia, and who would transmit that attitude to his young team. The result was probably the greatest Test series ever played.

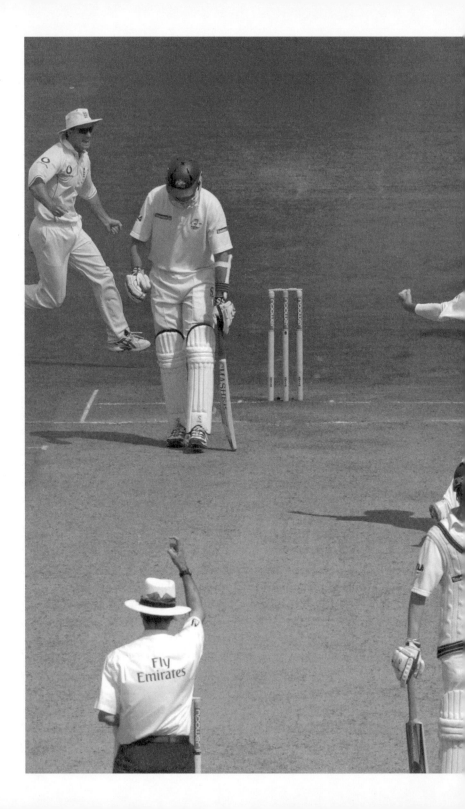

2005 AND
ALL THAT

2005

'This really is a war out here, isn't it?'

[JUSTIN LANGER TO ANDREW STRAUSS, FIRST TEST, LORD'S, 21 JULY 2005]

JUSTIN LANGER LOOKED LIKE A MAN with three elbows. It was barely seconds since he had been hit by a short delivery from Steve Harmison, yet his elbow was already grotesquely swollen. Only two balls of the series had been bowled. Later in that morning session Matthew Hayden was hit on the helmet, and then Harmison drew blood when he hit Ricky Ponting below the eye. None of the England team bothered to ask if the Australian captain was okay. And so, with a bang to Ponting's cheek followed by a whimper from Langer, the much-anticipated 2005 Ashes were well and truly underway.

Before the war came the phoney war. It started almost a year earlier, when Michael Vaughan's young England side won all seven home Tests against New Zealand and West Indies. Then, either side of an excellent series victory in South Africa, came two significant statements of intent. In the Champions Trophy semi-final in 2004, they beat Australia comfortably by six wickets. And in the single T20 international at the start of the 2005 summer, on a giddy June evening in Southampton they thrashed the Aussies by 100 runs. At one stage Australia were 31 for seven.

These were, admittedly, not Test match victories, but they suggested that England were no longer afraid of Australia. England's hyper-aggressive approach revealed itself during a one-day match at Edgbaston, when Simon Jones accidentally threw the ball at Matthew Hayden's shoulder and the two squared up, with a

290 GENTLEMEN AND SLEDGERS

number of England fielders surrounding Hayden. But it was not just England's aggression that caught Australia cold. They started their tour shambolically.

In the week after that T20 defeat, they failed to defend 342 in a 50-over match against Somerset and were shockingly beaten by Bangladesh in the one-day international tournament. The next day Kevin Pietersen, a spectacular addition to England's ODI side the previous winter, mangled 91 not out from 65 balls to pull off an unlikely victory at Bristol. Andrew Flintoff later recalled Pietersen sitting in the dressing-room saying: 'Not bad, am I?'

Australia were not just bad; they had become a laughing stock. When it was reported that Shane Watson, part of the one-day squad, had been sufficiently spooked by a ghost at Lumley Castle in Durham that he spent the night in Brett Lee's room, Gough shouted 'wooooooo' and pretended to be a ghost during the next match.

'A team full of dobbers and crap fielders?' wrote Mike Atherton in the *Telegraph*. 'It has been said about every England touring team to Australia in the past fifteen years. It's nice to be able to return the compliment.' Australia inevitably improved, and eventually shared the ODI tournament after a thrilling tie in the final against England. Another three-match series between the sides was akin to having about twelve hors d'oeuvres.

Australia won 2–1. In the final match, Pietersen played with such majesty that England decided to take a gamble on him for the Test series. It meant omitting Graham Thorpe, a brutally hard decision given that Thorpe had played superbly in the previous year.

> **A team full of dobbers and crap fielders? It has been said about every England touring team to Australia in the past fifteen years. It's nice to be able to return the compliment**

Australia had regained their strut. 'We find it both amusing and amazing how they always talk it up with about twelve months to go, telling everyone that they've finally got the team to beat us,' said Glenn McGrath on the eve of the first Test at Lord's, which was hyped to breaking point.

'I'd never heard an old man roar before,' said Flintoff of the reception as England walked through the Long Room at Lord's on the first morning. He also said Harmison was 'foaming at the mouth'. Australia were whipped out for 190, with Harmison taking five wickets, but before you could say 'open-top bus tour', he had been trumped and gazumped by Glenn McGrath. He took five for two in 31 deliveries, including his 500th Test wicket, to reduce England to

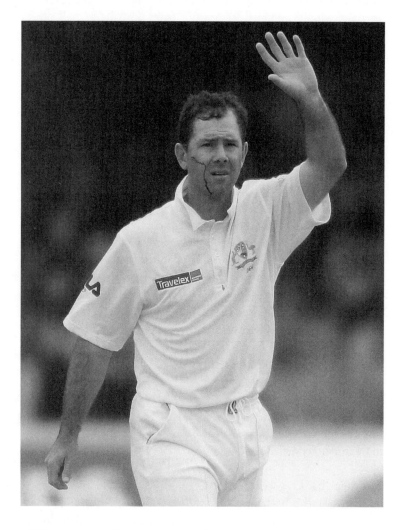

Ricky Ponting calls for treatment after taking one on the cheek from Steve Harmison; first Test, Lord's, 21 July 2005.

21 for five. If he had ever bowled better, nobody could remember it. For the third consecutive Ashes in England, the first day of the series was beyond the most fertile imagining: 17 wickets fell for 282 runs.

England eventually trailed by 35 on first innings, despite a splendid 57 on debut from Pietersen that included thrillingly disrespectful sixes off McGrath and Shane Warne. It was high-octane stuff. At one point Pietersen met Geraint Jones mid-pitch between overs. 'Sorry, China,' he said. 'Can't talk now. Too pumped.' With the aid of dropped catches, a piercing reminder of times past that furthered the sense that this would be the same old story, Australia built a huge lead. England slipped to defeat by 239 runs, collapsing from 80 for nought to 180 all out, despite another arrogant half-century from Pietersen. The manner and margin of Australia's victory were utterly familiar. As the ground cleared that evening, Australia sang their team song in the England dressing-room.

I've seen nothing to make me change my 5-0 prediction

'I've seen nothing to make me change my 5–0 prediction,' said McGrath. Many England fans agreed with him, and started crying over milk that hadn't even been spilt yet. It was the Groundhog Ashes, and the series was going to end 4–1 or 5–0.

Vaughan's team were savaged by the press, with widespread calls for change. Flintoff, their banker, had a shocker: he scored three runs and took four wickets for 173. 'I bottled it,' he later said. The former Zimbabwe captain Dave Houghton said that playing with the spinner Ashley Giles was akin to playing with ten men, adding to Terry Alderman's pre-series suggestion that any Australian dismissed by Giles should hang themselves. The England selectors kept their nerve and stuck with the same side. They deserve the highest praise, and maybe even an MBE, for doing so.

With hindsight, there were enough signs – in the bowling of Harmison and the batting of Pietersen in particular – to suggest that this wasn't necessarily the same old England. Yet even their biggest cheerleaders could not have imagined how spectacularly they would prove it.

2005

'It's 1–1, you Aussie bastard.'

[ANDREW FLINTOFF JOKES ABOUT
WHAT HE SAID TO BRETT LEE AT
THE END OF THE SECOND TEST,
EDGBASTON, 7 AUGUST 2005]

THE BIGGEST TURNING POINT OF THE greatest cricket series ever played came during a game of rugby. Australia were warming up on the morning of the second Test at Edgbaston, playing touch rugby, when Glenn McGrath trod on a stray cricket ball and badly injured his ankle. As word spread that McGrath would miss the match, the whole of England celebrated like a dictator had been overthrown.

Although the pitch looked good, Australia had planned to bowl first if they won the toss in an attempt to further expose the wounds opened by McGrath at Lord's. In his absence, Ricky Ponting took the same decision to the surprise of almost everybody at the ground. The video of the toss shows his opposite number Michael Vaughan having to work exceptionally hard to retain his poker face at the moment Ponting says Australia will bowl. 'He's a lovely guy, that Ricky Ponting,' said Geoffrey Boycott later. 'He likes the English so much he changed the series with the most stupid decision he'll ever make in his life.'

Normally a captain is savaged if he bowls first and a side makes 600. England made 407 at Edgbaston, a good score but no more, yet the manner in which they did so changed the mood of the series. They scored those runs in just 79.2 overs, at a staggering 5.13 per over, with 10 sixes. It was an outrageously aggressive response to the crushing humiliation of Lord's.

Marcus Trescothick set the tone with a coruscating 90, and after lunch Kevin Pietersen and Andrew Flintoff had a game of unspoken one-upmanship during a partnership of 103. Pietersen made 71 and Flintoff returned to form with 68 from just 62 balls. That included five sixes, one hooked blind off Brett Lee, an unwitting homage to Ian Botham in 1981. Flintoff said he bottled it at Lord's; if he could have bottled the freedom with which he played for the rest of the series, he would have been one of the greatest players of all time.

In the most important game of their lives, England batted with happy abandon. It was their captain Vaughan who imbued the entire side with the same aggressive approach he demonstrated in Australia in 2002–03. 'He's the best liar I ever met,' said Steve Harmison of Vaughan's ability to make his team believe everything was or was going to be okay.

He's a lovely guy, that Ricky Ponting. He likes the English so much he changed the series with the most stupid decision he'll ever make in his life

He didn't need to lie on the second day, as England took a significant first-innings lead of 99. Giles' dismissal of Ponting – who moved ominously to 61, determined to make up for his decision at the toss – was a key moment, one of three important top-order wickets for a player who had been heavily criticised after the first Test.

Any sense of English comfort soon started to dissipate, however. Warne bowled Andrew Strauss with a staggering delivery on the Friday evening – his Ball of the Twenty-First Century. On the eve of the match, Warne was asked about his famous delivery to Mike Gatting in 1993. 'I'd give up sex to bowl a few more of those balls this summer, that's for sure.' The delivery to Strauss, and the grainy pictures of Warne in a hotel room with two blondes and an inflatable, suggested there was no need for such a trade-off.

On the third morning at Edgbaston, Warne and Brett Lee reduced a jittery England to 75 for six. Flintoff then continued his exceptional match with 73 from 86 balls, including four more sixes. The third, a bunt down the ground off Lee provided one of Mark Nicholas's many memorable commentaries during the series on Channel 4 in England. 'Oh, hello! Massive! MASSIVE!' All the while his co-commentator Boycott could be heard cackling with disbelief and joy. Flintoff added 51 for the last wicket with Simon Jones. Warne, bowling imperiously, ended with six for 46 in the innings and ten in the match. As Flintoff walked off, Warne shouted after him. When Flintoff turned round, Warne mouthed 'well played' and applauded.

Australia were left needing 282 to win. Matthew Hayden and Justin Langer moved so easily to 47 for none that, even at that early stage, it felt like it was Flintoff or bust. In his first over, he dismissed both Langer and Ponting. It was the moment an ordinary human being became SuperFred. Langer was bowled off his elbow, and then Ponting received the most exhilarating working-over since Michael Holding blew away Geoff Boycott in 1981.

A no-ball from Flintoff actually helped England, because it gave him an extra delivery – from which Ponting was dismissed. 'They were five of the most vicious deliveries you could ever see,' said Gilchrist. 'And then Ricky was somehow good enough to get his bat on the last ball to nick it to Geraint Jones. Flintoff stood there like Hercules and his team-mates mobbed him. I remember, in the rooms, watching and thinking, "We are in big strife."'

Flintoff stood there like Hercules and his team-mates mobbed him. I remember thinking, 'We are in big strife'

The third day was one for the ages: there were 332 runs, 17 wickets, and approximately four million momentum shifts. It ended with Australia surely beaten: they were 175 for eight after Harmison bowled Michael Clarke with an outrageous slower ball in the final over of the day.

The fourth day was apparently a simple case of England turning up and taking the last two wickets. There was a slight scare when Warne and Lee added 45, but when Warne comically kicked his own stumps down against Flintoff, everyone relaxed again. For about twenty minutes. Then it became apparent that, not only were Lee and Kasprowicz adding runs at speed, they were doing so with alarming comfort. It all happened so fast that, before anyone knew it, Australia needed only 15 to win. That was when Jones, diving forward at third man, dropped a sharp chance offered by Kasprowicz.

The target moved into single figures. By now an entire nation had stopped its day of rest. 'Physically sick but still watching,' texted the England coach Duncan Fletcher's daughter to her mother. You know sport is truly special when you feel nervous even when you watch replays, and Edgbaston 2005 retains that quality. With four needed, Lee smashed Harmison through the covers; there was a fleeting yelp of triumph from the Australian fans, before they realised Vaughan had a cover sweeper in place and it would only be one run. Two balls later, Kasprowicz fended a short ball from Harmison down the leg side, where the much-maligned wicketkeeper Geraint Jones took an excellent tumbling catch.

England's celebrations were joyously uncoordinated, with players running in different directions before they eventually came together. Harmison broke off from the celebrations to console Lee and then Flintoff did the same, his face a picture of compassion, respect and empathy. The result was one of cricket's iconic photographs, a pictorial code for sportsmanship at its finest.

The cricket world often wonders what Flintoff said, as if he dispensed one of the great pearls of wisdom. The reality was more mundane. 'It came out of my mouth, it's nothing profound is it?!' said Flintoff. 'It's not gonna be something life-changing!' Lee has a vague recollection. 'It was something like, "Awesome game, bad luck, I thoroughly enjoyed it."'

Lee cried in the shower area after the game, his batting gloves still on, and then had a beer with Flintoff in the dressing-room. Flintoff sometimes jokes that the sympathetic expression was a smokescreen for an earthy reminder to Lee that England had just made the score 1–1. The reality was far more generous in spirit, of course. Although the essential point of Flintoff's joke is correct: Lee may not be an Aussie bastard, but it was 1–1 rather than 2–0, and the Ashes were ablaze. In no small part thanks to a stray cricket ball.

Freddie Flintoff consoles
Brett Lee, Edgbaston,
7 August 2005.

2005

'I knew I'd hit rock bottom when one night I rolled over in bed to give my wife Mel a kiss goodnight and all I saw was Freddie bloody Flintoff.'

[ADAM GILCHRIST, 2005]

THE WORLD'S SCARIEST BATSMAN HAD FAILED again and nobody was surprised. Not Adam Gilchrist, who briskly exited the arena after being dismissed by Andrew Flintoff as if he knew it had been coming. Not the England captain Michael Vaughan, who simply clapped rather than punching the air as he did with most wickets. Not Richie Benaud, commentating on Channel 4; he quietly said 'Goddim!' as if Flintoff had routinely dismissed a tail-ender.

In a sense, he had. By that stage, the second innings of the third Test at Old Trafford, Gilchrist had become Flintoff's rabbit. Nothing so neatly summed up the change in the relationship between England and Australia in 2005 as that of the relationship between Gilchrist and Flintoff; after two series of being slaughtered by Gilchrist, now England were spooking the bogeyman. He couldn't even kiss his wife without seeing Fred.

The Old Trafford Test confirmed that Edgbaston was not a one-off and that, for the first time in a generation, Australia were in significant danger of losing the Ashes. The match came only four days after the heart-stopping second Test, although there was time for Glenn McGrath to make an unlikely recovery and return to the side.

There had been no centuries thus far in the series but, after another fast start from Marcus Trescothick, Michael Vaughan returned spectacularly to form with a dominant 166. There were moments of fortune, most notably in consecutive deliveries from McGrath when Gilchrist dropped a routine chance and he was bowled by a no-ball, but he played throughout with a resounding authority and aggression.

Gilchrist caught Trescothick to give Shane Warne his 600th Test wicket, but otherwise had a desperate day. 'I walked out of the hotel, up a strip of cafés,' he said. 'I sank my head into my collar. I'm sure no one there would have cared if they'd seen me, or knew who I was, but I was so low I covered up the team shirt: I was wearing the Australian shirt and I was ashamed of myself.'

England eventually reached 444 and, in what was becoming a recurring theme, took decisive control of the match on the Friday

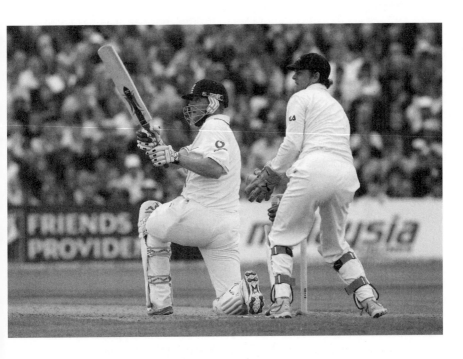

Flintoff hits out, watched by Gilchrist; third Test, Old Trafford, 12 August 2005.

afternoon. Ashley Giles took care of the top order, including his own Ball of the Century to bowl a startled Damien Martyn, and Simon Jones ran through the middle order with his in-your-face 90mph reverse swing.

A breezy 90 from Warne ensured Australia would not follow on, and rain took plenty of time out of the match on the third day. Andrew Strauss made his first Ashes century on the fourth, despite being bloodied early on when Brett Lee hit him on the ear, and England were able to enjoy the rare luxury of a declaration against Australia just before the close.

The equation for the last day was deliciously simple: England needed 10 wickets, Australia 399 runs. Old Trafford was full by 9am, with more than 20,000 people locked out. England chipped away throughout an unforgettable day, with Flintoff at his most talismanic. 'That's the overriding positive feeling about having retired from international cricket – not having that big bugger charging in at me,' said Justin Langer later. While others crumbled under the pressure, most notably Gilchrist and Matthew Hayden, Ricky Ponting played perhaps his greatest innings: 156 in 411 minutes of jutting-jawed defiance.

> **That's the overriding positive feeling about having retired – not having that big bugger charging in at me**

When he was caught down the leg side off Harmison, however, there were twenty-four balls remaining and England needed only one wicket. Somehow Lee – back in the firing line just eight days after Edgbaston – and McGrath held on, leading McGrath to boast cheerily that he still didn't have an average in the series because he hadn't been dismissed.

Australia were delirious after the game. In the aftermath of the final ball, they celebrated wildly on the balcony. Vaughan drew his weary, frustrated team into a huddle and pointed out that the great Australia were now celebrating draws against England. All the momentum was with England; now they had to actually win the urn.

'All the palaver caused me to burn my toast.'

RICKY PONTING WAS CHUNTERING TO everyone and no one, his face a picture of affronted dismay. As he walked off the field, absent-mindedly removing his gloves while swearing in all directions, it was as much as he could do not to grit his teeth to breaking point. When he reached the pavilion steps, Ponting – still with his helmet on, as if he couldn't quite bring himself to take off his work clothes and fully acknowledge his innings was over – snapped his head and started shouting abuse in a specific direction, and at a specific person on the England balcony. In a series full of symbolic moments, this was the biggest of all; the moment England knew Australia had cracked.

The tourists were under enormous pressure at the start of the fourth Test at Trent Bridge, after their narrow escape at Old Trafford. Glenn McGrath was absent for the second time in three Tests, this time with an elbow injury. With Jason Gillespie also put out of his misery, having been taken apart by England's batsmen, Australia's pace attack was led by Brett Lee and Michael Kasprowicz, with support from the debutant Shaun Tait, the rawest of fast bowlers.

England, for the third Test in a row, got first use of a good pitch and got off to a flyer. Marcus Trescothick, the unsung hero of the series, and Andrew Strauss added 105 in just 21.4 overs – a better scoring rate than many an England one-day innings of the time – and England ended a rain-affected first day on 227 for four.

The second day was their most dominant of the series. A clinical, controlled 102 from Andrew Flintoff, easily the best innings of his career, and 85 from the wicketkeeper Geraint Jones took England to an imposing total of 477 all out. By the close Australia were 99 for five and in disarray. Matthew Hoggard, relatively quiet in the first three Tests, came into his own in the swinging conditions of Nottingham and took the vital wickets of Justin Langer, Matthew Hayden and Damien Martyn.

The beauty of England's 'Fab Four' – as Flintoff, Steve Harmison, Simon Jones and Hoggard were christened – was that between them they covered every base: bounce, pace, aggression, quiet diligence, orthodox and reverse swing. Australia did not reach 400 in the series.

Australia's lower order swung with angry defiance on the third morning, but England's increasing supremacy was reflected by Andrew Strauss's astonishing diving catch at slip to dismiss Adam Gilchrist off the bowling of Flintoff. Australia were made to follow on for the first time in seventeen years.

What England – not to mention Ponting – did not know at the time was that Simon Jones, who ran through the tail to take another five-for in the first innings, was struggling with injury. He bowled only four second-innings overs before leaving the field and never played for England again.

With the pitch still good, England endured an increasingly hard time getting through Australia second time round. They were 155 for two, 104 behind, and Ponting was looking ominously set on 48. Damien Martyn called Ponting for a tight single on the off side, and the substitute Gary Pratt – on for Jones – threw down the stumps with dead-eyed certainty. Ponting's exasperation at getting out in such a manner at such a time was great enough, even before he realised he had been run out by a substitute.

Australia had been irritated throughout the series by England's habit of using substitute fielders, apparently to give their bowlers a rest after a long spell; it was a legitimate complaint – England clearly bent the rules – but in this case Jones was genuinely injured.

Ponting did not know that, and all the frustration and pressure came out in five seconds of ranting at Fletcher on the balcony. Fletcher was sufficiently distracted by events that he burnt his toast in the dressing-room, though it was clear he loved every second of Ponting's outburst. 'If you want to take a run to the cover fielder and get out, whose fault is that?' he said at the close of play.

The tourists battled on to 387 – Simon Katich got an appalling lbw decision after resisting over four hours for 59 – which left

If you want to take a run to the cover fielder and get out, whose fault is that?

England needing 129 to go ahead in the series. It turned into the kind of run-chase that ages people by ten years. Shane Warne raged majestically against the dying of the light, reducing England to 57 for four. Kevin Pietersen and Flintoff calmed things down with a partnership of 46 before Lee dismissed both, with Flintoff bowled by a stunning delivery. England, in control throughout the match, now faced the very real prospect of losing the match – which would have ended the drama at a stroke, because Australia would have gone 2–1 up and retained the urn.

When Geraint Jones skied Warne to mid-off, England were 116 for seven, 13 short of victory. Hoggard loafed out to join Ashley Giles and said, 'Come on, let's me and you get it done.' Giles' reply – 'It's reversing at 95mph' – did not quite maintain the mood of cheery certainty. But they did get it done, just about. The crowd greeted Hoggard's cover-driven four off Lee like the announcement of world peace, and soon after Giles hit the winning runs. 'Whether we win or lose, we relish creating a bit of an arse-nipper,' he said. The biggest of them all, the series decider, was yet to come.

2005

'I'm fed up with blocking it, I'm just going to whack it instead.'

[KEVIN PIETERSEN TO MARCUS TRESCOTHICK, FIFTH TEST, THE OVAL, 12 SEPTEMBER 2005]

KEVIN PIETERSEN WAS SICK AND TIRED of being Brett Lee's punchbag. He had been hit all over the body, and dropped twice as well. He was trying to bat time, to secure the draw that would win the Ashes for England, but it was as unnatural and uncomfortable as holding his breath. Runs were just as important, because of a complex time/runs equation, and Pietersen decided to start scoring some. He informed his partner Marcus Trescothick about the imminent change in tactics and then launched Shane Warne for two sixes in an over.

The fact England only needed to draw the final Test at The Oval put them in a tricky stick-or-twist position, especially as aggression had been their default setting throughout the series. They played safe by replacing the injured Simon Jones with Paul Collingwood rather than Jimmy Anderson. Australia resisted calls to drop the out-of-form Matthew Hayden, though Glenn McGrath returned in place of Michael Kasprowicz.

On a good pitch, England's first-innings score of 373 felt below par. Andrew Strauss made a superb 129, and Andrew Flintoff maintained his rich all-round form with an authoritative 72. But the inevitable Warne, disgusted at the thought of surrendering the urn, took six for 129, including a wonderful spell of four quick wickets either side of lunch on the first day.

With the match played in mid-September, rain was a factor for parts of the next three days. So was bad light – which Australia surprisingly accepted on more than one occasion, even though they needed as much time as possible if they were to square the series and retain the Ashes. Hayden and Justin Langer both made centuries, and at one stage Australia were 264 for one. But Flintoff and Matthew Hoggard bowled so well in helpful conditions on the fourth morning that England secured an improbable first-innings lead of six. More rain meant that England started the last day on 34 for one. Duncan Fletcher, their usually serene coach, started retching involuntarily in his hotel room before he left for the ground.

The start went well for England, so well that you suspected trouble had to be around the corner. It was. McGrath, summoning one last effort, dismissed Michael Vaughan and Ian Bell with consecutive deliveries and nearly made it a hat-trick with a vicious bouncer to Pietersen that ended in the hands of gully. Billy Bowden correctly judged that it had hit the shoulder rather than the shoulder of the bat.

Pietersen was dropped twice, first by a combination of Adam Gilchrist and Hayden off Warne, and then a routine chance at first slip offered to Warne off the bowling of Lee. It was then that Pietersen decided to play his natural game. Warne carried on regardless, quickly dismissing Trescothick and Flintoff to leave England in the perilous position of 127 for five – a lead of 133 – at lunch.

After lunch, Pietersen savaged the pace bowling of Lee and Shaun Tait, hooking sixes with abandon, and calmly milked Warne and McGrath for low-risk ones and twos. Given the context – and the later criticism that he could only play one way – it was an admirably two-faced innings.

In that decisive afternoon session he scored at a strike rate of 228 runs per 100 balls against Lee and Tait, and 32 per 100 balls against McGrath and Warne. Pietersen's assault on the pace bowlers took the game away from Australia, and his partnership of 109 with Ashley Giles effectively secured the urn. After tea, when the match was essentially over, Pietersen decided to take McGrath and Warne to the cleaners as well. Has there ever been a more important maiden Test century? Pietersen finished with 158 from 187 balls, including 15 fours and seven sixes. 'I'll love him forever,' said Giles. Even a decade on, the audacity of the innings boggles the mind.

So does his haircut, which Sir Ian Botham described as being like 'a dead mongoose'. By the end of the series Pietersen had a big blue stripe through his hair. 'He sent me a message asking what I thought of his hair,' said his mother, 'and I replied that a mother will always love her son, no matter what the circumstances.'

As Pietersen walked off, Warne ran after him and said, 'Savour this moment.' Pietersen achieved so much in his career, but it was never that good again. Warne's gesture summed up the goodwill of the final day, which was reciprocated when the England fans sang 'We wish you were English' at him. Warne's performance – 249 runs and 40 wickets – was even more admirable because of the collapse of his marriage just before the tour. Mike Atherton wrote of 'the many tales of midnight fun and frolics which made it on to the front, rather than back pages of interested newspapers – making him if not the greatest Test cricketer of all time, then certainly the greatest text cricketer of all time.' It's easy to imagine Warne as the plumber coming to the rescue in the kind of movie not renowned for subtlety of dialogue, but it was not all lad larks in 2005. 'I cried a fair bit when I was by myself,' he said. 'I feel like I'm on *The Truman Show*.'

> **To be honest, I wouldn't wanna bump into me later. I fancy being a nuisance tonight**

More rain and bad light ensured that the series ended in slightly farcical circumstances, with the umpires Bowden and Rudi Koertzen striding out self-importantly to formally signal that England had won the Ashes. Not that the whiff of anti-climax mattered; England had ended sixteen years of pain by winning a series that may never be bettered. After two months of the highest intensity, it was time to celebrate. Flintoff sounded a warning to the cameras: 'To be honest, I wouldn't wanna bump into me later. I fancy being a nuisance tonight.'

2005

'To be honest, Mark, I'm struggling. I've not been to bed yet and behind these sunglasses is a thousand stories.'

[ANDREW FLINTOFF TO MARK NICHOLAS,
13 SEPTEMBER 2005]

ENGLAND CELEBRATED THEIR ASHES VICTORY with a heroic, Homeric bender. Andrew Flintoff led the way, just as he had on the field. He did not sleep at all on the night of 12 September 2005, and when he was interviewed during an open-top-bus parade the following day he needed subtitles.

Matthew Hoggard feared the bus tour, which started at Mansion House and ended in Trafalgar Square, would be an embarrassment, in front of 'three men and a dog'. In fact there were tens of thousands, an outpouring of affection to mark the end of cricket's summer of love. Pietersen says it was the summer in which 'cricket went viral'.

The players ended up at 10 Downing Street, where Flintoff sneaked into a private room to conduct his own imaginary cabinet meeting before being told off by security. He also, so legend has it, urinated in the garden. Later came the MBEs, for all the squad including Paul Collingwood, who played the final Test.* 'Nice place, Buckingham Palace. The Queen has clearly done very well for herself,' said Hoggard.

---

* During the final Test of the 2006–07 series, Shane Warne rounded on Collingwood: 'You're an embarrassment! How can you get an MBE for getting just 17 runs? That's embarrassing. Maybe you should give it back.'

'I've never seen a man so drunk as Fred that day,' said Simon Jones. 'Fair play to him, he was in a hell of a tangle. The way we got absolutely obliterated and then had to go to 10 Downing Street the next day wasn't ideal. The twelve drunkest people in England had to go to the most important place in London. We all looked like we slept in a bush.'

I've never seen a man as drunk as Fred that day

When the dust and the alcohol settled, England had to work out how they might follow such a defining achievement. In a sense, a young team achieved the ultimate too early. In another, it's a good job they did: a series of unexpected problems meant they never played together again.

For Australia, the way forward was pretty clear. Shane Warne was due to retire had Australia won the 2005 Ashes, but now he and the rest of the team were ominously set on revenge.

Vaughan, Pietersen and Flintoff enjoy England's celebratory bus ride, 13 September 2005.

2006–07

'I reckon it will be 5–0 this time.'

[GLENN McGRATH, NOVEMBER 2006]

BRISBANE, NOVEMBER 2006. ONE OF the most eagerly anticipated moments in Ashes history. England's Steve Harmison roared in to bowl the first ball of the Ashes rematch – and let fly a hopeless wide that went straight into the hands of his captain Andrew Flintoff at second slip. It was a bit like waiting to take delivery of a brand-new, turbo-charged SUV, only for the garage to deliver a second-hand Mondeo with 100,000 miles on the clock and a dodgy rear axle.

Australia, aided by Harmison's sweaty palms and helter-skelter heartbeat, got off to a flying start and ended up piling up 600 in their first innings. It was a statement of intent to go alongside the one made by their premier new-ball bowler before the series.

From the mid-2000s, Glenn McGrath announcing that Australia would win the Ashes 5–0 became an essential part of the phoney war before each series. Given McGrath's ability to walk the talk, it had the ominous certainty of a tax bill. When England won 2–1 in 2005, McGrath was ridiculed for his perceived hubris. It did not stop him making exactly the same prediction eighteen months later.

Australia had responded to their 2005 Ashes defeat with terrifying purpose, thrashing allcomers, including a decent South Africa side. England had not, as many predicted, ascended to greatness – though that was largely down to a series of injuries that meant the 2005 Ashes side would never play together again.

The injured Vaughan was replaced by Flintoff as captain, while Marcus Trescothick flew home from the 2006–07 tour because of depression. The fast-bowling quartet were also broken up because of a series of ankle and knee injuries suffered by Simon Jones.

That put even greater pressure on Harmison; a combination of that, and the unbearable hype, were too much. As Harmison ran in to bowl the first ball of the series, Troy Cooley, England's bowling coach in 2005, who was now working with Australia, turned to Ricky Ponting and said: 'Watch this. This'll go straight to second slip.'

It did, and it set the tone just as much as Harmison's fierce assault on the first morning of the 2005 series. 'I think I'm allergic to my passport,' said Harmison of his habitual woes overseas. He took one for 177 in the first test, with Australia ruthlessly dismantling England. Nobody oozed more purpose than Ponting, who made 196, and then McGrath – who had been written off by many as too old – demolished England's batting yet again, taking six for 50 as the tourists subsided for just 157 runs on a flat pitch.

Instead of enforcing the follow on, Ponting decided to crush England's spirit to such an extent that, when he finally declared on 202 for two, courtesy of a Justin Langer hundred, the fourth-innings target was a modest 648. Despite fine innings from Kevin Pietersen and Paul Collingwood, it was all over early on the fifth day. The sight of Langer at long-on, clenching his fists in celebration even before he had caught an errant blow from Flintoff, demonstrated how up for the fight Australia were.

For a few mad seconds I thought, 'mates or not, I'm never gonna speak to that dickhead again'

The mateship of the 2005 series, symbolised by Flintoff's handshake with Brett Lee, was evidently a thing of the past. Australia made a point of calling England's players by their first names rather than their nicknames. At one stage in the first Test Warne threw the ball straight back at Pietersen. 'You f****** arsehole, Shane, f*** you,' said Pietersen. 'Who the f*** do you think you are, fatso?' 'For a few mad seconds I thought, "mates or not, I'm never gonna speak to that dickhead again".' The whole England side would be speechless after the next Test.

2006-07

'You don't like being called the Shermanator, do you?'

[SHANE WARNE TO IAN BELL,
SECOND TEST, ADELAIDE,
4 DECEMBER 2006]

SHANE WARNE WAS GETTING IRRITATED. He had taken the worst figures of his Test career two days earlier, and now England were not rolling over in their second innings as he thought they might. Even Ian Bell, his bunny, was playing nicely. Both teams had posted first-innings totals in excess of five hundred, and the second Test appeared to be heading for a draw. Warne, remembering a lesson taught him by Allan Border, started to pick fights to get himself going. The night before, he and Michael Clarke had been eating when the film *American Pie* came on TV, when they perceived a likeness between Bell and a character called the Shermanator.

It was not a flattering comparison. The Shermanator was a goofy, ginger-haired virgin who invented stories about his sex life and attempted to seduce girls by quoting *The Terminator*. Warne decided to share his observation with Bell, and suggested his opponent did not like it. 'I've been called worse,' said Bell. 'Mate,' sniggered Warne, 'I'm not sure you have.'

If the idea was to get inside Bell's head, it didn't work. He and Andrew Strauss comfortably survived a tricky spell before the close, with England 59 for one; in doing so, they appeared to have ensured that the match would peter out as a draw on the final day. At the post-play press conference, Matthew Hoggard and other England players were able to laugh off Warne's comments. They all seemed in rather good spirits. They had no idea of the trauma that awaited them.

Ian Bell and Alastair Cook leave the field at close of play on the fourth day of the third Test match at the WACA; 17 December 2006.

The Adelaide Test was the bore draw that became a once-in-a-generation thriller. England came back superbly from their thrashing at Brisbane, with Paul Collingwood's 206 – the first double hundred by an Englishman in Australia since Wally Hammond in 1928–29 – and Kevin Pietersen's 158 allowing them to declare on 551 for six. During Pietersen's innings, Warne was reduced to bowling defensively into the rough outside leg stump; he ended the innings with figures of one for 167.

Look at that timid little creature Ian Bell

Ricky Ponting was dropped early in his innings, a relatively straightforward chance for a fielder as good as Ashley Giles, and went on to make another century. 'You can't bring it back. . . it's gone,' said Giles. 'I'll just spend the next twenty years worrying about it.'

Australia reached 513 and left England facing a tricky stick-or-twist session on the fourth evening. When they got through that for the loss of only their young opener Alastair Cook, the match was all but over with a day to spare.

The final morning began serenely. And then it happened: a collapse as shocking and resounding as any in English cricket history. It started when Warne got a dodgy decision against Strauss, fortune favouring the knave again; then Bell was needlessly run out, and then Pietersen – who had released a book a couple of months earlier in which he said it was impossible for him to be bowled round his legs by Warne – was bowled round his legs by Warne.

That was the moment a walk in the park became a desperate fight for survival. England were rendered strokeless by the situation, not to mention by the wiles of Warne and the reverse swing of Brett Lee. They could barely score a run, and endured the slowest of tortures before eventually being dismissed for a paltry 129 in 73 overs just before tea.

Warne took a respectable four wickets rather than a hatful, but his figures do not reflect his impact. He got inside the England batsmen's heads to such an extent that he dictated the events of an extra-ordinary day. Australia, left to chase an ostensibly tricky target of 168 against the clock, knocked the runs off with contemptuous ease.

I find it difficult to describe just how pissed off I felt

One moment England were 1–0 down in the series, and expecting to have had the better of a draw at Adelaide; the next it was 2–0 and they were mentally shattered. 'I find it difficult to describe just how pissed off I felt,' said Hoggard. 'It changed the lives and careers of quite a few people, especially me,' said the England coach Duncan Fletcher, who resigned a few months later.

After Adelaide, it was somehow inevitable that McGrath's prediction would come to pass. England started the third Test at Perth well, but were eventually overwhelmed. Adam Gilchrist, no longer in Flintoff's pocket, smacked a staggering century from 57 balls in Australia's second-innings 527 for five.

Flintoff fell to earth spectacularly during the series. He struggled with bat and ball, suffered from depression and found solace in the bottle. Matters came to a head at the World Cup soon afterwards when he capsized a pedalo in the small hours.

The struggles of England's younger players, including Bell, Cook and Jimmy Anderson, were almost as dramatic. Bell played well at times, hitting four half-centuries and using his feet confidently against Warne, yet in Australian eyes he symbolised England's eternal mental fragility. 'Look at that timid little creature Ian Bell,' said the former Australian batsman Stuart Law.

Warne wrote his own script on Boxing Day, taking his 700th Test wicket in front of his home crowd. A now rampant Australia won the fourth Test by an innings and 99 runs, and the first whitewash since 1920–21 was completed at the SCG. It was the final Test for Warne and McGrath, two men who were the definition of the word 'champion'. They saved one of their greatest tricks for last. As they walked off the ground, arms round each other's shoulders, even thousands of Poms had a lump in their throat.

Glenn McGrath and Shane Warne leave the field at the end of their final Test match for Australia; fifth Test, Sydney, 5 January 2007.

2009

'Not another one!'

[MARK KERMODE, DURING HIS FILM
REVIEW ON BBC FIVE LIVE, AS ANOTHER
AUSTRALIAN WICKET FALLS,
FIFTH TEST, THE OVAL,
21 AUGUST 2009]

AS HE SENT THE BALL DOWN JUST outside off stump, Stuart Broad
had no idea that, in sporting terms, he was about to become a man.
Ricky Ponting, the Australian captain, tried to force the ball through
the off side, and dragged it back onto his stumps. At a key moment of
an Ashes decider, Broad had taken the most important wicket of his
life. A week earlier, many in the media wanted him to be dropped;
two weeks later he was a guest on *The Jonathan Ross Show*.

Ponting's wicket was the second of five in a life-changing spell on
the Friday afternoon at The Oval. He and Graeme Swann struck
so regularly that the BBC's film reviewer Mark Kermode, who was
doing his show with Simon Mayo live from The Oval, became sick of
being interrupted as he offered his acerbic opinions on *Dance Flick*
and *I Love You, Beth Morris*.

The dramatic swing in Broad's fortunes was an apt reflection of a
tempestuous 2009 series which, while not always high on quality,
was consistently thrilling. England were tentatively rebuilding under
their new management team of Andrew Strauss and Andy Flower,
having been humiliated in the Caribbean when they were bowled
out for 51 a few months earlier. Since the previous Ashes, Australia
had lost almost half a team of greats, including McGrath, Warne,
Gilchrist and Hayden. Despite losing a series at home for the first
time in sixteen years when South Africa triumphed in 2008–09,

2005 AND ALL THAT   317

they were clinging on to their official No.1 world ranking by their fingertips. They were particularly struggling to replace Shane Warne. 'I expect all of the English batsmen to target me pretty heavily,' said the off-spinner Nathan Hauritz before the series. 'I would, if I was facing me.'

English hopes of a close series looked misplaced when Australia completely dominated the first Test. Hundreds from Simon Katich, Ponting, Marcus North and the new wicketkeeper Brad Haddin took them to 674 for six, a lead of 239. On a nerve-shredding final day, England lost wickets at regular intervals until an improbable last-wicket partnership between Jimmy Anderson and Monty Panesar saved the game. 'I wouldn't have given 'em tuppence!' shrieked the Sky commentator David Lloyd.

The pair survived 11.3 overs, and the situation became tinged with farce when England, in an attempt to waste time, sent their physio onto the field with no specified purpose. He was Steve McCaig, a large Australian whose hero was Ricky Ponting. 'What the f*** are you doing here?' were Ponting's first words to his No.1 fan. Never cheat your heroes.

What the f*** are you doing here?

Before the second Test at Lord's, Andrew Flintoff announced his decision to retire from Test cricket at the end of the series because of his increasing injury problems. 'I was having problems dressing myself,' he said later. He undressed Australia on the final day in the second Test at Lord's, producing one last demonstration of his greatness. The captain Strauss had set the tone with a brilliant 161 on the first day, and England took a huge first-innings lead. Eventually Australia were left to chase 522; they recovered from 128 for five to end day four on 313 for five, with Michael Clarke and Haddin playing beautifully. On the last morning, Flintoff took four of the last five wickets in an immense, extended spell of fast bowling to bring England victory by 115 runs. The messianic pose he assumed after his fifth wicket, that of Peter Siddle, felt pretty apt.

The third Test was a rain-affected draw, though Graham Onions and Graeme Swann both had moments to tell the grandchildren. Onions dismissed Shane Watson and Michael Hussey with the first two balls of the second day, while Swann bowled Ponting through the gate in classical style to conclude a wonderful over on the fourth evening.

England went to Headingley for the fourth Test knowing they were one win or two draws away from regaining the Ashes. They had got hopelessly ahead of themselves, and were effectively beaten by Friday afternoon – a particularly ignominious state of affairs given that the match started on the Friday, rather than Thursday as was usually the case before the advent of back-to-back Tests.

An overnight fire alarm, the controversial omission of the unfit Flintoff and a fitness scare over the wicketkeeper Matt Prior contributed to a scrambled start from England, who were bowled out for 102 and thrashed by an innings. Stuart Clark, restored to the Australian side, bowled immaculately. The *Mirror* launched into England's 'FREDLESS CHICKENS'.

The decider at The Oval brought intriguing selections on both sides; England replaced the struggling Ravi Bopara with Jonathan Trott, who became the first England debutant in an Ashes decider since the nineteenth century; Australia omitted the spinner Nathan Hauritz despite a dusty wicket.

England's 332 seemed around par – until Broad, on that giddy Friday afternoon, reduced Australia from 73 for none to 111 for seven and then 160 all out. For most of the series Broad's pretty features and long blond hair had been ridiculed by the Australian fans, who sang 'Dude (Looks Like a Lady)' by Aerosmith every time he fielded near them. But he had the last laugh with the spell that decided the series. There was a bit of luck involved, too; Broad later wrote that the key wicket of Ponting came from a delivery that slipped out of his hand and landed far shorter than he had wanted. The sense of a life-changing spell was confirmed when Broad picked up his mobile phone at the end of the day's play, switched it on and watched it fire seventy-five messages of congratulations at him.

Trott, who played with indecent composure to make 119 on debut, pushed home England's advantage to such an extent that Strauss was able to declare and set Australia a target of 546. It seemed impossible on a pitch that had started crumbling on day two, but at

217 for two, with Ponting starting to put together one of his defiant masterpieces and with a day and a half's play remaining, thoughts of an astonishing victory entered some minds – and not just optimistic Australian ones. Then Mike Hussey took a sharp single to mid-on. It seemed safe, given that the fielder was the crocked Flintoff. But in one lumbering movement, Flintoff ran round the ball, picked up and whistled a direct hit to run out Ponting. It was a shoo-in for Test Match Special's champagne moment. 'If I had known you got a bottle of champagne for run-outs I would have practised more!' said Flintoff.

When we were bad we were awful, but when we were good we managed to be just good enough

The wicket broke Australia, and England regained the Ashes later that day. Australia had dominated the series for large parts, but two Friday afternoon batting collapses at Lord's and The Oval were decisive. 'When we were bad we were awful, but when we were good we managed to be just good enough,' said the England captain Andrew Strauss. It was largely an apt summary of the series, though Strauss got one thing wrong. On the second day at The Oval, England, and especially Broad, were exceptional. Just ask Mark Kermode.

2010–11

'Stop the clocks! Hold the front pages! Shout it from the rooftops! Australia are in utter disarray.'

[THE *GUARDIAN*'S ANDY BULL LIVEBLOGS THE DRAMATIC START TO THE SECOND TEST AT ADELAIDE, 3 DECEMBER 2010]

THE DELIVERY TEMPTED MICHAEL CLARKE like a femme fatale. He knew what he wanted to do was risky; he also knew it was irresistible. The ball from James Anderson was full, right in the slot to drive; to drive through the covers and begin to reassert Australia's authority after a desperate start to the match. Clarke had only a split-second to instinctively process all those thoughts and plenty more. He threw his hands into the drive with such vigour that, when the ball started to swing, it was too late for him to soften his hands. He edged the ball to slip, and England whooped and hollered like they had never whooped and hollered before. 'To say I was happy,' said Anderson, 'would be one of the understatements of the decade.' Australia were two for three on one of the best batting pitches in the world.

For the second time in a week, it was as if an English computer nerd had hacked into all of Australia's electronic scoreboards. At Brisbane it read that England were 517 for one. Now Australia were two for three at Adelaide. Later in the match, as England passed 600 with ease, the former Australian leg-spinner Kerry O'Keeffe suggested during his radio commentary that the scoreboard needed salt tablets because it was cramping up.

It was difficult to comprehend that an Australian cricket team could be in quite such disarray. Even during their chaotic build-up to the

Kevin Pietersen pulls a boundary during his Adelaide double-hundred, 4 December 2010. Mike Hussey looks on.

series, there was a sense that, this being Australia, it would probably be alright on the night. Australia named a seventeen-man squad for the first Test, whereas England's XI was obvious even before the tour started. Not that it impressed everyone. 'It should be the Empire XI,' said the former Australian captain Allan Border, referring to the fact that Kevin Pietersen, Jonathan Trott, Andrew Strauss and Matt Prior were all born in South Africa. 'They got any Poms in the side?'

For English fans, there was the sense that their ultra-smooth build-up had gone too well. This lot had only three virtues: they could bat, they could bowl, and they could field, and the precedent of 1986–87 (see page 218) suggested that might not necessarily be a good thing.

The captain Andrew Strauss was out to the third ball of the first Test at Brisbane, and a poor first day for England suggested the series might go the way of all the others in Australia in modern times. Peter Siddle, on his twenty-sixth birthday, took a hat-trick as England were bowled out for 260. Australia built a huge lead thanks to centuries from Mike Hussey and Brad Haddin, despite some excellent bowling from Anderson and Stuart Broad in particular. They somehow picked up only two wickets between them, while the less impressive Steven Finn made off with a six-for.

England, trailing by 221 on first innings, had a serious scare when Strauss offered no stroke to the first ball of the second innings and just about survived an lbw referral. Strauss went on to score 110, and then Alastair Cook and Jonathan Trott set about the kind of partnership that has everyone reaching for their *Wisdens*. Cook made 235 not out and Trott 135 not out in a partnership of 329. England declared on 517 for one; few Australians or Englishmen could recall ever seeing such a Himalayan score.

It should be the Empire XI. They got any Poms in the side?

And they saw a pretty unusual one a few days later when Australia were reduced two for three at the start of the second Test at Adelaide. In response to Australia's below-par 245, England simply continued the run feast they had started in their second innings at Brisbane. By the time he had made 136 not out at the end of the second day, Cook – whose very place in the side had been questioned the previous summer – had made 371 runs without being dismissed in 1022 minutes of play. Pietersen stormed his way to 227, during which he manhandled Australia's left-arm spinner Xavier Doherty into a two-year Test match exile. England declared at 620 for five.

Pietersen also took the vital wicket of Michael Clarke with the final ball of the fourth day's play, at a time when Australia were fighting hard for a draw. England wrapped up a thumping innings victory on the final morning, with Graeme Swann taking five for 91 in the second innings. Anderson's match figures of six for 143 did not do justice to another wonderful performance. But the memories of the moment he dismissed Clarke, and reduced Australia to two for three, will last forever.

2010–11

'Why aren't you chirping now, mate? Not getting wickets?'

[MITCHELL JOHNSON TO
JIMMY ANDERSON, THIRD TEST,
PERTH, 16 DECEMBER 2010]

JIMMY ANDERSON DELIVERED THE ultimate conversational put-down without saying a word. Seconds after Mitchell Johnson wondered why Anderson had nothing to say to the Australian batsmen, he bowled Ryan Harris with a beauty. Anderson turned round to Johnson, spread his arms in triumph and pointedly kept his mouth shut. It was a reflection of England's almost embarrassing superiority. Even one of Australia's oldest friends, the well-timed sledge, was letting them down. They were 201 for eight on the first day of the third Test at Perth, and in significant danger of losing the Ashes with two matches to spare.

They had made a number of changes to their side: Johnson and Ben Hilfenhaus, dropped for the second Test, returned in place of Doug Bollinger and the Pietersen-damaged Xavier Doherty. The young batsmen Steve Smith and Phil Hughes replaced Marcus North and Simon Katich. England were far more settled, and their only change was enforced: with Stuart Broad injured, Chris Tremlett came in for his first Test since 2007.

Tremlett and England started the third Test excellently and, as at Adelaide, dismissed Australia cheaply on the first day. At one stage the Aussies were 137 for six; even their recovery to 268 did not seem a problem. Not for a side who, in their previous two innings, had scored 1137 runs for the loss of six wickets.

The continuation of Ricky Ponting's poor form, when he was caught wonderfully by a flying Paul Collingwood for 12, aptly reflected the status of the two sides. When England proceeded easily to 78 for none on the second morning, knowing that a win would mean they retained the Ashes with two matches to spare, Australia were sucking on a lemon in the last-chance saloon. Then Johnson started swinging.

With the ball beginning to shape back into the right-handers, an uncontrollable phenomenon that makes Johnson nigh-on unplayable, he shredded England's top order: Jonathan Trott, Kevin Pietersen and Collingwood were all lbw to deliveries that tailed back in, and England lost five wickets for 20 in eight overs. It was a stunning twist, and a reminder of Johnson's enormous unpredictability.

After a brief recovery, Matt Prior was bounced out by Peter Siddle and, according to reports at the time, suggested the pair should settle their differences in a manner not found in the MCC coaching manual. In his autobiography, *The Gloves are Off*, Prior denies offering Siddle a fight, though reports at the time said he was overheard suggesting they go outside.

England, so serene a few hours earlier, had lost their heads. Johnson finished with six for 38, a spectacular return to form. Mike Hussey, in the form of his life, rammed home Australia's advantage with another century. England collapsed again second time round, this time for 123, with Harris – a supremely skilful fast bowler seizing the chance of a Test career in the evening of his playing days – taking six for 47. As was often the case with Andy Flower's England, a fast pitch had been their total undoing. They had been well and truly duffed up on the Perth trampoline. Only forty-eight hours earlier they were in total charge of the series, and on the brink of retaining the Ashes. Now it was 1–1 with two to play, and it was Australia who were chirping.

2010–11

> 'He bowls to the left,
> he bowls to the right.
> That Mitchell Johnson,
> his bowling is shite.'

[THE BARMY ARMY, PASSIM]

MITCHELL JOHNSON WOULD RATHER HAVE been anywhere else on the planet. It was near the end of play on day four of the final Test at Sydney and Australia were facing an almost unprecedented humiliation at English hands. Johnson had to walk out to bat and face a fired-up Chris Tremlett, not to mention thousands of England fans who had taken almighty pleasure in his poor form since the third Test at Perth.

As Johnson entered the pitch, the crowd started singing their paean to his bowling. Even Kevin Pietersen joined in at mid-off. Tremlett galumphed in to wild cheers – and bowled Johnson first ball. 'What a nut!' screamed the commentator David Lloyd on Sky. For England, it was the arguably the champagne moment in a series full of them.

The extent of England's dominance had seemed impossible two weeks earlier. The Boxing Day Test at the MCG began with the series 1–1, and the momentum with Australia after their victory at the WACA. England won the toss and, after plenty of deliberation given how badly the decision had gone at Perth, decided to bowl first.

What followed has a strong case for being the greatest day in modern English cricket history. Australia were bowled out for 98, as batsman after batsman obligingly snicked outswingers to Matt Prior, the towering Tremlett, Anderson and Bresnan sharing the wickets, and

England then finished on 157 for none. The Ashes were effectively decided in a single day's play. In icy England, cricket fans awoke to a blissful dawn, relishing the turning of the tide after so many winters of Ashes discontent.

Jonathan Trott's unbeaten 168 took England to 513, an unimaginable lead of 415, and then England got into their work on a flat pitch. Bresnan, brought in to replace Steven Finn, who was the leading wicket-taker thus far in the series but deemed too expensive by England, gave a superb demonstration of reverse swing to take four for 50.

It was Bresnan who took the decisive wicket when Ben Hilfenhaus was caught behind. Australia were thrashed by an innings and 157 runs in little over three days. England cavorted joyously around the MCG, and celebrated by demonstrating their infectiously naff 'sprinkler dance' (see below).

For a cricketer, defeating Australia is the equivalent of a rock band cracking America; even though they went to No.1 in the ICC Test rankings by thrashing India 4–0 the following summer, and won the World Twenty20 in 2010, this was the defining triumph of Andy

Graeme Swann leads the 'sprinkler dance' after England's victory in the fourth Test at Melbourne, 29 December 2010.

Flower's England side. It had been planned like a military campaign. Coaches normally talk about the '1 percenters' that make a difference; in 2010–11, England took care of the 0.00001 percenters.

It was the first time England had won the Ashes in Australia since 1986–87, and a more mature companion piece to the wonderful melodrama of 2005. This time, England were far better than Australia, and they confirmed as much in the final Test at Sydney by making it 3–1 with their third innings victory. English delight at the series' outcome was intensified by the sheer scale of their victory. Johnson's ambush at the WACA excepted, Australia had been royally stuffed by Strauss's men.

Alastair Cook's 189 completed a monumental series in which he scored 766 runs, the second highest total by an Englishman in an Ashes series after Wally Hammond in 1928–29 (see pages 59–61). There were also centuries for Ian Bell and Matt Prior as England racked up another huge score, 644 this time. England averaged 51.14 runs per wicket over the five Tests, their highest in any Ashes series. 'They've really showed us how to bat in Test match cricket,' said Ricky Ponting. 'They've out-batted us, out-bowled us and pretty much out-fielded us right the way through the series.'

Anderson took seven wickets to complete an outstanding performance, which obliterated the pre-series perception that he needed helpful bowling conditions to be truly effective. On flat pitches, Anderson had become a master of 'bowling dry': denying impatient batsmen the oxygen of runs with tight bowling and passive-aggressive fielding. 'Areas is the way forward,' said Anderson's new-ball partner Stuart Broad, who missed the last three Tests because of injury, of the approach that served Flower's England so well for so long. If England bowled dry, then Australia's attack – and particularly Johnson – leaked runs.

In the delirium of their Ashes triumph at Sydney, England players and fans could hardly be expected to have glimpsed a shadow, the size of a giant Western Australian bowler's left mitt, moving slowly towards the brightly shining sun. . .

2013

'I hope the public get stuck into him. That was blatant cheating.'

[DARREN LEHMANN ON STUART BROAD'S DECISION NOT TO WALK DURING THE FIRST TEST, TRENT BRIDGE, 16 JULY 2013]

IT WAS THE SORT OF MOMENT FOR which the Decision Review System was invented. Stuart Broad had obviously edged Ashton Agar to slip, via the body of the wicketkeeper Brad Haddin, yet Aleem Dar had given him not out. Broad was standing his ground. Then it suddenly dawned on Australia: the DRS was not an option because they had frivolously used both their reviews earlier in the day. On the third evening of the first Test at Trent Bridge, the 2013 Ashes series had its defining event.

Australia bristled with injustice, even more so as Broad moved towards an important 65. The fuss over Broad's non-walking was a strange one given that scarcely anybody in cricket walked anyway, least of all Australian batsmen. Australia cited the obviousness of the snick, with some disingenuously pointing out that it went to first slip – but it only got there via a deflection off Haddin. In fifty years' time, the story will probably be told that Broad middled one to cover, refused to walk and then punched Agar in the face.

It all had the feel of a media construction, or perhaps a social-media construction. Before the return series in 2013–14, the Australian coach Darren Lehmann suggested Australian fans should attempt to reduce Broad to tears with their barracking.

Lehmann came in as Australian coach just before the first of the two back-to-back series, when Mickey Arthur was surprisingly sacked. Australia were dismissed as a rabble. They had just lost 4–0 in India, during which four of their players were banned from a Test for failing to complete a homework 'assignment' set by Arthur. One of those, the pugnacious opener David Warner, was then banned from the first Test in England by his own board after punching England's young batsman Joe Root in a Birmingham bar.

England, despite losing their place at No.1 in the world to South Africa by losing to them at home in 2012, had won outstandingly in India the previous winter and retained their authority under the new captain Alastair Cook. Sir Ian Botham raised Glenn McGrath's traditional prediction (see page 309), suggesting England would win the back-to-back series 10–0.

The first Test at Trent Bridge was an unexpected epic, with more incident in five days than there are in most five-Test series. The eighteen-year-old Agar, batting at No.11 on his Test debut, stroked an astonishing 98 to take Australia from 117 for nine to 280 all out, a lead of 65. Agar's score was the highest by a No.11 batsman in a Test, and his ninth-wicket partnership of 163 with Phillip Hughes was also a record.

Ian Bell's exceptional 109, on a pitch where no batsmen was truly 'in', and Broad's controversial innings enabled England to set Australia a target of 311. The match seemed over at 231 for nine after a brilliant performance from James Anderson; then, in an echo of Edgbaston 2005, Australia's last pair gave England a collective Sunday-morning coronary. Brad Haddin and James Pattinson put on 65 before Haddin was given out caught behind off Anderson after a review. England won a thriller by 14 runs and Anderson, with five wickets in each innings, had produced a career-defining performance.

Had this match been a series decider it would be regarded as one of the greatest ever played. Instead, harshly, it has been a little forgotten because of what followed. England romped to victory by 347 runs at Lord's, where Root made 180 and Australia's performance plumbed new depths. Cliché says that things are darkest before the dawn, and, in retrospect, the Lord's débâcle could be seen as the moment that Australia began to turn things round.

Even though their hopes of regaining the Ashes were over after the drawn third Test at Old Trafford, they completely dominated the match. Michael Clarke's 187 was the bedrock of Australia's imposing 527 for seven; while Pietersen's studious 113 was his twenty-third hundred for England, who were probably saved by the rain. Australia should have won the fourth Test at Chester-le-Street, but were overwhelmed by one of Broad's hot spells on the fourth evening. He took six for 50 as the Aussies lost their last eight wickets for 56 to lose by 74 runs.

With the Ashes long gone, the series became a kind of public-relations war, with criticism of England's perceived negativity and aloofness, and Clarke's 'funky fields' celebrated by all. The fifth Test at The Oval, in which the Lancashire left-arm spinning debutant Simon Kerrigan had a meltdown with the ball, was a strange match in that Australia were the dominant side yet England should have won. Clarke declared in both innings, the second time more of a county declaration than a Test match one, setting England 227 in 44 overs. They were well on course after a lordly 66 from Pietersen, and required just 21 from 24 balls when bad light ended the match and the series.

England had won 3–0, yet there was a powerful sense that one side was on the up and the other on the way down. There was a feeling before the return series that they would meet in the middle and produce a classic, hard-fought contest. It did not exactly pan out like that.

MITCHELL JOHNSON WAITED AT THE END of his mark. And waited some more. James Anderson, the batsman in his sights, moved out of his crease to prepare himself for the imminent assault. As he did so, he began to exchange unpleasantries with George Bailey, Australia's short leg. Michael Clarke, the Australian captain, walked towards the incident and was met halfway by Anderson, where they had a full and frank exchange of views. After a few seconds, Clarke began to walk backwards to his position and uttered the words that would shape an Ashes series.

Clarke's threat to Anderson, which was picked up by the stump mic, cost him 20 per cent of his match fee. It was worth every penny. It changed the way he was perceived by many among the Australian public; more importantly, it told England that Australia would stop at almost nothing to regain the Ashes. They were about to go 1–0 up in the series, and Clarke sensed the opportunity to score some points for the four remaining Tests.

The tenor of the contest had changed so much from the previous series that Clarke wanted to ram home the point that England were now on Australia's manor, and were playing by their rules. It might have backfired; Anderson might have taken ten-for in the next Test, but Clarke's instinct told him that England were vulnerable.

Shane Warne later said that the stump mic was switched off – but still accessible for the commentators – seconds earlier when Anderson told Bailey that he wanted to punch him in the face. 'Anderson brought it on himself,' said the Australian bowler Peter Siddle after the game, without going into specifics. 'So fair's fair.'

If England are expecting the old Mitchell Johnson to walk out onto the pitch, they're in for a big shock

Australia's pre-series promise of aggression had been largely ignored by England. They heard the spook stories about a revitalised Johnson and hostile crowds, smiled politely and satisfied themselves there was nothing to worry about. They had won the summer series 3–0 without being at their best; just imagine what would happen when they hit top form. The impression was that England thought Australia were full of hot air and bluster. Many in the English media adhered to

James Anderson and Michael Clarke exchange words on day four of the first Test, Brisbane; 24 November 2013.

that view, predicting a comfortable win for the tourists. Things were so bad for Australia that even Glenn McGrath did not predict a 5–0 whitewash, though he did say they would win the series and warned that 'If England are expecting the old Mitchell Johnson to walk out onto the pitch, they're in for a big shock.'

The first day of the series only seemed to confirm England's superiority: Australia were picked apart by Stuart Broad, who walked into the press conference pointedly holding a copy of the Brisbane *Courier Mail* that had attempted to demonize him for not walking in England during the previous series (see page 329). In reply to Australia's 295, England reached 82 for two. The flustered manner of Jonathan Trott's dismissal to Johnson was disconcerting, but no more than that. Broadly speaking, things were going to plan.

Then England turned the corner and were caught a glancing blow by a swinging axe. It takes years to build a very good cricket team, and an hour to destroy it. That's how long it took for England to slip from 82 for two to 91 for eight in a jaw-dropping collapse. Six wickets for nine runs, but this was not tailenders being destroyed by reverse swing or uneven bounce: the men out were Michael Carberry, Kevin Pietersen, Ian Bell, Matt Prior, Joe Root and Graeme Swann. All six could bat, and the pitch was essentially flat. Only three of those six wickets went to Johnson, yet his pace unquestionably sparked the mayhem.

After England were dismissed for 136, aggressive centuries from David Warner and Clarke allowed Australia to declare at 401 for seven and set England a target of 561. They were routed for 179, with Johnson taking five more wickets. That included Trott, who looked horribly unsettled as he made nine in the second innings. Johnson had got inside his head first, during the one-day series in England between the back-to-back Ashes, and now he was about to get inside everyone else's.

Johnson ended the match with figures of nine for 103. His performance was not just about pace. He peaked at around 95mph, but there have been faster in recent times. Johnson had something just as important as pace, however: force, which overwhelmed England from the first innings of the series at Brisbane.

He took four for 61 in that innings. Good figures, no more than that, but the manner in which he did so – particularly the way he harassed Trott and the lower order – traumatised England. The phrase 'shock bowler' has become a cliché for those who bowl short, sharp spells, but Johnson fulfilled the role in the truest sense. An experienced, battle-hardened side were so shocked that they never recovered. Before he was a shock bowler, Johnson had been not a stock bowler but a laughing stock, certainly to the Barmy Army.

The team which played that first Test were the second most experienced in England's history. They had 649 caps and around 649GB of data based on those appearances and on study of the Australians. This was a grizzled, gnarled team, who thought they had seen everything and were prepared for anything. They had no idea. No computer could have prepared them for the way Johnson spooked them. He no longer bowled to the left and the right; he bowled at the stumps and the head. Modern batsmen, not just England's, were lulled into a false sense of security by years of mollycoddling; when they were then exposed to extreme pace and aggression, they had about as much idea how to survive as rich kids dropped into the meanest streets of the Bronx.

Everybody has a plan, until they get punched in the face

Johnson's impact was similar to that of the West Indian quicks in the 1980s – but there were four of them. He had emphatically got his mojo back, and a combination of his surname and Movember moustache made MoJo an inevitable nickname. And though he never appeared with a low-buttoned shirt exposing enormous clumps of chest hair, his moustache was an inadvertent tribute to the hirsute brutes of 1974–75, the last time England were assaulted so extremely in Australia.

The *Guardian*'s Andy Bull, in reference to Johnson's impact, cited the old Mike Tyson line: 'Everybody has a plan, until they get punched in the face.' Bull's *Guardian* colleague Mike Selvey referred to Johnson's as 'bare-knuckle bowling'. And yet in this game there was no merciful knockout or stoppage. England had to continue to take the blows for five whole Test matches.

2013–14

'It does look like they have scared eyes, and the way Trotty got out was pretty poor and weak.'

[DAVID WARNER, FIRST TEST, BRISBANE, 23 NOVEMBER 2013]

FOR A SPLIT-SECOND IT LOOKED PERFECT. Jonathan Trott flick-pulled Mitchell Johnson off the hip so languidly that the ball seemed to have gone exactly where he wanted. But that burgeoning thought was quickly shattered by a collective shout of 'catch!' The ball flew straight into the hands of Nathan Lyon at deep backward square leg, and Trott had failed once more against his new nemesis. England's most reliable, secure cricketer had turned into a fly-by-night who couldn't stand the heat.

Trott's second failure of the first Test came just before the close of the third day's play. At the press conference a few minutes later, the Australian opener David Warner put the boot in in his inimitable style. When Trott then flew home with what was described as a 'stress-related illness', Warner was heavily criticised. That seemed a little disingenuous – unless Warner knew about Trott's illness, his comments were legitimate trash talk.

The departure of Trott, and the way in which he was harassed by Johnson, symbolised the dramatic change of fortune. He had been England's implacable No.3, who made runs in all weathers against all bowlers, including bucketloads in Australia in 2010–11. Johnson reduced him to a scatterbrained mess at the crease. Trott's departure hit England extremely hard, both on a human and a professional level. If Trott was vulnerable, all bets were off and nobody was safe.

As the series developed, England acquired the glazed look of trauma victims, all kitted out with million-yard stares. With the Tests so close together – they needed ten months after the first Test at Brisbane to process what had happened, not ten days – they were unable to recover from that inaugural shock. The second Test at Adelaide was another drubbing, this time by 218 runs, though in reality the margin of victory was much greater: Australia declared in both innings and only lost 12 wickets in the match. Clarke made another hundred, and the wicketkeeper Brad Haddin tucked into Graeme Swann on the way to a rapid century.

They led by 398 on first innings after Johnson scorched England with figures of seven for 40 on a slow pitch, including the wickets of Ben Stokes, Matt Prior and Stuart Broad in one awesowe over. He was too fast, too straight, too much. Before then there was the lingering hope for England that Brisbane might have been a miserable one-off, like Perth four years earlier (see pages 324–25); one hour of Johnson at Adelaide – in which they collapsed from 111 for three to 135 for nine – confirmed that he had set up camp in their subconscious. Dennis Lillee's comment a decade before that Johnson was a 'once-in-a-generation bowler' suddenly made perfect sense. The England lower order, in particular, were terrorised by Johnson.

Australia regained the Ashes at the earliest opportunity by winning the third Test at Perth with their most brutal all-round display yet. The batsmen, taking Johnson's lead, assaulted England's bowlers, hitting fifteen sixes in the match. In the second innings, as they set up yet another declaration, Shane Watson hit Swann into retirement while George Bailey took a Test-record-equalling 28 off one over from Anderson, a metaphorical punch in the face if ever there was one. Warner made another century, and reversed the usual rules of sledging during it by openly ridiculing the wicketkeeper Matt Prior for missing a stumping chance. A stirring maiden Test century from the young all-rounder Ben Stokes was England's only consolation. He was the only England batsman to average as much as 30 in the series.

Swann retired from all cricket after the game, citing his ever-worsening elbow injury, while Prior was dropped. He had been

England's Player of the Year only seven months earlier. There were also increasing whispers about the role of Kevin Pietersen, who was heavily criticised for some of his dismissals during the series – not least being caught at long on when England were theoretically trying to save the Perth Test. At the end of the series, Pietersen was effectively sacked by England, the start of an increasingly tedious public slanging match between him and the ECB.

Swann said England had been 'arse raped', attracting no little criticism for his choice of metaphor. Prior said they 'finished third in a two-horse race'. The extent of the devastation will never truly make sense. This was one of England's finest sides, dismantled mercilessly by a very good but not great Australian side. And they were probably the most stable side England had ever had, with a core of eight senior players. Selection meetings were a formality. Then, after a few weeks of mayhem, the selectors had to find almost an entirely new team.

2013–14

'We've f****** got 'em back!'

[BRAD HADDIN AFTER AUSTRALIA
REGAINED THE ASHES WITH
VICTORY IN THE THIRD TEST AT
PERTH, 17 DECEMBER 2013]

IT HAD BEEN A SERIOUSLY LONG TIME COMING. The Ashes had been in England's possession for 1577 days when, on the final day of the third Test at Perth, Mitchell Johnson rammed in a short ball that James Anderson could only fend to short leg. Australia had regained the urn with the most comprehensive demolition job it was possible to recall. As the players celebrated in a huddle out in the middle at Perth, one voice was heard above the others on the stump mic: 'We've f****** got 'em back!'

It's not clear which player was responsible for that joyous shriek, though Brad Haddin gave the pre-watershed version of the quote when he was interviewed a few minutes earlier. Even for someone in his career dotage like Haddin, this represented fulfilment. Of the Australian team, only the captain Michael Clarke had previously won an Ashes series.

After regaining the urn, they turned their attention to an even rarer feat: trying to secure only the third Ashes whitewash. It was pretty clear from early in the series that, while England had not suffered a broken f****** arm, their spirit had been smashed to smithereens by Johnson and friends. They could not even get up for the two dead rubbers at the end of the series, so often England's best chance in recent Ashes contests. Stuart Broad – the only England player to emerge from the series in credit apart from Ben Stokes – and Anderson secured an unlikely first-innings lead in the Boxing Day

Mitchell Johnson bowls to Michael Carberry on the first day of the fourth Test match; Melbourne, 26 December 2013.

Test at the MCG, but another miserable collapse proved decisive. England lost their last five wickets for six runs to Nathan Lyon and Johnson, and Australia eased to a target of 231 to win by eight wickets. Chris Rogers – the quiet achiever of the Australian side, who was the highest scorer on either side across the ten Ashes Tests of 2013–14 – shepherded the run-chase with a fine century.

Australia were in early trouble in the last Test at Sydney, reduced to 97 for five. As so often in the series, Haddin got them out of trouble with a furious counter-attack from No.7. He made 75, while the fast-improving Steve Smith played beautifully for his second century of the series in a total of 326. Haddin, at the age of thirty-six, had the best series of his career: he ended with 493 runs at 61.62 and routinely rescued Australia from a first-innings score of around 150 for five with strokeplay of such authority that it soon became self-perpetuating.

England made 155 in reply – a triumph given that they were 23 for five at one stage. By now the batsmen had almost completely given up bar the impressive, feisty Stokes. In the second innings, facing a nominal target of 448, England lasted a pathetic 31.4 overs. Effectively, they were bowled out twice in a day during the match; both their innings combined lasted exactly 90 overs. I'm an England cricketer, get me out of here.

Australia, you f****** beauty!

Australia just wanted to stay where they were, out in the middle of the SCG, singing their team song. Lyon did not know the stump mic was still on. Even if he had known, he probably wouldn't have cared. 'Australia, you f****** beauty!' he shouted. Australia, a team who were widely ridiculed only a few months earlier, had completed only the third-ever Ashes whitewash.

Their XI, unchanged throughout the series, had achieved immortality. In future years, this will be the answer to a popular trivia question: Warner, Rogers, Watson, Clarke, Smith, Bailey, Haddin, Johnson, Siddle, Harris, Lyon. They were the team who played all five Tests.

They should really be known as the Mental Disintegrators. This was the definitive example of mental disintegration, beyond even

Steve Waugh's most sadistic dreams. Johnson was the main weapon, of course, but Ryan Harris (22 wickets at 19.31) and Peter Siddle (16 at 24.12) gave him outstanding support with bowling of such aggressive accuracy that at times England had to beg, steal or borrow almost every run. Pietersen said it was the best collective bowling performance he had ever faced.

With the bat, David Warner and Haddin in particular captured the mood of merciless enforcement. After the series, Haddin praised a return to an 'Australian type of cricket'. If in doubt, take the attacking option. If not in doubt, ask yourself whether you should be in doubt. Australia hit 40 sixes, a world record for a Test series. This was one of the great thrashings: shocking in its scale, brutal in its manner, an assault without precedent in over 130 years of Ashes cricket. It was also a case of Australia emphatically reasserting the natural order of Ashes cricket. The little urn stays in the MCC museum, but even the most partisan Pom would have to concede that their spiritual home is in Australia. For now, at least, Australia have got 'em back.

APPENDIX

**THE ASHES
1882-2014**

THE ASHES 1882–2014

SERIES RESULTS AND LEADING BATSMEN AND BOWLERS

1882–83
Australia 1–2 England (3 Tests)
Captains
Aus: Billy Murdoch
Eng: Ivo Bligh
Most runs
Aus: Alec Bannerman 182 @ 36.40
Eng: Walter Read 210 @ 42.00
Most wickets
Aus: Joey Palmer 17 @ 16.82
Eng: Billy Bates 16 @ 13.12
A fourth Test was won by Australia, but the Ashes had been awarded to England after the third Test

1884
England 1–0 Australia (3)
Captains
Eng: A. N. Hornby and Lord Harris
(one and two Tests)
Aus: Billy Murdoch
Most runs
Eng: Allan Steel 212 @ 53.00
Aus: Billy Murdoch 266 @ 66.50.
Most wickets
Eng: George Ulyett 11 @ 17.63
Aus: Joey Palmer 14 @ 18.57

1884–85
Australia 2–3 England (5)
Captains
Aus: Billy Murdoch, Tom Horan,
Hugh Massie and Jack Blackham
(two Tests for Horan, one each for
Murdoch, Massie and Blackham)
Eng: Arthur Shrewsbury
Most runs
Aus: Percy McDonnell 230 @ 57.50
Eng: Billy Barnes 369 @ 52.71
Most wickets
Aus: Frederick Spofforth 19 @ 16.10
Eng: Bobby Peel 21 @ 21.47

1886
England 3–0 Australia (3)
Captains
Eng: Allan Steel
Aus: Henry Scott
Most runs
Eng: Arthur Shrewsbury 243 @
60.75
Aus: Sammy Jones 145 @ 24.16
Most wickets
Eng: Johnny Briggs 17 @ 7.76
Aus: Frederick Spofforth 14 @ 18.57

1886–87
Australia 0–2 England (2)
Captains
Aus: Percy McDonnell
Eng: Arthur Shrewsbury
Most runs
Aus: Harry Moses 116 @ 29.00
Eng: Dick Barlow 82 @ 27.33
Most wickets
Aus: J. J. Ferris 18 @ 13.50
Eng: George Lohmann 16 @ 8.56

1887–88
Australia 0–1 England (1)
Captains
Aus: Percy McDonnell
Eng: Walter Read
Most runs
Aus: Jack Blackham 27 @ 27.00
Eng: Arthur Shrewsbury 45 @ 22.50
Most wickets
Aus: Charlie Turner 12 @ 7.25
Eng: George Lohmann 9 @ 5.77

1888

England 2–1 Australia (3)
Captains
Eng: Allan Steel and W. G. Grace
(one and two Tests)
Aus: Percy McDonnell
Most runs
Eng: Billy Barnes 90 @ 22.50
Aus: Percy McDonnell @ 11.66
Most wickets
Eng: Bobby Peel 24 @ 7.54
Aus: Charlie Turner 21 @ 12.42

1890

England 2–0 Australia (3)
Captains
Eng: W. G. Grace
Aus: Billy Murdoch
Most runs
Eng: W. G. Grace 91 @ 30.33
Aus: John Lyons 122 @ 30.50
Most wickets
Eng: Fred Martin 12 @ 8.50
Aus: J. J. Ferris 13 @ 13.15

1891–92

Australia 2–1 England (3)
Captains
Aus: Jack Blackham
Eng: W. G. Grace
Most runs
Aus: John Lyons 287 @ 47.83
Eng: Andrew Stoddart 265 @ 53.00
Most wickets
Aus: Charlie Turner 16 @ 21.12
Eng: Johnny Briggs 17 @ 15.76

1893

England 1–0 Australia (3)
Captains
Eng: Andrew Stoddart and W. G.
Grace (one and two Tests)
Aus: Jack Blackham
Most runs
Eng: Arthur Shrewsbury 284 @
71.00
Aus: Harry Graham 170 @ 34.00
Most wickets
Eng: Johnny Briggs 16 @ 18.31
Aus: George Giffen 16 @ 21.37

1894–95

Australia 2–3 England (5)
Captains
Aus: Jack Blackham and George
Giffen (one and four Tests)
Eng: Andrew Stoddart
Most runs
Aus: George Giffen 475 @ 52.77
Eng: Albert Ward 419 @ 41.90
Most wickets
Aus: George Giffen 34 @ 24.11
Eng: Tom Richardson 32 @ 26.53

1896

England 2–1 Australia (3)
Captains
Eng: W. G. Grace
Aus: Harry Trott
Most runs
Eng: Kumar Ranjitsinhji 235 @ 78.33
Aus: Harry Trott 206 @ 34.33
Most wickets
Eng: Tom Richardson 24 @ 18.29
Aus: Hugh Trumble 18 @ 18.83

1897–98

Australia 4–1 England (5)
Captains
Aus: Harry Trott
Eng: Archie MacLaren and Andrew
Stoddart (three and two Tests)
Most runs
Aus: Joe Darling 537 @ 67.12
Eng: Archie MacLaren 488 @ 54.22
Most wickets
Aus: Ernie Jones 22 @ 25.13
Eng: Tom Richardson 22 @ 35.27

1899

England 0–1 Australia (5)
Captains
Aus: Joe Darling
Eng: W. G. Grace and Archie
MacLaren (one and four Tests)
Most runs
Eng: Tom Hayward 413 @ 68.83
Aus: Monty Noble 367 @ 52.42
Most wickets
Eng: Jack Hearne 13 @ 24.69,
Wilfred Rhodes 13 @ 26.23
Aus: Ernie Jones 26 @ 25.26

1901–02
Australia 4–1 England (5)
Captains
Aus: Joe Darling and Hugh Trumble (three and two Tests)
Eng: Archie MacLaren
Most runs
Aus: Clem Hill 512 @ 52.10
Eng: Archie MacLaren 412 @ 45.77
Most wickets
Aus: Monty Noble 32 @ 19.00
Eng: Len Braund 21 @ 35.14

1902
England 1–2 Australia (5)
Captains
Eng: Archie MacLaren
Aus: Joe Darling
Most runs
Eng: Stanley Jackson 311 @ 44.42
Aus: Clem Hill 258 @ 36.85
Most wickets
Eng: Wilfred Rhodes 22 @ 15.27
Aus: Hugh Trumble 26 @ 14.26

1903–04
Australia 2–3 England (5)
Captains
Aus: Monty Noble
Eng: Pelham Warner
Most runs
Aus: Victor Trumper 574 @ 63.77
Eng: Reginald 'Tip' Foster 486 @ 60.75
Most wickets
Aus: Hugh Trumble 24 @ 16.58
Eng: Wilfred Rhodes 31 @ 15.74

1905
England 2–0 Australia (5)
Captains
Eng: Stanley Jackson
Aus: Joe Darling
Most runs
Eng: Stanley Jackson 492 @ 70.28
Aus: Reggie Duff 335 @ 41.87
Most wickets
Eng: Walter Brearley 14 @ 19.78
Aus: Frank Laver 16 @ 31.87,
Warwick Armstrong 16 @ 33.62

1907–08
Australia 4–1 England (5)
Captains
Aus: Monty Noble
Eng: Frederick Fane and Arthur Jones (three and two Tests)
Most runs
Aus: Warwick Armstrong 410 @ 45.55
Eng: George Gunn 461 @ 52.33
Most wickets
Aus: Jack Saunders 31 @ 23.09
Eng: Jack Crawford 30 @ 24.73

1909
England 1–2 Australia (5)
Captains
Eng: Archie MacLaren
Aus: Monty Noble
Most runs
Eng: Jack Sharp 188 @ 47.00
Aus: Warren Bardsley 396 @ 39.60
Most wickets
Eng: Colin Blythe 18 @ 13.44
Aus: Albert 'Tibby' Cotter 17 @ 21.47

1911–12
Australia 1–4 England (5)
Captains
Aus: Clem Hill
Eng: Johnny Douglas
Most runs
Aus: Warwick Armstrong 324 @ 32.40
Eng: Jack Hobbs 662 @ 82.75
Most wickets
Aus: Herbert 'Ranji' Hordern 32 @ 24.37
Eng: Sydney Barnes 34 @ 22.88

England, Australia and South Africa took part in the Triangular Tournament of 1912, with England winning the tournament.

1920–21
Australia 5–0 England (5)
Captains
Aus: Warwick Armstrong
Eng: Johnny Douglas
Most runs
Aus: Herbie Collins 557 @ 61.88
Eng: Jack Hobbs 505 @ 50.50
Most wickets
Aus: Arthur Mailey 36 @ 26.27
Eng: 'Ciss' Parkin 16 @ 41.87

1921
England 0–3 Australia (5)
Captains
Eng: Johnny Douglas and Lord
Tennyson (two and three Tests)
Aus: Warwick Armstrong
Most runs
Eng: Frank Woolley 343 @ 42.87
Aus: Charles Macartney 300 @ 42.85
Most wickets
Eng: 'Ciss' Parkin 16 @ 26.25
Aus: Ted McDonald 27 @ 24.74

1924–25
Australia 4–1 England (5)
Captains
Aus: Herbie Collins
Eng: Arthur Gilligan
Most runs
Aus: Johnny Taylor 541 @ 54.10
Eng: Herbert Sutcliffe 734 @ 81.55
Most wickets
Aus: Arthur Mailey 24 @ 41.62
Eng: Maurice Tate 38 @ 23.18

1926
England 1–0 Australia (5)
Captains
Eng: Arthur Carr and Percy
Chapman (four and one Tests)
Aus: Herbie Collins and Warren
Bardsley (three and two Tests)
Most runs
Eng: Jack Hobbs 486 @ 81.00
Aus: Charles Macartney 473 @ 94.60
Most wickets
Eng: Maurice Tate 13 @ 29.84
Aus: Arthur Mailey 14 @ 42.28

1928–29
Australia 1–4 England (5)
Captains
Aus: Jack Ryder
Eng: Percy Chapman and Jack
White (four and one Tests)
Most runs
Aus: Jack Ryder 492 @ 54.66
Eng: Wally Hammond 905 @ 113.12
Most wickets
Aus: Clarrie Grimmett 23 @ 44.52
Eng: Jack White 25 @ 30.40

1930
England 1–2 Australia (5)
Captains
Eng: Percy Chapman and Bob Wyatt
(four and one Tests)
Aus: Bill Woodfull
Most runs
Eng: Herbert Sutcliffe 436 @ 87.20
Aus: Don Bradman 974 @ 139.14
Most wickets
Eng: Maurice Tate 15 @ 38.26
Aus: Clarrie Grimmett 29 @ 31.89

1932–33
Australia 1–4 England (5)
Captains
Aus: Bill Woodfull
Eng: Douglas Jardine
Most runs
Aus: Don Bradman 396 @ 56.57
Eng: Wally Hammond 440 @ 55.00,
Herbert Sutcliffe 440 @ 55.00
Most wickets
Aus: Bill O'Reilly 27 @ 26.81
Eng: Harold Larwood 33 @ 19.51

1934
England 1–2 Australia (5)
Captains
Eng: Cyril Walters and Bob Wyatt
(one and four Tests)
Aus: Bill Woodfull
Most runs
Eng: Maurice Leyland 478 @ 68.28
Aus: Don Bradman 758 @ 94.75
Most wickets
Eng: Hedley Verity 24 @ 24.00
Aus: Bill O'Reilly 28 @ 24.92

1936–37
Australia 3–2 England (5)
Captains
Aus: Don Bradman
Eng: Gubby Allen
Most runs
Aus: Don Bradman 810 @ 90.00
Eng: Wally Hammond 468 @ 58.50
Most wickets
Aus: Bill O'Reilly 25 @ 22.20
Eng: Bill Voce 26 @ 21.53

1938
England 1–1 Australia (5)
Captains
Eng: Wally Hammond
Aus: Don Bradman
Most runs
Eng: Len Hutton 473 @ 118.25
Aus: Bill Brown 512 @ 73.14
Most wickets
Eng: Ken Farnes 17 @ 34.17
Aus: Bill O'Reilly 22 @ 27.72

1946–47
Australia 3–0 England (5)
Captains
Aus: Don Bradman
Eng: Wally Hammond and Norman
Yardley (four and one Tests)
Most runs
Aus: Don Bradman 680 @ 97.14
Eng: Bill Edrich 462 @ 46.20
Most wickets
Aus: Ray Lindwall 18 @ 20.38, Colin
McCool 18 @ 27.27
Eng: Doug Wright 23 @ 43.04

1948
England 0–4 Australia (5)
Captains
Eng: Norman Yardley
Aus: Don Bradman
Most runs
Eng: Denis Compton 562 @ 62.44
Aus: Arthur Morris 696 @ 87.00
Most wickets
Eng: Alec Bedser 18 @ 38.22
Aus: Ray Lindwall 27 @ 19.62, Bill
Johnston 27 @ 23.33

1950–51
Australia 4–1 England (5)
Captains
Aus: Lindsay Hassett
Eng: Freddie Brown
Most runs
Aus: Lindsay Hassett 366 @ 40.66
Eng: Len Hutton 533 @ 88.83
Most wickets
Aus: Bill Johnston 22 @ 19.18
Eng: Alec Bedser 30 @ 16.06

1953
England 1–0 Australia (5)
Captains
Eng: Len Hutton
Aus: Lindsay Hassett
Most runs
Eng: Len Hutton 443 @ 55.37
Aus: Lindsay Hassett 365 @ 36.50
Most wickets
Eng: Alec Bedser 39 @ 17.48
Aus: Ray Lindwall 26 @ 18.84

1954–55
Australia 1–3 England (5)
Captains
Aus: Ian Johnson and Arthur Morris
(four and one Tests)
Eng: Len Hutton
Most runs
Aus: Neil Harvey 354 @ 44.25
Eng: Peter May 351 @ 39.00
Most wickets
Aus: Bill Johnston 19 @ 22.26
Eng: Frank Tyson 28 @ 20.82

1956
England 2–1 Australia (5)
Captains
Eng: Peter May
Aus: Ian Johnson
Most runs
Eng: Peter May 453 @ 90.60
Aus: Jim Burke 271 @ 30.11
Most wickets
Eng: Jim Laker 46 @ 9.60
Aus: Keith Miller 21 @ 22.23

1958–59
Australia 4–0 England (5)
Captains
Aus: Richie Benaud
Eng: Peter May
Most runs
Aus: Colin McDonald 519 @ 64.87
Eng: Peter May 405 @ 40.50
Most wickets
Aus: Richie Benaud 31 @ 18.83
Eng: Jim Laker 15 @ 21.20

1961
England 1–2 Australia (5)
Captains
Eng: Colin Cowdrey and Peter May
(two and three Tests)
Aus: Richie Benaud and Neil Harvey
(four and one Tests)
Most runs
Eng: Raman Subba Row 468 @ 46.80
Aus: Bill Lawry 420 @ 52.50
Most wickets
Eng: Fred Trueman 20 @ 26.45
Aus: Alan Davidson 23 @ 24.86

1962–63
Australia 1–1 England (5)
Captains
Aus: Richie Benaud
Eng: Ted Dexter
Most runs
Aus: Brian Booth 404 @ 50.50
Eng: Ken Barrington 582 @ 72.75
Most wickets
Aus: Alan Davidson 24 @ 20.00
Eng: Fred Titmus 21 @ 29.33

1964
England 0–1 Australia (5)
Captains
Eng: Ted Dexter
Aus: Bobby Simpson
Most runs
Eng: Ken Barrington 531 @ 75.85
Aus: Bob Simpson 458 @ 76.33
Most wickets
Eng: Fred Trueman 17 @ 23.47
Aus: Garth McKenzie 29 @ 22.55

1965–66
Australia 1–1 England (5)
Captains
Aus: Brian Booth and Bob Simpson
(two and three Tests)
Eng: M. J. K. Smith
Most runs
Aus: Bill Lawry 592 @ 84.57
Eng: Ken Barrington 464 @ 66.28
Most wickets
Aus: Neil Hawke 16 @ 26.18, Garth
McKenzie 16 @ 29.18
Eng: Jeff Jones 15 @ 35.53

1968
England 1–1 Australia (5)
Captains
Eng: Colin Cowdrey and Tom
Graveney (four and one Tests)
Aus: Bill Lawry and Barry Jarman
(four and one Tests)
Most runs
Eng: John Edrich 554 @ 61.55
Aus: Ian Chappell 348 @ 43.50
Most wickets
Eng: Derek Underwood 20 @ 15.10
Aus: Alan Connolly 23 @ 25.69

1970–71
Australia 0–2 England (7)
Captains
Aus: Bill Lawry and Ian Chappell
(six and one Tests)
Eng: Ray Illingworth
Most runs
Aus: Keith Stackpole 627 @ 52.25
Eng: Geoff Boycott 657 @ 93.85
Most wickets
Aus: John Gleeson 14 @ 43.21
Eng: John Snow 31 @ 22.83

1972
England 2–2 Australia (5)
Captains
Eng: Ray Illingworth
Aus: Ian Chappell
Most runs
Eng: Tony Greig 288 @ 36.00
Aus: Keith Stackpole 485 @ 51.10
Most wickets
Eng: John Snow 24 @ 23.12
Aus: Dennis Lillee 31 @ 17.67

1974-75
Australia 4–1 England (6)
Captains
Aus: Ian Chappell
Eng: Mike Denness and John Edrich
(five and one Tests)
Most runs
Aus: Greg Chappell 608 @ 55.27
Eng: Tony Greig 446 @ 40.54
Most wickets
Aus: Jeff Thomson 33 @ 17.93
Eng: Bob Willis 17 @ 30.70, Derek
Underwood 17 @ 35.00, Tony Greig
17 @ 40.05

1975
England 0–1 Australia (5)
Captains
Eng: Mike Denness and Tony Greig
(one and three Tests)
Aus: Ian Chappell
Most runs
Eng: John Edrich 428 @ 53.50
Aus: Ian Chappell 429 @ 71.50
Most wickets
Eng: John Snow 11 @ 32.27
Aus: Dennis Lillee 21 @ 21.90

*The Ashes were not at stake in the
Centenary Test of 1976–77, which
Australia won by 45 runs.*

1977
England 3–0 Australia (5)
Captains
Eng: Mike Brearley
Aus: Greg Chappell
Most runs
Eng: Geoff Boycott 442 @ 147.33
Aus: Greg Chappell 371 @ 41.22
Most wickets
Eng: Bob Willis 27 @ 19.77
Aus: Jeff Thomson 23 @ 25.34

1978-79
Australia 1–5 England (6)
Captains
Aus: Graham Yallop
Eng: Mike Brearley
Most runs
Aus: Graham Yallop 391 @ 32.58
Eng: David Gower 420 @ 42.00
Most wickets
Aus: Rodney Hogg 41 @ 12.85
Eng: Geoff Miller 23 @ 15.04, Ian
Botham 23 @ 24.65
*Australia beat England 3–0 in a 3-Test series,
1979–80, but the Ashes were not at stake.*

1981
England 3–1 Australia (6)
Captains
Eng: Ian Botham and Mike Brearley
(two and four Tests)
Aus: Kim Hughes
Most runs
Eng: Ian Botham 399 @ 36.27
Aus: Allan Border 533 @ 59.22
Most wickets
Eng: Ian Botham 34 @ 20.58
Aus: Terry Alderman 42 @ 21.26

1982-83
Australia 2–1 England (5)
Captains
Aus: Greg Chappell
Eng: Bob Willis
Most runs
Aus: Kim Hughes 469 @ 67.00
Eng: David Gower 441 @ 44.10
Most wickets
Aus: Geoff Lawson 34 @ 20.20
Eng: Bob Willis 18 @ 27.00, Ian
Botham 18 @ 40.50

1985
England 3–1 Australia (6)
Captains
Eng: David Gower
Aus: Allan Border
Most runs
Eng: David Gower 732 @ 81.33
Aus: Allan Border 597 @ 66.33
Most wickets
Eng: Ian Botham 31 @ 27.58
Aus: Craig McDermott 30 @ 30.03

1986–87
Australia 1–2 England (5)
Captains
Aus: Allan Border
Eng: Mike Gatting
Most runs
Aus: Dean Jones 511 @ 56.77
Eng: Chris Broad 487 @ 69.57
Most wickets
Aus: Bruce Reid 20 @ 26.35
Eng: John Emburey 18 @ 36.83

1989
England 0–4 Australia (6)
Captains
Eng: David Gower
Aus: Allan Border
Most runs
Eng: Robin Smith 553 @ 61.44
Aus: Mark Taylor 839 @ 83.90
Most wickets
Eng: Neil Foster 12 @ 35.08
Aus: Terry Alderman 41 @ 17.36

1990–91
Australia 3–0 England (5)
Captains
Aus: Allan Border
Eng: Allan Lamb and Graham
Gooch (one and four Tests)
Most runs
Aus: David Boon 530 @ 75.71
Eng: Graham Gooch 426 @ 53.25
Most wickets
Aus: Bruce Reid 27 @ 16.00
Eng: Devon Malcolm 16 @ 41.56

1993
England 1–4 Australia (6)
Captains
Eng: Graham Gooch and Mike
Atherton (four and two Tests)
Aus: Allan Border
Most runs
Aus: David Boon 555 @ 69.37
Eng: Graham Gooch 673 @ 56.08
Most wickets
Eng: Peter Such 16 @ 33.81
Aus: Shane Warne 34 @ 25.79

1994–95
Australia 3–1 England (5)
Captains
Aus: Mark Taylor
Eng: Mike Atherton
Most runs
Aus: Michael Slater 623 @ 62.30
Eng: Graham Thorpe 444 @ 49.33
Most wickets
Aus: Craig McDermott 32 @ 21.09
Eng: Darren Gough 20 @ 21.25

1997
England 2–3 Australia (6)
Captains
Eng: Mike Atherton
Aus: Mark Taylor
Most runs
Eng: Graham Thorpe 453 @ 50.33
Aus: Matthew Elliott 556 @ 55.60
Most wickets
Eng: Andy Caddick 24 @ 26.41
Aus: Glenn McGrath 36 @ 19.47

1998–99
Australia 3–1 England (5)
Captains
Aus: Mark Taylor
Eng: Alec Stewart
Most runs
Aus: Steve Waugh 498 @ 83.00
Eng: Nasser Hussain 407 @ 45.22
Most wickets
Aus: Stuart MacGill 27 @ 17.70
Eng: Darren Gough 21 @ 32.71

2001
England 1–4 Australia (5)
Captains
Eng: Nasser Hussain and Mike
Atherton (three and two Tests)
Aus: Steve Waugh and Adam
Gilchrist (four and one Tests)
Most runs
Eng: Mark Butcher 456 @ 50.66
Aus: Mark Waugh 430 @ 86.00
Most wickets
Eng: Darren Gough 17 @ 38.64
Aus: Glenn McGrath 32 @ 16.93

2002–03
Australia 4–1 England (5)
Captains
Aus: Steve Waugh
Eng: Nasser Hussain
Most runs
Aus: Matthew Hayden 496 @ 62.00
Eng: Michael Vaughan 633 @ 63.30
Most wickets
Aus: Jason Gillespie 20 @ 24.60
Eng: Andy Caddick 20 @ 34.50

2005
England 2–1 Australia (5)
Captains
Eng: Michael Vaughan
Aus: Ricky Ponting
Most runs
Eng: Kevin Pietersen 473 @ 52.55
Aus: Justin Langer 394 @ 43.77
Most wickets
Eng: Andrew Flintoff 24 @ 27.29
Aus: Shane Warne 40 @ 19.92

2006–07
Australia 5–0 England (5)
Captains
Aus: Ricky Ponting
Eng: Andrew Flintoff
Most runs
Aus: Ricky Ponting 576 @ 82.28
Eng: Kevin Pietersen 490 @ 54.44
Most wickets
Aus: Stuart Clark 26 @ 17.03
Eng: Matthew Hoggard 13 @ 37.38

2009
England 2–1 Australia (5)
Captains
Eng: Andrew Strauss
Aus: Ricky Ponting
Most runs
Eng: Andrew Strauss 474 @ 52.66
Aus: Michael Clarke 448 @ 64.00
Most wickets
Eng: Stuart Broad 18 @ 30.22
Aus: Ben Hilfenhaus 22 @ 27.45

2010–11
Australia 1–3 England (5)
Captains
Aus: Ricky Ponting and Michael
Clarke (four and one Tests)
Eng: Andrew Strauss
Most runs
Aus: Mike Hussey 570 @ 63.33
Eng: Alastair Cook 766 @ 127.66
Most wickets
Aus: Mitchell Johnson 15 @ 36.93
Eng: Jimmy Anderson 24 @ 26.04

2013
England 3–0 Australia (5)
Captains
Eng: Alastair Cook
Aus: Michael Clarke
Most runs
Eng: Ian Bell 562 @ 62.44
Aus: Shane Watson 418 @ 41.80
Most wickets
Eng: Graeme Swann 26 @ 29.03
Aus: Ryan Harris 24 @ 19.58

2013–14
Australia 5–0 England (5)
Captains
Aus: Michael Clarke
Eng: Alastair Cook
Most runs
Aus: David Warner 523 @ 58.11
Eng: Kevin Pietersen 294 @ 29.40
Most wickets
Aus: Mitchell Johnson 37 @ 13.97
Eng: Stuart Broad 21 @ 27.52

*The 1890, 1938 and 1970–71 series
included one Test that was abandoned
without a ball being bowled.*

THE ASHES 1882–2014

BATTING AND BOWLING RECORDS

HIGHEST TEAM SCORES

England 903 for seven declared,
The Oval, 1938
Australia 729 for six declared,
Lord's, 1930
Australia 701, The Oval, 1934
Australia 695, The Oval, 1930
Australia 674 for six declared,
Cardiff, 2009
Australia 659 for eight declared,
Sydney, 1946–47
England 658 for eight declared,
Trent Bridge, 1938
Australia 656 for eight declared,
Old Trafford, 1964
Australia 653 for four declared,
Headingley, 1993
Australia 645, Brisbane, 1946–47

LOWEST TEAM SCORES

Australia 36, Edgbaston, 1902
Australia 42, Sydney, 1887–88
Australia 44, The Oval, 1896
England 45, Sydney, 1886–87
England 52, The Oval, 1948
England 53, Lord's, 1888
Australia 53, Lord's, 1896
Australia 58, Brisbane, 1936–37
Australia 60, Lord's, 1888
England 61, Melbourne, 1901–02
England 61, Melbourne, 1903–04

HIGHEST INDIVIDUAL SCORES

Len Hutton (E) 364, The Oval, 1938
Don Bradman (A) 334, Headingley,
1930
Bob Simpson (A) 311, Old Trafford,
1964
Bob Cowper (A) 307, Melbourne,
1965–66
Don Bradman (A) 304, Headingley,
1934

Reginald 'Tip' Foster (E) 287,
Sydney, 1903–04
Don Bradman (A) 270, Melbourne,
1936-37
Bill Ponsford (A) 266, The Oval,
1934
Ken Barrington (E) 256,
Old Trafford, 1964
Don Bradman (A) 254, Lord's, 1930

BEST BOWLING (innings)

Jim Laker (E) 10–53,
Old Trafford, 1956
Jim Laker (E) 9–37,
Old Trafford, 1956
Arthur Mailey (A) 9–121,
Melbourne, 1920–21
Frank Laver (A) 8–31,
Old Trafford, 1909
George Lohmann (E) 8–35,
Sydney, 1886–87
Glenn McGrath (A), 8–38,
Lord's, 1997
Albert Trott (A), 8–43,
Adelaide, 1894–95
Hedley Verity (E), 8–43,
Lord's, 1934
Bob Willis (E), 8–43,
Headingley, 1981
Bob Massie (A), 8–53,
Lord's, 1972

BEST BOWLING (match)

Jim Laker (E), 19–90,
Old Trafford, 1956
Bob Massie (A) 16–137,
Lord's, 1972
Hedley Verity (E) 15–104,
Lord's, 1934
Wilfred Rhodes (E), 15–124,
Melbourne, 1903–04

Frederick Spofforth (A), 14–90,
The Oval, 1882
Alec Bedser (E), 14–99
Trent Bridge, 1953
Billy Bates (E), 14–102,
Melbourne, 1882–83
Monty Noble (A), 13–77,
Melbourne, 1901–02
Frederick Spofforth (A), 13–110,
Melbourne, 1878–79
Bruce Reid (A), 13–148,
Melbourne, 1990–91

MOST APPEARANCES
For Australia:
Syd Gregory 52 (1890–1912)
For England:
Colin Cowdrey 43 (1954–75)

MOST MATCHES AS CAPTAIN
For Australia:
Allan Border 29 (1985–93)
For England:
Archie MacLaren 22 (1897–1909)

MOST RUNS

Australia
Don Bradman 5028
Allan Border 3548
Steve Waugh 3200
Clem Hill 2660
Greg Chappell 2619
Mark Taylor 2496
Ricky Ponting 2476
Neil Harvey 2416
Victor Trumper 2263
David Boon 2237

England
Jack Hobbs 3636
David Gower 3269
Geoff Boycott 2945
Wally Hammond 2852
Herbert Sutcliffe 2741
John Edrich 2644
Graham Gooch 2632
Colin Cowdrey 2433
Len Hutton 2428
Kevin Pietersen 2158

MOST CENTURIES

Australia
19 Don Bradman
10 Steve Waugh
9 Greg Chappell
8 Allan Border, Arthur Morris,
Ricky Ponting
7 David Boon, Michael Clarke,
Bill Lawry, Michael Slater

England
12 Jack Hobbs
9 David Gower, Wally Hammond
8 Herbert Sutcliffe
7 Geoff Boycott, John Edrich,
Maurice Leyland
5 Ken Barrington, Denis Compton,
Colin Cowdrey, Len Hutton,
Stanley Jackson, Archie
MacLaren

BEST BATTING AVERAGE
(minimum 10 innings)

Australia
Don Bradman 89.78
Sid Barnes 70.50
Mike Hussey 59.27
Steve Waugh 58.18
Allan Border 56.31
Matthew Elliott 55.60
Greg Matthews 53.54
Dean Jones 50.76
Arthur Morris 50.73
Keith Stackpole 50.60

England
Eddie Paynter 84.42
Herbert Sutcliffe 66.85
Ken Barrington 63.96
Chris Broad 59.00
Maurice Leyland 56.83
Len Hutton 56.46
Jack Hobbs 54.26
Charles 'Jack' Russell 52.66
Phil Mead 51.87
Wally Hammond 51.85

MOST WICKETS

Australia
Shane Warne 195
Dennis Lillee 167
Glenn McGrath 157
Hugh Trumble 141
Monty Noble 115
Ray Lindwall 114
Clarrie Grimmett 106
George Giffen 103
Bill O'Reilly 102
Charlie 'Terror' Turner 101

England
Ian Botham 148
Bob Willis 128
Wilfred Rhodes 109
Sydney Barnes 106
Derek Underwood 105
Alec Bedser 104
Bobby Peel 101
Johnny Briggs 97
Tom Richardson 88
John Snow 83
Maurice Tate 83

BEST BOWLING AVERAGE (minimum 10 innings)

Australia
J. J. Ferris 14.25
Charlie 'Terror' Turner 16.53
Rodney Hogg 17.00
Frederick Spofforth 18.41
Harry Boyle 20.03
Bruce Reid 20.40
Ryan Harris 20.63
Stuart Clark 20.63
Hugh Trumble 20.88
Shane Warne 20.92

England
George Lohmann 13.01
Billy Barnes 15.54
Billy Bates 16.42
Bobby Peel 16.98
Jim Laker 18.27
Bill Lockwood 20.53
Johnny Briggs 20.55
George Ulyett 20.66
Allan Steel 20.86
Wilf Flowers 21.14

MOST DISMISSALS AS WICKETKEEPER

Australia
Rod Marsh 148
Ian Healy 135
Adam Gilchrist 96
Bert Oldfield 90
Wally Grout 76

England
Alan Knott 105
Dick Lilley 84
Alec Stewart 78
Godfrey Evans 76
Matt Prior 63

MOST CATCHES (outfielder)

Australia
Greg Chappell 61
Allan Border 57
Mark Taylor 46
Hugh Trumble 45
Mark Waugh 43

England
Ian Botham 57
Wally Hammond 43
Colin Cowdrey 40
W. G. Grace 39
Len Braund 37
Tony Greig 37

BIBLIOGRAPHY

Arlott, John, *Jack Hobbs: Profile of 'The Master'*, Readers Union, 1981

Atherton, Mike, *Opening Up*, Hodder & Stoughton, 2002

Berry, Scyld, and Peploe, Rupert, *Cricket's Burning Passion*, Methuen, 2006

Booth, Lawrence (ed.), *'What Are The Butchers For?' And Other Splendid Cricket Quotations*, A. & C. Black, 2009

Botham, Ian, *The Incredible Tests*, Pelham, 1981

Bradman, Don, *Farewell to Cricket*, Hodder & Stoughton, 1950

Brearley, Mike, *Phoenix from the Ashes*, Hodder & Stoughton, 1982

Brearley, Mike, *The Art of Captaincy*, Hodder & Stoughton, 1985

Briggs, Simon, *Stiff Upper Lips and Baggy Green Caps*, Quercus, 2006

Craig, Edward (ed.), *Story of the Ashes*, Wisden Cricketer Publishing, 2009

Foot, David, *Wally Hammond: The Reasons Why*, Robson, 1998

Fingleton, Jack, *Brightly Fades the Don*, Collins, 1949

Fingleton, Jack, *Cricket Crisis*, Pavilion, 1985

Frith, David, *Bodyline Autopsy*, Aurum Press, 2002

Frith, David, *Thommo*, TBS, 1980

Gower, David, *Gower: The Autobiography*, CollinsWillow, 1992

Haigh, Gideon, *Ashes 2005*, Aurum Press, 2005

Haigh, Gideon, *The Big Ship*, Aurum Press, 2002

Haigh, Gideon, *The Book of Ashes Anecdotes*, Mainstream, 2006

Hamilton, Duncan, *Harold Larwood*, Quercus, 2009

Hopps, David (ed.), *Great Cricket Quotes*, Robson, 2006

Hughes, Simon, *Cricket's Greatest Rivalry*, Cassell, 2013

Jardine, Douglas, *In Quest of the Ashes*, Methuen, 2005

Knox, Malcolm, *Bradman's War*, The Robson Press, 2013

Lynch, Steven (ed.), *Wisden on the Ashes*, John Wisden & Co., 2011

McLellan, Alastair and Steen, Rob, *500–1: The Miracle of Headingley '81*, BBC Books, 2001

Mailey, Arthur, *10 for 66 and All That*, Phoenix, 1959

Ponting, Ricky, *At the Close of Play*, HarperSport, 2013

Quelch, Tim, *Bent Arms and Dodgy Wickets*, Pitch Publishing, 2012

Rae, Simon, *W. G. Grace: A Life*, Faber & Faber, 1998

Rajan, Amol, *Twirlymen*, Yellow Jersey, 2012

Ryan, Christian, *Golden Boy: Kim Hughes and the Bad Old Days of Australian Cricket*, Allen & Unwin, 2010

Smith, Robin and Crace, John, *Quest for Number One*, Boxtree, 1993

Tyson, Frank, *A Typhoon called Tyson*, Heinemann, 1961

Waters, Chris, *Fred Trueman: The Authorised Biography*, Aurum, 2011

Waugh, Steve, *Out of my Comfort Zone*, Michael Joseph, 2006

INDEX

Bold numbers indicate that the person is the speaker or writer – or subject of – a chapter-opening quotation.

Italic numbers indicate that the person appears in a photograph.

Afzaal, Usman 281

Agar, Ashton 329, 330

Agnew, Jonathan 245

Alderman, Terry 195, 199-201, 206, 210, 212, 215, 236–8, 240, 293

Aldred, Tanya 277

Allen, Gubby 70, 75, 80, 87, **89**, 90, 131

Amiss, Dennis 173, 176, 179

Anderson, Jimmy 306, 316, 318, 320–23, 324, 326, 328, 330, 332, 333, 339

Appleyard, Bob 131

Arlott, John 31, 55, 107, 110, **148**

Armstrong, Warwick 40, 41, 43, **46**, 47, *48*, *52*, 53

Arnold, Geoff 179

Arthur, Mickey 330

Atherton, Mike 120, 140, 233, 241, 243, 250, 254–5, 257–9, 266, *267*, 269, 270, 277, 279, 282, 287, 291, 308

Athey, Bill 220

Bailey, George 332, 333, 337

Bailey, Trevor 115, 119, 123, 134, 136

Bairstow, David 82

'Ball of the Century' (Shane Warne) 245, *246*

Bannerman, Charles 5

Barber, Bob 146–7

Bardsley, Warren 41, 43, 46, 56

Barlow, Dick 11

Barmy Army 285, **326,** 335

Barnes, Billy 7

Barnes, Sid 100, 106

Barnes, Sydney 27, 29, 40, **42,** 43–4, *45*

Barnett, Ben 96

Barnett, Charlie 91, 93

Barrington, Kenny *112–13*, 140–41, 143, 283

Bates, Billy 11

Beal, Charlie 8

Bedser, Alec 102, 105, 106–7, 110, 116–17, 118, 121, **194**, 196, 197

'Alec Bedser Calypso' **118**

Bell, Ian 307, 313, *314*, 315, 316, 328, 330, 334

Benaud, Richie 119, 123, 134, 136, **137**, *139*, 161–2, 199, 300

Berry, Scyld 20, 214

Bichel, Andy 284, 287

Bird, Dickie 249, 250

Blackham, Jack 18

Blewett, Greg 257, 263

Bligh, Ivo **10**, 11–13

Blythe, Colin 40

Bodyline bowling 69–72, 74–7, 80–86, 99, 114

Bollinger, Doug 324

Lehmann, Darren **329**, 330
Lever, Peter 154, 160
Lewis, Chris 250
Leyland, Maurice 75, 90–91, 97
Lillee, Dennis 155, 160, 164–5,
    168–73, *174*, 175–6, 179–82,
    186, **187**, 189, 193, 195, 198,
    201, 206–8, 210–12, 256, 337
Lilley, Dick 29, 30, 35
Lindwall, Ray 99–100, *104*,
    106–7, 109, 116, 123, 125,
    136
Lister, Simon 245
Lloyd, David *152–53*, 177, **178**,
    319, 326
Loader, Peter 134
Lock, Tony 123–4, 129–30, 132,
    134
Lockwood, Bill 29
Lohmann, George 13
Loxton, Sam 107
Luckhurst, Brian 154, 159
Lush, Peter 242–3
Lyon, Nathan 336, 342
Lyttleton, Alfred 7

Macartney, Charles 41, 46, 49,
    50, 51, 56
MacGill, Stuart 271, 272, 273
Mackay, Ken 131
MacLaren, Archie 20, 27, 28, 30,
    42
Mailey, Arthur 47–8, *52*
Malcolm, Devon 232, 243, 254,
    256, 258
Malone, Mick 190
Manning, J.L. 143
Marks, Vic 168
Marlar, Robin 245
Marsh, Geoff 234, 241, 263
Marsh, Rodney 155, 159, 164,
    167, 168, 173, 175, 180–81,
    186, 198, 204, 226

Martin-Jenkins, Christopher 177
Martyn, Damien 275, 304
Mason, Ronald **50**
Massie, Bob 165–6
May, Peter 123, 126, 130, 136,
    139
May, Tim 250, 254
Mayne, 'Ernie' 52
McAlister, Peter 44
McCabe, Stan 60, 65, 72, 90–93,
    95
McCague, Martin 82, 253–4,
    255, 256
McCaig, Steve 318
McConnell, Peter **239**, 241
McCool, Colin 103
McCosker, Rick 186
McDermott, Craig 215, 242, 249,
    256, 258
McDonald, Colin 130–31, 136
McDonald, Ted 51
McGrath, Glenn 120, 262–3,
    265–6, 270, 273, 276–8, 280,
    282, 285–7, 291–4, 300–301,
    303, 306–7, **311**, 312, 315,
    316, 317, 330, 334
McKenzie, Graham 'Garth'
    112–13, 137, 143, 144, 156
Meckiff, Ian 134–6
Menzies, Pattie **56**, 58
Menzies, Robert 56
Miandad, Javed 249
Miller, Geoff 213
Miller, Keith 98–9, **102**, 103, *104*,
    105–7, 116, 119–20, 123, 127,
    129, 130, 174–5
Milne, A.A. **39**
'miracle of Adelaide' xvi
Mitchell, Leslie 107
Morley, Fred 10
Morphy, Florence 11–12
Morris, Arthur 103, 106, 108,
    111, 116, 121, 123

ACKNOWLEDGEMENTS

I'd like to thank everyone at Head of Zeus, especially my editor Richard Milbank for his patience, advice and knowledge – and for having the idea for the book in the first place. Thanks also to Cris Freddi, Rob Bagchi, Daniel Harris, Scott Murray, Alex Netherton, Jonathan Hungin, Andrew Miller, Simon Barnes, Steve Busfield, Richard O'Hagan, Gary Naylor, Simon Farquhar, Ian Smyth, Olivia Gannon, Helen Francis and Ed Wilson for their help. And thanks to Jay and Royal for their love, support and 6am wake-up calls.

SECTION OPENERS

The Golden Age
(pages 2–3)
The Australians of 1882: the seated figure in the back row is captain W. L. Murdoch. Frederick 'The Demon' Spofforth is third from the right, back row.

The Age of Bradman
(pages 62–3)
Walter Hammond and Donald Bradman walking out for the toss, first Test, Trent Bridge, 10 June 1938.

The Age of Attrition
(pages 112–13)
Ken Barrington cuts Graham McKenzie, fifth Test, Sydney, February 1963. The Surrey batsman scored 101 and 94 in the drawn match.

The Age of the Fast Men
(pages 152–3)
David Lloyd is poleaxed by Jeff Thomson, second Test, Perth, 15 December 1974.

Australia Ascendant
(pages 224–5)
Shane Warne bowls Robin Smith, first Test, Old Trafford, 3 June 1993.

2005 and All That
(pages 288–9)
Michael Kasprowicz is given out, caught Jones bowled Harmison, Edgbaston, 7 August 2005. England captain Michael Vaughan, in the sun hat (centre), prepares to celebrate with his triumphant fast bowler.